All About **BASEBALL**

All About
BASEBALL

Leonard Koppett

Quadrangle / The New York Times Book Co.

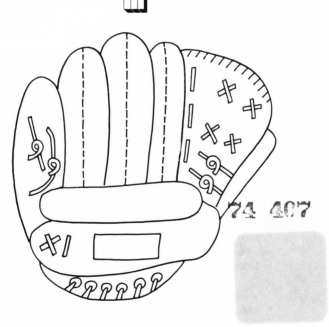

Library of Congress Catalog Card Number: 73-79917
International Standard Book Number: 0-8129-0408-7
DESIGN: VINCENT TORRE

Contents

SECTION 3

Personalities and Propositions

APPENDIXES

Preface

About six years ago, after some 20 years of covering baseball for three different New York City papers, and some 20 years before that of reading up to 10 of them daily, I decided to write a book about what I thought I had learned. My main motivation was to relieve a mind congested with acquired information that could not satisfactorily work its way into daily stories. My hope was that I could share some of the fascinating material my privileged position had exposed me to with people equally interested but not so fortunately placed.

I wanted to call it "The Intellectual's Baseball Book," but a horrified publisher explained to me how a nasty word like "intellectual" would put people off. We settled on "A Thinking Man's Guide to Baseball." Nevertheless, what came out was, truly, an intellectual's baseball book, for better or worse, because it approached every aspect of the game from an intellectual viewpoint.

Now, six years later, I have made a startling discovery: most of what I wrote then I don't want to change. This may mean, simply, that my views fossilized six years ago. Or it may mean (I hope) that the fundamentals dealt with here don't change very much in six years, although many other aspects of baseball have changed a lot.

Nevertheless, neither the fundamentals nor my view of them has been completely static, and the present version of the book is different in many details. Four new chapters have been added, and every chapter has been updated or revised. This is, then, essentially all I know about baseball on my 50th birthday, or at least all I can put down coherently.

I wish it were more, but I'm glad I've been able to get off

my chest as much as I have. Every sector of the baseball world has its special satisfactions: players and managers have victories and statistics; scouts and general managers have the success of young men they picked; fans have the emotional ups and downs that make it all worth while. The writer's special kick—and privilege—is one all the others envy: he gets to express his ideas about it publicly, again and again. This is my turn, one more time. Thanks for listening.

September 15, 1973
Palo Alto, California

All About **BASEBALL**

Introduction

This book has an ambitious title but a modest aim. It hopes to fill in the gaps, and expand some horizons, for those who feel any degree of interest in Baseball—baseball with a capital B, which derives from its official name, "Organized Baseball." Organized Baseball is a structure that has evolved over more than a century, and it comprises, through a series of interlocking agreements, all professional baseball in the United States. Anything outside of O.B. is automatically classified as semipro or amateur. Through its offices, Organized Baseball also exerts controls over American players in the Caribbean, South America, and Japan.

This structure forms the context for the mass-entertainment commercial enterprise that has enabled the game itself to be developed to such a high degree.

Accordingly, several assumptions have been made about you, the reader:

That you would enjoy knowing more about Baseball, as it exists in the middle 1970s, than daily newspapers and broadcasts can convey.

That you would prefer the realities, even if they seem complicated and sometimes incomplete, to myths and clichés, however neat.

That you take baseball fairly seriously—but never too seriously—and feel some curiosity about its techniques as well as its personalities.

And that, no matter how familiar you may be with certain aspects of this complex industry and fascinating sport, there are other aspects that haven't come to your attention.

It is not, in any sense, a "How To" book, or a "Who Did,"

1

or a "Who Will Win," or a "What Happened," or a "Who Said What" book. It contains no secrets and no startling revelations. In fact, it directly reproduces one of the underlying modes of thought of the baseball world: repeat the obvious, repeat the well known, remind your men of what they probably are perfectly aware of—in order to make sure that the appropriate thought is firmly in mind at the appropriate moment. The catcher reminding his fielders of the number of outs, the coach reminding the runner to tag up, the manager telling the pinch hitter to make sure he gets a good pitch to hit—these are the day-to-day, moment-to-moment actualities of baseball's mental processes, not some sort of mystical flashes of brilliance. Perspective, context, relevance: those are the attributes being emphasized.

The themes that will arise again and again are interaction, human fallibility, and unpredictability, and above all dynamics. Like all reality, baseball is a dynamic process, with many related forces at work simultaneously. Words, which are unavoidably static, need the help of imagination if some approximation of the true picture is to arise.

In real life, the mood and ailments of a man affect his performance. The intent of a maneuver is always an intrinsic part of its execution. Confidence and concentration, the two perpetual intangibles, often determine results to a far greater degree than physical abilities and the hallowed "percentages." There is a great tendency, in dealing with baseball, to get bogged down in statistics and history—to treat numbers as if they were things, instead of mere records of something already finished; to fantasize about mathematical laws and averages, instead of recognizing them to be rather simple probabilities derived pragmatically from decades of accumulated experience.

This book will try, then, to give the reader the raw material for such a viewpoint, in the hope that his continuing baseball interest will be enriched by such perspective. Every element will be touched upon—the techniques of play and strategy, the way of life of the participants, the business and how it is run, the peripheral people (like writers and broadcasters and peanut venders and road secretaries), the rules, the customs, and the outlook.

Certain people, like Sandy Koufax and Casey Stengel, will be quoted more often than others. This is not because they have any special wisdom, but because they happen to be the ones who gave expression to various points in my presence. Others could have taught the same lessons just as well. Everyone who has learned baseball has had particular teachers, and the ones quoted in this book represent general knowledge rather than special intelligence.

Above all, baseball is entertaining. That's why it exists (in organized form): people are willing to pay to be entertained by it. But it is a special kind of entertainment. Through rooting interest in a team's fortunes, and personal identification with its players, baseball offers the fan an emotional experience rather than mere diversion. In reading and listening, as well as watching, the dedicated follower is involved in an active (albeit vicarious) pursuit. Beyond the mental and emotional satisfactions it can provide, it has no meaning to the follower.

But to those performing, or working in its business areas, Baseball is a serious matter—a livelihood, a battle, a profession. Their approach is more cold-blooded, less starry-eyed, more concerned with realistic details—and yet much more involved emotionally than that of most people's toward their businesses.

These attitudes, the periodic rise and fall of intensity of feeling, the ritualistic definitions of right and wrong, are also part of the total picture. They influence the words and actions of those "in baseball," and help paint the picture for those outside it.

In this book, too, everything said is subjective, from the

particular (and peculiar) vantage point of the daily baseball writer. The consensuses are authoritative enough, but the distillations of them are my own.

It is customary to refer to baseball as a "science," but to me this conjures up an image of animated chess pieces, and I have found the game to be nothing like that. "Art" seems a better metaphor. "Science" suggests natural, automatic, unchanging forces, which always lead to the same result when applied the same way. "Art" implies intuitive and purposeful manipulation of material for a special result. "Natural" laws can't be broken, but the "rules" of art can be, productively, if the artist is great enough; and baseball players seem to me to fall into the latter category. Stan Musial broke all the "rules" of a correct batting stance, and Casey Stengel violated all sorts of "percentages" in strategy and tactics, and both succeeded mightily.

In all the theories and anecdotes that follow, therefore, one Stengelism will prove to be the underlying (often unstated) principle: "What's the use," Casey once said, when asked why he didn't order a bunt, "of askin' a man to execute if he can't execute?"

This sums up my view, my bias, about the game we are to discuss. No theory is valid unless you can execute—unless you can make it work, physically, in competition; and any theory at all is wonderful if you *can* make it work.

Let's see how they go about it.

The Game
on the Field

- The art of hitting is the art of getting your pitch to hit.

> Dr. Robert William Brown, 1949

- Aarghh! How kin ya t'ink an' hit atta same time?

> Lawrence Peter Berra (Dr. Brown's roommate), 1949

The Artist at Bat

Fear.

Fear is the fundamental factor in hitting, and hitting the ball with the bat is the fundamental act of baseball.

The fear is simple and instinctive. If a baseball, thrown hard, hits any part of your body, it hurts. If it hits certain vulnerable areas, like elbows, wrists or face, it can cause broken bones and other serious injuries. If it hits a particular area of an unprotected head, it can kill.

A thrown baseball, in short, is a missile, and an approaching missile generates a reflexive action: get out of the way.

This fact—and it is an unyielding fact that the reflex always exists in all humans—is the starting point for the game of baseball, and yet it is the fact least often mentioned by those who write about baseball.

All the tactics employed by pitchers, and all the problems faced by batters, are rooted in this reflex. Even historically, baseball evolved into recognizable form only when this fact was taken into account. In most primitive forms of the game, a runner between bases could be put out by being hit with a thrown ball. This meant that only a fairly soft ball could be used, or the players would soon be maimed; and a soft ball cannot be hit very far or very fast. Only when the tag play, with the ball held in a fielder's hand, was substituted did it become possible to use a ball that was hard enough to behave in a way familiar to us. There has been no basic change in the size, weight, or consistency of the ball since 1872.

The act of hitting, therefore, encompasses what seems like an emotional contradiction. It is simultaneously pleasurable and dangerous. The batter's primary desire is to hit the ball as hard as he can, and this requires "stepping into" the approaching ball with the rear foot very firmly planted. But self-preservation demands that the body move away from a ball that is going to hit it, or that *seems* to be going to hit it.

This interplay between executing a productive swing and resisting the built-in desire to dodge is the reality of every time at bat.

And the tactical consequence is, at bottom, rudimentary: throw close, and drive the batter back; then throw over the outside part of the plate. Then, if you can alternate pitches that seem to be headed for the batter but aren't (curves) with pitches that have a straighter trajectory, you can keep the batter off balance most of the time.

Why, then, is there so little talk of fear? Why is this subject a sort of myth of omission?

One reason is that it is taken for granted. The process of becoming a capable batter begins with learning to overcome this specific fear—but it is never eliminated; it is mastered. By the time a man has become proficient enough to play professionally, he has mastered his fear to such a degree that he has nothing to discuss in such direct terms.

Another reason is that "fear" implies cowardice or lack of manliness, and as such is a loaded word. Therefore, the subject really is much discussed among professionals, but in circuitous language. They talk of "hanging in there," "standing up to the plate," "bearing down," "challenging," "fighting back."

All these are euphemisms for conquering the fear of being hit—but many of the professional eavesdroppers who communicate to the public don't bother to translate. If knowledgeable, they, like the players, take it so much for granted that they don't think of being explicit; if not knowledgeable, they don't realize what the references really are.

There are also deeper reasons for glossing over the naked truth. In all athletics, conquest of fear of pain is an essential element. One must learn to carry out the proper action *despite* the possibility of getting hurt. A professional football player, or boxer, or hockey player, isn't less susceptible to pain than other people; he doesn't hurt less; prick him and he bleeds. His special quality is that he is *willing* to endure the pain to gain his objective. It's true that he has conditioned himself physically to withstand some type of beating and strain—but the conditioning in itself involved self-inflicted pain.

It is no help, however, to remain conscious of the feeling of fear that one is trying to conquer. Very quickly, then, and very firmly over a long period of time, *awareness* of fear is pushed aside. A man doesn't go to bat saying to himself, This time I will not be afraid; he stopped thinking in such terms long ago. But the fact remains that he is, on the instinctive level, afraid, and how he performs in spite of this is the measure of his success.

So the participant has pushed the subject out of his conscious mind, while the spectator has either forgotten his own feelings, or never experienced them.

It is revealing, however, that once a participant passes out of the line of fire, once he has retired, the awareness surges up and becomes prominent in conversation.

Listen to Dizzy Dean, reminiscing about his great days with the Gas House Gang of the St. Louis Cardinals in the early

1930s: "I'm pitchin' against Hubbell," says Diz, "and I knock down eight men in a row. I skip Hub. Then I knock down the lead-off man again, to make an even nine."

"They'd never dare dig in the way they do now," declares Frankie Frisch, who was Dean's manager then. "If our pitchers saw a guy diggin' a ditch with his spikes the way some of these fellows do, you know where that next pitch would be."

"I remember Fitz pitching one time to Johnny Mize," says Leo Durocher, in his best flamboyant storytelling mood. "I'm managing the Dodgers, and Fitzsimmons is pitching for me, and Mize is with the Cardinals. He looks down and he yells to Mize, 'The first one is coming right here'—and he throws it *right here!*" (Leo points to his head.) "Then the next pitch is that big slow curve, right on the outside corner. Now it's one and one. 'Again,' yells Fitz, and throws it right here for ball two. Then the curve, and it's two-two. 'One more time!' Fitz hollers at him, and sure enough, he goes flying. And then strike three."

Every gathering of old baseball people is guaranteed to produce reminiscences of this sort as the evening, and the booze, wear on.

But if it all begins with fear, it doesn't end there. That is merely the beginning.

The second fundamental fact about hitting is so self-evident that it is mentioned only as a cliché, when clichés are being derided. It's a round ball and a round bat.

Yet this unique problem in physics is what gives baseball its particular character. It doesn't come up in any other widely played game.

In all the tennis-family games (including squash and even handball), a moving ball is struck by some flat surface that is large in relation to the ball. In hockey, a sliding or rolling disc is hit or guided by a flat blade. A cricket bat has three plane surfaces (and the ball may be hit in any direction). In golf, the striking surface is flat and, what's more, the ball is stationary. Even in billiards (where the balls are stationary), the striking tip of the cue is relatively flat.

In all these other games, therefore, the margin for error is much greater than in baseball. A hockey or tennis shot can be reasonably effective even if the point of contact is not quite centered on the blade. But to hit a baseball into fair territory, hard enough to have any reasonable chance of the ball falling safe, one must connect almost perfectly. A line drive can result only if the line from the center of the ball, through the point of contact, to the center of the bat cylinder is practically straight. The height of the area in which the bat and ball can meet squarely is something less than half an inch.

Consider the dimensions: a baseball's diameter is 2.868 inches; the bat's diameter, at its fattest part, cannot exceed 2.75 inches. A major-league fast ball can approach 100 miles an hour, which means that the distance from the pitcher's hand to home plate (less than 60 feet, since the ball is released in front of the rubber) is covered in something less than half a second.

To hit the ball, of course, the batter must begin swinging his bat before the ball arrives. In other words, he must decide on the basis of the first portion of the pitch's trajectory what its final path will be, and he has approximately one-quarter of one second in which to make this decision. Then he must start the bat, judge height, lateral placement and velocity, adjust the swing, and make contact no more than a quarter of an inch above or below the center of the ball. And while doing all this, he must keep his body from flinching if the ball seems to be coming too close.

Put that way, hitting seems impossible. It would be impossible if it were a conscious process. By and large, it is a trained reflex, the product of hundreds of thousands of swings taken from childhood on. But it is easy to see why the pitcher has so big an advantage, and why outstanding batters are so few, and why even the greatest of all never succeeded in hitting safely as much as 40 percent of the time. And that's why, at major-league levels, batting ability is considered an inborn gift.

"No batting coach," says Harry Walker, one of the best and most studious of all batting coaches, "can do anything to make a man a better hitter than he is. He may, once in a while, teach a man to overcome some basic flaw in his technique, a flaw which had been robbing him of the benefits of his natural ability. Mostly, though, all the coach can do is observe a man when he's hitting well, spot what he's doing differently when he's not hitting well, and get him back to his own correct groove as quickly as possible."

And why does a hitter lose his "groove"? There may be any variety of reasons, but the basic one brings us right back to the underlying fear. If he never had to worry about avoiding a close pitch, he would simply find his best spot (close enough to the plate to have the fattest part of the bat cover the width of the strike zone, with his feet firmly planted) and depend on a grooved swing to do the work. This is what a basketball player does on the free-throw line, or a golfer in addressing the ball. But the pitcher makes sure he does have to worry, so the batter can't dig his spikes in too firmly: he must remain ready to dodge.

Each time up, and often after each pitch, the batter must find his "right" spot all over again—not only the right spot for his feet, but for his whole body position. It is easy to lose the rhythm of one's own best swing in such circumstances, especially since being ready to dodge can be a mental distraction as well. And it doesn't matter much whether the pitch comes close unintentionally (if the pitcher is wild) or intentionally. The result is the same, and the batter must be "ready."

"The legs go first." That's one of the most universal sports clichés. Obviously, it does not apply to hitters. What goes first, as a man ages, is the hair-trigger reflex needed to control the bat properly—and, at just about the same time, the *confidence* in one's dodging reflex. Most players would never admit it, and some perhaps don't even realize it, but when a man reaches a certain age (or a certain state of satisfaction), the fear he originally conquered comes back. He becomes afraid, not (as the fans and writers assume) that he won't be able to move the bat quickly enough to hit the good pitch, but that he won't be able to move himself quickly enough to get out of the way of the bad pitch.

And this is what happens when teams get "complacent," or "tired," or in any other way lose the fine edge of highest motivation. It shows up in poor hitting. Any decrease in concentration not only makes a batter susceptible to being fooled, tactically; it loosens a little bit of the perpetual control on the fear. The defensive reflex breaks through. The head turns; the rear end moves backward; the arms hesitate; the step forward is unsure. These things may happen to an infinitesimal degree—but that's all it takes to turn a line drive into a pop-up or a foul.

Traditionally, fans think of a team as "fighting back" when it scores in the late innings to come from behind—and this vague terminology is precisely correct. That's exactly what it takes to score: added determination to stand up to the plate, with maximum concentration and minimum defensiveness.

So hitting is a tricky mechanical problem. Psychologically, it requires nerve and concentration. Is there a third basic factor? Yes indeed—luck.

It is unfashionable to talk about luck in baseball. To losers, it implies alibi; to winners, it detracts from self-esteem; to spectators and strategists, luck is an unwelcome intrusion into the illusion of an ordered universe and spoils the second-guesser's sensation of omnipotence. And to all those involved in baseball as a business—players, managers, executives—it is a wise policy to ignore luck, good and bad, in their own thinking. Their concern is always with next time—the next inning, the next game, the next season, the next pitch. To dwell on the chance factor in what has already happened undermines the will and disciplined thinking; in planning ahead, one must, by definition, exclude luck from his calculations.

Nevertheless, the reality is that luck plays an important role in almost every game. It could not be otherwise with round bats, round balls, and fields full of pebbles, ruts, clumps of grass, and odd-shaped boundary walls. Baseballs *do* take funny bounces; a ball hit weakly may drop between fielders who were properly placed; a ball may land fair or foul by a fraction of an inch; a roller may be beaten out for a hit; and the hardest possible line drive may go right into a fielder's glove instead of a foot to either side.

With these general observations out of the way, let's come to grips with the more specific aspects of hitting, as it occupies the minds of thousands of hard-thinking professionals and their eager followers.

The main concern of every hitter (and, of course, pitcher) is the strike zone. According to the rules, this is the portion of space directly above home plate (which is 17 inches wide) and bounded by the levels of the batter's knees and armpits "when he is in his natural stance."

Actually, that's a pretty flexible area. It differs with the height, and the degree of crouch, of every batter. It also varies, although it's not supposed to, with many umpires. But it is definite enough to work with, and it is the strike zone—his own strike zone—that each hitter must come to know. Its evolution is the key to its importance. Trial and error, in the early years, delineated which pitches could be hit solidly. If the batter has to reach out too far, or step away from a close pitch, or reach too high or too low with the bat, he doesn't have "a fair chance" to hit the ball with any degree of power. If it is in this "fair-chance" zone and the batter lets it go, he is penalized by a called strike; if it is outside it, he doesn't have to swing and the pitcher is penalized by a "ball," or one-fourth of a base on balls.

Anytime a batter swings at a ball outside the strike zone, he is hurting himself in three ways: he accepts a physical disadvantage, he saves the pitcher from an unfavorable count, and he weakens the accuracy of his own future responses to balls and strikes.

Hang around managers, and you'll hear the following observations over and over, in a variety of phrasings:

"If only he'd stop trying to kill the ball!"

"When he gets to know the strike zone—"

"If he'd go with the pitch once in a while, instead of trying to pull everything—"

These are three of the cardinal sins from a coaching or observing point of view: swinging too hard, swinging at bad pitches, and refusing to hit an outside pitch to the opposite field. As a general principle, major-league hitters are expected to avoid them (although there are plenty of specific exceptions, certain occasions when it is all right or even desirable to violate each of the three precepts).

Listen to individual hitters, and you'll hear a different set of preoccupations:

"I've been in a slump—I'm pressing."

"I don't feel comfortable up there."

"Since I opened up my stance, I pick up the ball better."

"I'm getting good wood on the ball."

The hitters seem more concerned with the mechanics of hitting the ball squarely than with intent and judgment stressed by managers. But this impression is only partly correct. It is true that the individual ball player thinks, and talks, more about the mechanics than the manager does, because each individual's mechanical problems are personal and peculiar. If he is a good ball player, however, he devotes a lot of thought to the intent-and-judgment business, too. Of course, thinking is a long way from doing, and many times the batter who knows perfectly well that he shouldn't swing at a bad pitch still finds himself unable to avoid doing it. In general, though, as long as a hitter smacks the ball with satisfying solidity a good proportion of the time, he feels content; a manager, on the other hand, may be dissatisfied with a player who is hitting the ball squarely but doing so on borrowed time because of the faults he is committing.

When coaching, the teacher—it may be the manager, or a special coach, or one player helping another—deals with a much finer collection of technicalities:

"You're jerking your head."

"You're overstriding."

"Your hands are being held too low."

"You're dropping your elbow."

"You're locking your hips."

These are specific prescriptions for specific problems of specific batters. No two men swing the bat exactly the same way. Each athlete has slightly different body proportions, slightly different relative strengths in various muscles, different eyesight, different rhythm, different lifelong experiences, and different habits.

In the final analysis, again, batting is a conditioned reflex, built up over tens of thousands of repetitions against a certain level of pitching. To begin with, a natural gift must exist, in the form of that special eye-to-arms-and-hands coordination that is rare. Practice—repetition—develops this ability to a degree high enough, in a few hundred men, to get the opportunity to play in the majors at all.

Only then comes the real test: hitting in competition against the pitchers who have made a profession of foiling that reflex.

It is clear, therefore, that the mechanical side of hitting is largely habit: "good" habits acquired by practice, and "bad" habits slipped into unconsciously through fatigue, injury, carelessness, laziness, eagerness, complacency, worry, or experimentation. And it follows that the key psychological factor in success at bat boils down to confidence. The batter must have complete faith in his reflexes, in his ability to swing the bat exactly where and when he wants to, in his ability to hit *this* pitcher *this* time up. Only when he is convinced of these things emotionally can his conscious mind be free enough to concentrate on the mental problem of when and where to swing; and only then can he get the proper balance of tension and relaxation that allows the trained reflexes to move muscles by themselves.

One of Yogi Berra's most quoted remarks contains, simultaneously, the purest truth and the most misleading idea. Bill Dickey, one of Yogi's early coaches, tried to impress the young Yankee with the importance of thinking about what he was going to do at bat.

Yogi, always a malleable character, tried it, and popped up.

"Aarghh," he declared in disgust, "how kin ya t'ink an' hit atta same time?"

In one sense, Yogi was absolutely right. You can't. No rapid, reflexive action can be performed consciously. If you play the piano, just try thinking consciously about the next note, and the one after: it can't be done. The hands, once trained in a particular piece, go by themselves, and they stumble if thought intrudes. Or try reading a book one letter at a time and see how far you get. It's the same with hitting: you can't think *about hitting*—that is, about how you swing the bat, where it is to meet the ball, just how you will stride— while you're doing it in competition. You can, and should, remind yourself of little corrective details *just before*, and in practice, but not while doing it.

In another sense, though, a major-league hitter *must* think if he is to hit safely with any regularity. He must think about what the pitcher is likely to do, what the situation is in the inning and in the game, and what he wants to accomplish in this time at bat. In other words, he must have an *idea*, a positive approach to the immediate problem. When a hitter is simply hoping to avoid making an out—and that happens a lot—he is being "defensive." Good hitters are seldom on the defensive in this way.

Yogi, of course, could and did do this kind of thinking with the best of them; he simply didn't consider it "thinking." In his case, mental reflexes were as thoroughly attuned to baseball as his remarkable physical reflexes. He couldn't tell you how he knew what was right—but he knew, and his record reflected it.

But, if hitters have to think, *what* do they think? Do they say to themselves, Gee whiz, the score is tied and there are three men on—I gotta get a hit and win the game? Do they say, I'm gonna hit a homer into the third deck? Do they say, I see the shortstop is one step too near second, so I'll poke a single just out of his reach?

Not really—or, at least, not very often.

They think the following things, or they should, starting when they reach the on-deck circle:

1. What is this pitcher's best stuff, and what is his best *today?*
2. What sequence of pitches has he gotten me out with in the past?
3. Knowing my weaknesses—which he does—how does he usually try to exploit them with his particular equipment?
4. Which of his deliveries have been behaving properly the last couple of innings, and which haven't?
5. What is the situation in the game and what do I want to accomplish?
6. What is there about this ball park and this day—dimensions, wind strength and direction, visibility—that should affect my intentions?
7. What pitch do I *want* to hit?

That's not an all-inclusive list, but it will do. Let's elaborate.

Unless a pitcher is a newcomer, there is no excuse for an

experienced batter to be unfamiliar with the pitcher's equipment. The batter knows, from past experience, whether this opponent's basic strength is speed, or breaking pitches, or a combination; how well this pitcher usually changes speed on various deliveries; how reliable his control is; and whether he uses any of the trick pitches, like knucklers or screwballs. The batter should also be able to judge how well any single portion of that pitcher's repertoire is functioning in this particular game.

The second point is equally universal. A batter must be able to remember exactly what this pitcher did to him the last time they met, whether it was in an earlier inning of the same game or a month before. The pitcher (with the help of his catcher, his manager, and his coach) most certainly remembers it. He knows exactly how he got this batter out whenever he did get him out. The batter must be alert to the same information, so that if a recognizable pattern develops he can catch it—or so that he can draw intelligent conclusions from any variation of it.

Knowing his own weakness, the batter knows what he has to protect against. That every batter has a weakness is one of baseball's dogmas. The most general categories are "high-ball hitters" and "low-ball hitters"; almost every player will hit one better than the other, and experienced baseball men can spot which is which by watching even a few swings. But it gets broken down much finer than that: some men have more trouble with inside pitches, some with outside pitches; some can hit fast balls better than slow pitches, others the other way around; various kinds of curve balls bother some more than they bother other players, and all these factors can be combined. For instance, a batter may have trouble with an inside fast ball but not with an inside curve, but be able to murder a fast ball over the plate or away while acting relatively helpless when confronted with a curve that catches the outside corner.

Combining his knowledge of what the pitcher has available,

how it has been behaving most recently (particularly late in a game, when a pitcher may tire), how he likes to work on the batter's weakness, and how the pitcher has given him trouble in the past, the batter is in a position to make some reasonable estimate of what pitches will be thrown to him on this time at bat. Having arrived at his reasonable estimate, the batter must apply it to his own needs. Most important is the tactical situation at the time.

In general, a batter's duties are:

1. Avoid striking out—because this is a dead loss to the offense, especially if there is anyone on base. Once the ball is hit, however weakly, it has at least a slight chance of falling safely, taking a bad bounce, or being misplayed. For this reason, batters will usually cut down on their swing—not swing as hard—after the count has reached two strikes. The harder one swings, the more chance of missing the ball. With two strikes, the batter concentrates on "getting a piece of the ball" on any pitch that looks like a possible strike. Even a foul will preserve the batter's life.

2. If there is anyone on base, advance the runner. This is a primary rule of team play, often unappreciated even by knowledgeable baseball fans and ignored by selfish players. Of course, a base hit would advance the runner, but it's not an all-or-nothing proposition. No manager can expect even his best hitter to hit safely 40 percent of the time—but he does expect everyone to try to move the runner along 90 percent of the time.

This can be accomplished in various ways, some of which are the manager's prerogative. If he wants a sacrifice bunt, he'll signal the batter. If he wants a hit-and-run play (with the runner breaking for the next base and the batter committed to trying to get his bat on the pitch wherever it is, and to try to poke it through the infield if possible), he'll call the play from the bench.

Certain situations, however, are standard, and every batter

is supposed to know them without special instructions. If there is a runner on third with less than two out, the batter's job is to get him home by hitting a deep enough fly. If there is a runner on second with nobody out, the batter is supposed to produce at least a grounder to the right side of the infield, so that the runner can get to third with only one out. (This particular situation is really an uncredited sacrifice, and the best team players often give up their chance for a hit by making sure they make this sort of out. It doesn't show in the statistics, but managers remember and appreciate it.) If there's a runner on first, it is also better to hit the ball to the right side, because it's harder to start a double play from there, but it is better still not to hit a grounder at all.

3. If there's nobody on, get on. This is the situation, usually, in which "a walk is as good as a hit." Especially with nobody or one out, in a close game, the main idea is to get an attack started. Once there's a base runner, the pitcher and defense are confronted by new problems. With nobody on, the batter can be more choosy about taking pitches right on the borderline of the strike zone, or of his own weakness, than he can when there is an obligation to move a runner along. With a man on second and nobody out, for instance, a walk most definitely is not as good as a hit; it creates a double-play possibility with the next batter, without moving the potential run any closer to home. In that case a ground out, which moved the runner to third, from where he could score on an out or a wild pitch or an error, would be more valuable to the team than a walk—although less valuable to the batter's personal record. And, with nobody on base, the batter can be more selective about "getting his pitch to hit." His attention, however, is on hitting the ball sharply rather than setting tape-measure distance records. He wants a single or a double or a walk, to start something.

4. If the game situation demands or allows, go for distance. With two out, usually, a hitter who has even a moderate

amount of power is more justified in swinging for the fences than at other times. With two out, it would take three consecutive singles to score a run, and the chances are as much against that as they are against a 30-homer-a-year man hitting one out of the park.

More specifically, the score, inning, and identity of the batter have a lot to do with justifying a big swing, even after two strikes. Suppose we are back in old Yankee Stadium, under the old rules, the Yankees are losing, 3-2, in the home half of the ninth, and Graig Nettles is at bat with two out and nobody on. Let's say the next batter is Gene Michael, and the one after that is the pitcher, and the good pinch hitters have been used up. Furthermore, let's assume the opposing pitcher is a right-hander, and the left-handed Nettles always has a good shot at the accessible right-field stands. Obviously, the pitcher will do all he can to prevent Nettles from hitting a homer that will tie the score—but for Nettles and the Yankees, it's worth the attempt, even if it means swinging at a pitch that in other circumstances would be taken for a ball. In fact, if Nettles does accept a walk on a reachable pitch at this time, he is evading responsibility, because the chances of Michael and a weak pitch hitter getting him around are also very small.

This kind of thing comes up all the time for the better hitters. Only a limited number of men, on every team, are consistent power hitters. Late in a game, with the score close, they must try to cash in on their special ability while they have the chance, rather than leave the decision to less talented hitters who follow them.

A prime example—actual, not hypothetical—was Ted Williams. One of the greatest of all batters, this left-handed slugger was usually confronted by a lopsided defensive alignment (called the "Boudreau Shift" when Lou Boudreau, managing Cleveland, made it popular, but now a standard procedure against certain power hitters). This is an extreme shift toward the right-field foul line, with the second baseman playing back in short right, the right fielder close to the foul line, the center fielder in deep right-center, the shortstop on the second-base side of second, and the third baseman halfway between second and third.

It was an invitation to Williams to poke the ball to the left side for an almost certain single. Most of the time, Williams refused to accept it, and kept swinging for the right-field fence. He was often criticized for this by all segments of base-ball society from bleacher fan through Ty Cobb, and un-doubtedly he did act a bit stubbornly at times. But his argu-ment made sense, too: after all, one reason for the shift was that the defense was more afraid of a homer than a single, and by taking the single, Williams would be playing the defense's game. He might be robbed of some hits to right if he hit his normal way, but he would also hit at least some homers; if he went to the left, he wouldn't hit any homers. A homer could win a game better than a single—and if the hitter were as good as Williams was, it was worth the try.

On the other hand, Williams was also criticized for taking walks on border-line pitches when one of his extra-base hits could have done more good. In isolated strategic situations, this criticism was justified—but Williams' attitude sheds a lot of light on the nature of hitting, and is worth pondering. He insisted that "good habits" were the primary consideration for a hitter, and that the best habit was knowing exactly what the strike zone was and absolutely refusing to swing at any-thing outside it.

If you gave in once, Williams believed, and compromised swinging at a pitch just a little outside the strike zone, you would do it again, and then again at a pitch a little farther outside. You might hit some of those pitches safely, but you would be undermining your self-discipline and your reflexes, which were more important in the long run. You would eventually be seduced into swinging at bad pitches, and would be giving the pitchers a bigger target to throw at.

Williams, of course, was exceptional in all sorts of ways. The point is that the good hitter must make deliberate and intelligent decisions about what's needed, and try to carry them out. The situations that arise are not met by automatic, textbook-listed rules, but by trying to cope with all factors involved at that particular time.

All these decisions about the batter's intentions have to be tempered by the physical surroundings and weather conditions. In a big ball park, for instance, where it is harder to hit a home run, looking for the pitch that can be hit out of the park is self-defeating: pitchers love long, high flies if they have capable outfielders with plenty of room behind them. In a smaller park, or with a strong wind blowing straight out, free-swinging may be more profitable, and a pitcher aware of such handicaps may be worked for more walks. Far and away the most important thought of all, however, is: What pitch do I *want* to hit? This is where the artists are separated from the purposeless stick-wavers.

Just as every batter has a weakness, every batter—if he's in the majors—has a strength. And just as every batter is human, so is every pitcher. If a pitcher were able, every single time, to throw each pitch exactly where he wanted to, with the appropriate amount of force and spin, the batter would be out of business. Fortunately for baseball, no pitcher can be that consistent; sooner or later, the pitcher makes a mistake, physically if not mentally, but usually both.

Now: our hypothetical artistic hitter knows what he wants (let's say, "a ball I can pull," because it's late in the game and he has to try for an extra-base hit or even a homer). He knows that, in his case, this means any inside pitch above the waist, since he's pretty good at hitting curves as well as fast balls. He has a pretty good idea, by now, of how fast today's pitcher's fast ball is, and is geared to hit it; if the pitch turns out to be a curve, he'll have time to adjust. (If he set himself for a curve, on the other hand, a fast ball would catch him unprepared.) And he knows that this pitcher, in this game, has had trouble controlling his curve and has been relying on fast balls in the last few innings.

Our hypothetical hitter also knows that, ordinarily, this pitcher likes to throw him low-breaking balls, inside, a spot our hitter has trouble with. And the hitter, since he respects this pitcher, knows that the pitcher is just as aware as he is that the situation calls for a long hit.

The battle begins. The pitcher, despite past success, may not want to risk that unreliable curve; if he misses, and gets behind in the count, he will be in more danger when he has to make sure he throws strikes to avoid a walk. On the other hand, his fast ball may not have quite as much steam as it had earlier in the game.

From the hitter's point of view, then, the principles are:

Make sure you recognize the desired pitch (inside and above the belt) whenever it appears.

Avoid swinging at any other kind of pitch, even if it means taking two strikes.

If the count gets to two strikes, try to foul off possible strikes that are out of the desired area. (Only the real bat artist can try this; the rest must give in.)

All this time the pitcher is trying to keep the ball down and away. In doing so, he may miss the strike zone often enough to issue a walk—which isn't what the hitter wanted, but still useful. But he may also miss the other way: he may miss by throwing the ball into the zone the hitter has chosen. In that case, the hitter "got his pitch."

He still has to hit it—and a very large number of times, a hitter will pop up or ground out or even strike out on exactly the pitch he was looking for. That's the human element. And many a game-winning hit has been made off "a good pitch," one that was thrown just were the pitcher wanted, and one that the hitter ordinarily has trouble with. In fact, it's exactly this element of uncertainty that keeps baseball interesting. Nevertheless, the odds are in favor of the batter who "gets his pitch" to hit.

What if he doesn't get it? That's when he has to "give in" to the pitcher's skill, and to try to go with the pitch. If the pitcher, in our example, succeeds in making several good pitches low and away, the best the hitter can do is accept the fact and try to meet the ball, hoping to poke a single through the opposite side.

This question of "giving in" really lies at the heart of "getting one's pitch." No single time at bat exists in isolation. The same hitters face the same pitchers many times. The hitter who can hit the ball in several directions is more likely to find the pitches he wants than one who is always trying to do one thing. If a pitcher gets stung a few times by a single to left by the left-handed homerun slugger, he will try to do something about it—and, in the process, increase the slugger's chances of getting an inside pitch by accident or design. But if the slugger keeps trying to pull the outside pitch and, as a result, is hitting harmless flies to center, the pitcher can keep making a sucker out of him forever. So the batter's actions each time at bat affect his chances on subsequent turns.

Casey Stengel had his own way of expressing almost anything. On this subject—the unwillingness of many hitters to give up trying to hit homers off pitches that were not suitable for that—he used to say:

"They think they're bein' unlucky, but they'll be unlucky all their lives if they don't change."

And Hank Bauer, the right-handed bruiser who played for Stengel on the Yankees from 1949 through 1959 (on nine pennant winners in 11 years), learned the hard way. Yankee Stadium, of course, had an impossibly deep left center field. The left field foul line was only 301 feet long, but the angle it made with the stands was so wide that a point some 20 feet fair was 402 feet deep, and true left center ranged from 420 to 460 feet. Bauer could hit a ball hard and far, but if he got around on an inside pitch a little too much, it would go foul, and if he didn't pull the ball right down the foul line, he couldn't reach the stands. So pitchers would feed him nice, fat, appetizing-looking deliveries just out enough over the plate so that Hank couldn't pull too sharply. He'd hit the ball 410 feet or so, and the left fielder would catch it at an easy trot.

One day, after Hank had been a Yankee for seven years or so, he hit seven drives of 400 feet or more in one doubleheader. All were caught. After the games, he was sitting in front of his locker, shaking his head. A sympathetic newspaperman came by.

"Tough luck," said the reporter.

"How about that?" said Bauer, his hoarse voice a trifle hoarser than usual. "Seven of my best shots—seven. And not even a single."

"Well," the reporter (who had been indoctrinated by Stengel long ago) suggested politely, "can you draw a conclusion?"

Hank looked up, and started to smile slowly.

"Yeah," he said. "I know what you mean. Yeah. Maybe that's right."

Bauer was past his peak as a player when this happened, but the realization stayed with him. As a manager at Kansas City and Baltimore, he became an outspoken member of the Stop-Trying-To-Pull-Every-Pitch philosophy.

If it is so plain that hitting to all fields—going with a pitch—is advantageous, why do so many players fail to acquire the skill? After all, most players aren't idiots and their livelihood is at stake. There are three main reasons why players remain resistant: greed, insecurity, and difficulty. The last two reasons are, in all fairness, pretty good ones.

Greed is simple to explain: "Home-run hitters drive Cadillacs" is an irrefutable slogan. All of baseball's biggest money-makers (except pitchers)—Babe Ruth, Joe DiMaggio, Ted Williams, Willie Mays, Mickey Mantle, Stan Musial, Hank Aaron, and Richie Allen—were prolific home-run hitters. Home runs are hit, fundamentally, by pulling the ball, because a hitter's power is to the side he swings from, and fences are closer at the foul line. The trouble is, the ability to hit a lot of homers is a rare one. While it is true that those who can, "strike it rich," it is also true that those who try and can't, wind up with less lucrative careers than those who realize they must utilize their talents in more modest fashion. Since baseball players are not chosen for proficiency in freshman logic, the falsity of the mock syllogism "Home-run hitters drive Cadillacs; I want a Cadillac; therefore, I should try for homers" escapes many of them.

Even so great a slugger as Mantle, at the advanced age of 35, can be subject to this misplaced desire. About halfway through the 1966 season, Mickey went on a home-run spree. He hit eight home runs in a six-game swing through Boston and Washington, and was suddenly the hottest story in baseball.

The Yankees returned to their stadium, with its cozy right field, and played the Red Sox, the same team Mantle had slaughtered a week before in Boston. The same right-handed pitchers worked. But Mickey, now conscious of home-run heroism (and responding to its glory after a long period of injury-caused eclipse), started swinging for the fences deliberately. He tried to pull. He tried to hit it into the third deck. And he did nothing at all. He struck out six times in three games, popped up, got one opposite-field single. The Yankees lost three straight.

They went into the ninth inning of the fourth game of the series trailing, 2-0, about to lose their fourth in a row. But the Yankees rallied, tied the score, and had men on first and third with two out as Mantle came up.

Now it was a desperate situation for the team: the winning run was on third, and it didn't matter how it scored to end the losing streak. Any kind of hit would do it, but a long fly would be useless. All Mantle cared about was meeting the ball, poking it through the infield somehow, avoiding a strike-out at all costs.

Not concerned with distance or pulling the ball, Mickey belted it 12 rows deep into the right-field stands for a dramatic three-run homer. Having put aside home-run greed, he was able to swing naturally again—and got his homer.

Insecurity is a much more valid obstacle. Hitting is habit—reflex, groove, automatic reaction. Every player is wary of losing his timing, and therefore his confidence. Every player has a tremendous stake in doing things exactly the way he has always done them, because these have meant success. He got to the majors by hitting a certain way, and he is immensely reluctant to change any pattern as long as he continues to have a reasonable amount of success with it.

At this point, a question arises about degree of success. The manager constantly seeks improvement; the player tends to protect what he has. Hitting .280, he can be a regular. The manager thinks that, by making a few changes, that man might hit .300, but the hitter is more likely to feel that, in trying to make changes that feel unnatural or uncomfortable, he may drop to .250. In most professional athletes these days, the fear of a drop-off in record and earning power outweighs the hope of doing better.

And the thing that justifies the hitter's fear of change, in his own eyes and to a significant degree objectively, is the fact that it is not easy to change. With good intentions, and honest effort, a man may still fail to master the knack of hitting to all fields. Like power, this is a skill some men have naturally more than others. A man may have sufficient bat control to hit fairly well in his natural pattern, but not so much that he can also coordinate his actions for a more deliberate, less automatic way of hitting. So most major-league hitters, acknowledging the advantages of "going with the pitch," nevertheless fail to do it much of the time.

There's a slight relationship here to the subject of bunting. Everyone should be able to bunt, right? It's so simple: square around, face the pitcher, plant your feet, and just tap the ball out in front of the plate. (We're talking only about sacrifice bunts to advance runners, not surprise bunts to get on base.) Poor hitters above all, and especially pitchers, should be able to bunt. No single deficiency in baseball arouses as much indignation among intolerant old-timers as the inability to bunt.

Yet, a startling proportion of attempted sacrifice bunts fail. Why? Because today it is *not* easy to execute a bunt under game conditions. It's easy enough in practice, but not easy when the pitcher is throwing hard in an attempt to prevent exactly that, while the first baseman and third baseman tear in at top speed to field the ball. In the context of major-league baseball life, there is little opportunity to practice bunting under competitive conditions, and therefore, what is so simple in practice is difficult to carry out. Furthermore, in recent years, many fields consist of artificial turf, on which the ball moves quickly and far, and making the bunt soft enough becomes a new problem.

By now, another of baseball's unacceptable dirty words—like "luck"—is entering the picture. All we have said about hitting revolves around analyzing what the pitcher might do, and adjusting the batter's desires to the pitcher's actions. The word taking form is "guessing."

A "guess hitter," in baseball society, is one to be sneered at. But, obviously, all hitters are "guessing" all the time. The distinction is one of definition. To "guess" in one sense is fatal to good hitting—in the sense that a hitter says, I've got my mind made up that this next pitch is going to be a fast ball. And it is that sort of guessing that players have in mind when they criticize someone else for being a "guess hitter," or deny being one themselves.

In another sense, however, the "educated guess" is the basis of good hitting. Here the batter says to himself, For such-and-such a set of reasons, he might throw me a fast ball now, and if he does, I'm ready to hit it. In the first case, the hitter mentally committed himself to something that may not happen; in the second, he alerted himself for one thing but remained ready to cope with anything else that may happen.

So far, we have ignored one of the most obvious features of hitting—the fact that some players bat right-handed and some bat left-handed.

Batting left-handed is a major advantage. For one thing, the left-handed batter, at the end of his swing, is two steps closer to first base and moving in the right direction. The right-handed batter ends his swing with his body weight toward third. He must check his momentum and set off across home plate toward first. These two steps make a great deal of difference in beating out infield hits and in avoiding the second half of what would be a double play.

For another thing, most pitchers—about 75 percent of them in the majors—are right-handed, and it is a fundamental law of baseball that left-handed batters have a better shot at right-handed pitchers, and that right-handed batters have a better crack at left-handed pitchers. This is one popular theory that is absolutely true (as a generality, that is, with plenty of significant exceptions). There are two reasons why these lefty-righty opposites work in favor of the hitter: sight and spin.

Consider the right-handed batter facing a lefty. The arm delivering the ball is coming from the first-base side of the mound, and is in a field of vision that requires less turning of the head. As the ball approaches (imagine a straight fast ball), it appears to move toward the hitter laterally (as well as toward him from mound to plate). It is easier for a right-hander to judge the trajectory of such a pitch than one thrown from the third-base side of the mound. In that case, the ball's motion in the horizontal plane seems to be *away* from the batter, and the head must turn slightly to keep the ball in focus. In addition, the natural spin imparted to a baseball makes it tend to curve away from the side it was thrown from. A "normal" curve thrown by a right-hander breaks away from a right-handed batter, and toward a left-hander—and vice versa. Exceptions are numerous, because of individual styles and pitches given reverse spin, but that's a subject for the next chapter. The point is, left-handed hitters do have an advantage.

But, in that case, why doesn't everyone hit left-handed? Many players who throw right-handed bat left-handed, so it doesn't seem to be that closely tied to natural left-handedness. And why aren't all left-handed hitters better than right-handed hitters?

Here, again, human factors come into play. Most right-handed people automatically start to bat right-handed, and once the habits become set, they are too hard to change, especially since these habits begin in childhood. And the left-handers have some disadvantages, too, because of the prevalence of right-handers.

A right-handed hitter, to reach the majors at all, *must* learn to do reasonably well against right-handed pitchers. If he didn't, his record would be too poor. Then, when he faces a left-hander about one-fourth of the time, the unfamiliarity of the confrontation is compensated for by the natural advantages of righty-lefty oppositeness.

The left-handed batter faces the reverse problem. He has had the advantage, most of the time, of facing "opposite" pitchers. When he has to bat against a lefty, it is both difficult *and* relatively unfamiliar. And that's why, traditionally, left-handed batters have more trouble with left-handed pitchers than righties do with righties.

But then, it should be obvious, the greatest thing in the world must be to be a switch-hitter, like Mickey Mantle. If a man can hit from both sides of the plate, the confrontation with the pitcher is *always* in his favor. Or so it would seem. It turns out, though, that things aren't exactly what they seem. This point was made by Tom Tresh, one of the most successful of the young switch-hitters who blossomed in the wake of Mantle's example.

"It's an edge," Tresh explains, "but not as big an edge as you'd think. Hitting is rhythm, finding a groove, all that stuff. When you are a switch-hitter, you have two totally distinct batting styles. Something can go wrong with either one, independently of the other. And the constant changing may keep you from getting best set in either one. Now, every switch-hitter is better one way than the other. It's hard to say exactly how much better or worse a man might have done if he had concentrated all his life on his stronger side."

There's little incentive, of course, for a natural left-hander to learn to bat righty, since the left-handed hitter has the advantages already noted. Switch-hitters, then, are invariably natural right-handers who have learned to hit lefty also, and it is common practice to try to turn a weak-hitting but fast-running right-handed man into a switch-hitter. (It seldom works, but when it does, it saves a career—as it did for Maury Wills.)

Another long-accepted tenet of baseball lore is that the curve ball is the hardest pitch to hit. Traditionally, the minors are full of players who never made it in the majors because "they couldn't hit a curve." A surprising number of contemporary experts—that is, expert hitters—disagree with this idea. Red Schoendienst, who was one of the most skillful hitters of his day and subsequently manager of the St. Louis Cardinals, put it this way:

"The hardest pitch to hit is a fast ball, and anyone who doesn't realize that is kidding himself. I mean, of course, a real good fast ball. And it's hardest to hit for the simplest of reasons: you have the least time to react. A curve ball travels slower. You can learn to time and plot its course, and to adjust. But if the good fast ball is fast enough to keep you from getting all the way around on it, there's nothing you can do.

"What this means is that a hitter has to *set* himself for the pitcher's best fast ball. It may be true that if the pitcher threw nothing but fast balls in succession, the hitter might eventually time up to it—or the pitcher would get tired—but in practice that doesn't happen. The hitter, then, has to be ready to hit the fastest pitch that pitcher can throw.

"It is only then, working *off* the fast ball, that the curve becomes so hard to hit. It's not the curve itself, it's the contrast, in speed and direction, between the curve and the fast ball you have to be set for. It's when a pitcher mixes things up properly that a hitter finds it so hard to hit a curve ball. But if the fast ball isn't very fast, or if you know the curve is coming, the curve isn't that hard to hit."

The truth, then, is once again hidden by a common expression that contains a grain of it. It's true that many big-league hitters never learn to hit a curve—*while being set for a fast ball*. It's because they can't give up some degree of being set for the fast ball that the curve puts them out of business.

But now we are inching over into the pitcher's area of operation: the different deliveries, what they do, how they are used, and so forth. Before going on to that, we have to consider one final aspect of the hitter's viewpoint, one to which we will return in our discussion of pitching. This is the matter of the pitcher's "motion."

A hitter does not—cannot—see the ball approach in isolation, like some object on a radarscope. He sees it in a context: a pitcher winds up, goes through a complicated motion, and out of this motion the ball suddenly appears. All this, in turn, happens against a background that may or may not be a solid dark color. The hitter must react to the *totality* of windup, delivery, background, and trajectory, and this varies from pitcher to pitcher, from place to place. That is why a pitching machine has only limited usefulness in batting practice. It can reproduce, to any desired degree, the *actual* path of the ball as thrown by a pitcher, but it can't give the hitter any practice at all in identifying this actual path out of the welter of arm and leg motions produced by a live pitcher in a competitive game.

And, after all, that's the fellow who starts and controls the game—the pitcher.

2

- Pitching is 70 percent of baseball.

> Connie Mack, John McGraw, Branch
> Rickey, and 1,001 other baseball geniuses

- I make my living off the hungriness of the hitter.

> Lew Burdette, 1961

- I became a good pitcher when I stopped trying to make them miss the ball and started trying to make them hit it.

> Sandy Koufax, 1965

The Other 75 Percent— Pitching

Pitching is 75 percent of baseball—or 70 percent, or 90, or any other high number that pops into the mind of the speaker. The more popular current phrase, "pitching is the name of the game," reflects the fact that it is again more fashionable to speak in metaphors since high-powered computers have usurped the illusion of accuracy baseball statistics used to supply.

In any case, there is no disagreement about the point itself: pitching is the most important element in the game. As a rule, the team with better pitching wins the game, and the team with the better pitching staff wins the pennant, while many a heavy-hitting lineup winds up nowhere because its pitching is poor.

This may be obscured by the glamor of day-in, day-out slugging. Many outstanding teams, like the Yankees of 1927, 1936, and a dozen other winning years, had awesome power but they also had consistently fine pitching, and it was the combination that made them so great. On the other hand, teams like the 1930 Phillies (who had eight .300 hitters and finished eighth) and the 1947 Giants (who broke all home-run records and finished fourth) show how fruitless run-making can be if the pitching isn't there for the defensive half of the inning. Yet the Dodgers of 1963, 1965, and 1966 were able to win pennants with little else than superb pitching.

Such examples could be multiplied indefinitely.

Walter Alston, who managed the Dodgers to their victories, sums it up as well as anyone. "When you get consistently good pitching," he says, "you keep the score low, and you have a chance in every game. You can try to use all the ways there are to score a run, and benefit from any error or lucky break. You're never out of the game. But if your own pitching gives up a lot of runs, there will be lots of times when you're out of business early, where the only way to get back is with a lot of slugging of your own. So it's pretty hard to be lucky when your pitching is bad."

An axiom goes hand in hand with this truism: good pitchers usually stop good hitters, rather than the other way around. The good hitters fatten up on the mediocre pitchers, but the best pitchers often compile spectacular records against the best hitters. It isn't hard to see why all this should be so. It's an inherent condition of baseball, tactically and mathematically.

Tactically, the pitcher is the most important man on the ball field because he is, essentially, the aggressor. In the truest sense, he is the "offense," because he puts the ball in play and does so according to his intentions and ability. He has the initiative: he knows where he's going to throw the ball (provided his skill doesn't fail him) exactly when and how. His is the deliberate, calculated act, and the batter must react to it. In this sense, it is the batter who is on the defensive side of the action until and unless he hits the ball; only then does the team at bat become the attacker.

Mathematically, it's cut and dried. According to the rules, you can't win a game unless you get 27 men out; you *can* win by scoring only one run. The defensive side of baseball, therefore, requires great consistency: nine times a game, you must get three outs in an inning. The offensive side can, and almost always does, work in fits and starts. A lucky hit, one defensive lapse, one ball tagged just right, can produce one or more runs, and any one run can win a game; but a lucky bounce, a spectacular catch, or other exceptional defensive occurrence is only $\frac{1}{27}$th of the work needed—by definition—to complete a winning game.

That's what a pitcher thinks about—getting men out.

Let's examine some of his premises:

First, under major-league conditions, he accepts the fact that he cannot strike out every hitter. Therefore, the outs will have to be recorded by his fielders. Therefore, if he can prevent each hitter from hitting the ball too solidly, his fielders will have a chance to make the play in the vast majority of cases. The pitcher's job, then, is to do whatever he can to keep the batter from hitting the ball solidly.

How can he do this? The whole immense technique of pitching deals with this question, and we'll come back to it in detail a little further on. Suffice it to say that a pitcher can employ time (by varying the speed of his deliveries), space (by pitching high, low, inside, outside), trajectory (by making the ball curve or otherwise change direction on the way to the plate), deception (by making the hitter expect one thing while doing another), knowledge (of hitters' weaknesses and his own assets), and strategy (by limiting the batter's choice in particular situations, apart from deception).

A second premise is that pitching, physically, is an unnatural act. Hundreds of millions of years of human evolution did nothing to prepare the structure of the arm for the strain of 150 maximum-effort throwing motions in the space of a couple of hours. There are those who claim that any overhand throwing motion is contrary to nature; but whether it is or not, to use it as often and as hard as pitching requires is an abuse of normal body function. After all, the arm hangs down from the shoulder, the elbow joint turns in, and so many pitching motions require exertion in the opposite directions. All in all, pitching sets up tremendous strains in muscles, ligaments, tendons, joints, and even certain pieces of bone.

The consequence of this physical fact is that a pitcher must take care of his arm in some special fashion. He can work only so often (usually no more than once in four days, if he is a starter). He needs a trainer's assistance, in some form of rubdown or muscle-stretching massage, before he pitches and often afterward. He must be able to withstand a certain amount of inevitable pain without having his concentration suffer. He must stay in good shape in general because his whole body is involved in the rhythmic pitching motion, and because he must not succumb to fatigue late in a game. He must, in short, keep his arm physically sound in order to put into effect his knowledge of how to keep hitters from connecting.

It must seem confusing, in the light of this, to read about the pitching heroes of the nineteenth century, who posted won-lost records like 60-12 (Hoss Radbourne, in 1884) and regularly won more than 30 games. The mystery disappears, however, when one realizes how different the conditions were. Until 1884, overhand pitching wasn't even permitted; after that, until about the time of World War I, it was customary to use one baseball until it was lost, no matter how scarred or soft it became. In this dead-ball era, a complete game required perhaps half the number of pitches required today. And with little danger of a home run by any but the very best batters, pitchers didn't have to bear down as hard on every pitch, the way they do today. In short, they pitched more often because they didn't work as hard when they worked.

These physical limitations have tactical consequences. The full range of weapons available in theory is never at the disposal of any one pitcher. In individual cases, attempts to use the wrong type of delivery may hurt the arm, and very often minor injury or fatigue will prevent even a healthy pitcher from using a particular delivery as often as he would like that particular day. And, of course, the necessity for sufficient warm-up and proper rest determine every manager's thinking about who is to pitch and when.

Sandy Koufax is an example of a pitcher who ran into the first type of problem, while at the height of his powers. In 1963 and 1964, he developed a sidearm curve to use to left-handed hitters, and it gave his already overstocked arsenal an extra, especially unkind, torture weapon. But he found that using it made his elbow sore. It was only later that his arthritic condition was diagnosed, and it was clear that the sidearm pitch would have to be dropped permanently. This limited him so much that he could win only 53 games in the next two seasons —which is merely the largest number of victories posted in consecutive years by any National League left-hander in the modern era.

Sandy's teammate Maury Wills tells a story in his nightclub act that illustrates the kind of problem rest and warm-up cause for managers.

The Dodgers, Wills says, were playing a vital four-game series in San Francisco in August of 1965. The Dodger bullpen was slightly overworked and had to be stretched through the four-game set. Manager Walt Alston, therefore, was reluctant to order a reliever up any sooner than necessary.

In the fifth, Claude Osteen, the Dodger starter, lost his stuff abruptly, and Alston had to wave in Bob Miller.

"Look, Maury," Alston told Wills at the conference at the mound. "We need some extra time for Miller to warm up. When he gets here and takes his regular warm-up pitches, you go back to short, and then pretend you've got something in your eye. Make it good, really put on an act. Then, while we're trying to fix your eye, Miller can keep throwing."

It was a flawless plan, and Wills gave a great performance.

"I'm blinking, and staggering, and moaning," is the way Wills describes it. "The umpire is convinced, and doing his best to help. The trainer is working on me. Other players are gathering around. My act is so good that Miller has time not only to get warmed up but to get tired. And what does Miller actually do? Instead of warming up, he comes over with a towel to help them get something out of my eye!"

A third premise is that a pitcher must have control—and "control" is a tricky word. There are two kinds of control: one is the ability to throw strikes, to make every variety of pitch in that pitcher's repertoire go through the strike zone with great dependability (let's say, four out of five, or nine out of ten times). This kind of control—the broad-scale control—is an absolute must for a major-league pitcher. On the days he doesn't have it, there's nothing he can do.

The other kind of control is pinpoint control, the ability to throw each pitch not merely over the plate but to a very specific spot, just so high, just so much inside or outside, and at just exactly the desired speed. This is a much rarer accomplishment, and the pitchers who have it are the true maestros of their trade.

It is obvious enough why strike-zone control is essential and pinpoint control a blessing. Unless the pitcher can deliver the ball exactly where and how he wants to, his mental success in fooling the hitter is wasted.

The fourth basic premise of pitching is "stuff." The pitcher must be able to throw the ball hard enough to make reaction time a problem for the batter. A pitch perfectly placed, but thrown so softly that the hitter can readjust his sights, will be socked just as hard as if the hitter has guessed right in the first place. At the major-league level, there is a threshold of speed that must be maintained, and all talk of "slow" or "soft" or "junk" pitches refers to *relative* speed.

That's why, incidentally, slow-stuff pitchers are often effective. Hitters are geared to the average level of speed, a level that would catch most of us motionless, and a "slow" pitch (which would seem plenty fast if you or I were trying to hit it) is hard to adjust to. It requires a check on all those built-in reflexes it took years to set. But even these "slow" pitches can't be so slow that the batter gets a chance to check himself, and then start swinging again.

But with regular-speed pitches, the amount of stuff on them has to be sufficient. It's not enough to throw a curve or a fast ball to the right spot; it has to be a curve ball that really breaks, not gently bends, and a fast ball that has something on it. Otherwise, the correct intentions are nullified by physical failure.

Perhaps the most common of all pitching problems is the tendency, more often subconscious than conscious, to "ease up" or "aim the ball" in an effort to improve control. To "take something off it" as a deliberate change of speeds is one thing; to do it in an attempt to get a strike, or pitch to a particular spot, can lead to disaster. And it happens all the time, even to the best pitchers occasionally.

Our fifth and final pitching premise is the subject of "motion," touched on at the end of the chapter on hitting. The ball does not come toward the plate as an isolated object. The pitcher's windup, his kick, his arm motion, and the background all form part of the picture. Now, to the pitcher the motion has a positive and negative importance. On the positive side, it can be used to increase the deceptiveness of his delivery, by hiding the ball as long as possible, by distraction, and by intensifying some unusual angle of the trajectory (like a side-arm pitch thrown by a right-hander to a right-handed batter). On the negative side, a motion that is noticeably different for different types of pitches will tip off the alert opponent as to which pitch is coming.

Pitchers strive, therefore, to develop identical motions from which to throw all their basic deliveries, and to find a motion that strikes the best balance between their own comfort (which is the main consideration) and bewilderment of the batter.

Most pitchers whose repertoire is based on off-speed pitching —Stu Miller, Eddie Lopat, Jim Konstanty—rely on motion as much as on the actual pitch to fool the hitter. But it must be stressed, again, that even such pitchers have fairly respectable fast balls, fast enough to catch a hitter flat-footed when mixed in properly with the softer stuff.

Back in the 1950s, when New York still had three teams, Stu Miller worked for the Giants. They occupied the Polo Grounds, which had the shortest walls in the majors along the foul lines. This was early in Stu's career, and much was being made of his three speeds: "Slow, slower, slowest." Bill Roeder, a baseball writer for the then *World-Telegram and Sun*, decided he'd like to do a first-person story about how it felt to bat against Miller.

Roeder went to the manager, Bill Rigney, for permission.

"Nothing doing," said Rigney. "I can't afford to risk it."

Roeder, a good baseball man, could understand Rigney's reluctance.

"Look, I'm a young guy and I'm pretty agile," said Roeder. "I can get out of the way if he comes close, and you know he won't anyhow. Besides, we can fix it up so that my paper and I take full responsibility."

"It's not that," replied Rigney. "But what if you got lucky and hit one over that 257-foot fence? What happens to my pitcher then? How would he ever get his confidence back?"

Thus saved from possible psychological destruction by a solicitous manager, Miller went on to considerable success in both leagues over the next decade.

But there was a grain of truth to Rigney's apprehension. Miller's slow stuff, to an amateur, would not be a disturbing contrast but a handleable problem, and the fakes and twists of Miller's motion could not deceive someone who was not accustomed to reacting to ordinary motions. Of course, with his own fast ball, Miller could easily have overpowered a news-paperman, but if the experiment were performed in good faith, with Miller throwing easy, the kind of accident Rigney feared was not impossible.

Lopat, like Miller, promoted the idea that he was incredibly slow, but his real asset was a great variety of speeds with per-fectly placed curves. He could buzz one fairly hard, when he wanted to, and when he did—at a moment of his choosing—he looked like Walter Johnson just by contrast.

Almost all Lopat's pitching success came as a Yankee. When he was at the end of the line, however, he found himself pitching briefly for the Baltimore Orioles, whose manager was Paul Richards. Before managing Baltimore, Richards had man-aged Chicago White Sox teams that were repeatedly knocked out of contention by the Yankees, with Lopat's help. Richards, a proud Texan, had one point of pride above all others: his ability to teach pitching.

When Lopat arrived, Richards offered a suggestion.

"If you do this," said Richards, showing a certain grip and motion, "I'm sure it can help you."

"This?" asked Lopat. "I have that one here, here, here, and here," he said, rapidly displaying four different degrees of spin and arm location at the release of the ball. "What do you think I've been getting you out with all these years?"

Many years later, after Lopat had served as a manager and general manager and pitching coach and superscout himself, he once spoke of another dimension of truly artistic pitching.

"I could usually tell, by watching the hitter's reactions, how he would have hit a ball even if he didn't go through with the swing," he said. "You watch his legs, arms, body, eyes—every-thing. Sometimes, then, you may throw a pitch, outside the strike zone, just to watch his responses; it may tell you some-thing.

"Specifically, though, look at it this way. If you throw a fast ball and he fouls it off down the first base line (a right-handed hitter, I mean), you know he was a little late swinging at it. If he fouls it past third, you know he swung a little early. Now, if the thing you're doing is trying to prevent him from pulling the ball, you might try another one if you know he's been timing it late—if you've got that good a fast ball, of course —but you'd be absolutely crazy to try another one if he had just shown he was swinging at it too soon. So what he does with one pitch, or a series of pitches, can help you decide what to do with the next one."

The scientific element in pitching is considerably greater than the scientific element in hitting, according to our original definitions. The mechanics of pitching—grip, release of the ball, arm motion, body position—are dealt with much more consciously than the mechanics of hitting, and there are more of them to master. We are not concerned here with the mechanical details of how to grip and release various types of pitches, but this is a subject of vital interest to pitchers and their coaches.

The basic pitches used, however, do need description, and before they can be described, one of baseball's hoariest arguments must be dealt with.

Does a baseball, thrown over the distance of 60 feet 6 inches from the rubber to the plate, actually curve? Or is it just an optical illusion?

The real answer is: both. It most certainly does curve, but there is also an optical illusion involved that plays an important role.

Many, many treatises have been written proving mathematically that a baseball can't possibly curve under the forces applied. Many others have explained why it can and does. The explanation most widely accepted these days, at least among physics-minded baseball people, is this: the rotation of the ball, as determined by the way the pitcher releases it, sets up differences in air resistance and pressure on opposite sides of the ball, and this makes it veer to one side or the other. This deflection becomes greater as more of the forward force is spent. At the same time, gravity is working on the ball from the moment it leaves the pitcher's hand. The result is a fairly complicated path, but decidedly bent.

But what a batter, standing alongside home plate, sees is not an *actual* path but an *apparent* path. The actual path, plotted on a graph or photographed from directly above the field, is quite different from the illusion the batter must react to. The batter's illusion is a distorted one, because the ball is moving toward him while he is stationary. When it first leaves the pitcher's hand, any change in its direction appears relatively slight; by the time it is near the plate, exactly the same amount of horizontal or vertical deflection seems much larger.

But what does the batter actually swing at? After all, it takes a finite time—brief but finite—for muscles to respond to brain-and-eye directions. Whenever the swing actually begins, it must begin sometime *before* the ball reaches the plate if bat and ball are to collide flush in the area of home plate.

What happens, then, is this: the batter follows the flight of the ball for perhaps the first 40 of the 60 feet. On the basis of its apparent trajectory over that distance, he projects what the rest of the trajectory will be, and starts to swing accordingly. None of the process is conscious, of course. The human brain is still far the most efficient computer in existence, and experience has fed the batter's computer-brain, which does its work without bothering one's awareness. He may be able, as Ted Williams is supposed to have been, actually to see the ball hit the bat, but by then it's irrelevant. The bat action had to be started sometime before. The conscious decisions—to swing or not—and the unconscious decisions—where to swing—are made when the ball is approximately two-thirds of the way home.

For all these reasons, the *apparent* break of a curve ball is bigger (and more effective) from the hitter's point of view (and the catcher's and umpire's) than its actual break. This can be seen, sometimes, when television switches from a home-plate camera to a center-field camera on successive pitches. The shot from center field shows a curve breaking not as much as the shot from behind home plate. Since both cameras are relatively far from the action, however, the apparent difference is slight; to the batter on the scene, the scale of difference is much greater.

Jay Hook, one of the most personable and least successful of the original Met pitchers, is an engineer. He once provided *The New York Times* with a learned essay, complete with diagrams and formulas, showing why a baseball curves. This prompted the baseball writers to create the following parody, on the Rodgers and Hart song "I Could Write a Book," from *Pal Joey*. The actor depicting Hook sang:

> *If they asked me I could write a book,*
> *About the way a baseball's spin makes it hook.*
> *I know all the theories, the complex math,*
> *That explains a curving ball's path.*
> *I compute compression of the air,*
> *Count gravity as one-half times Gee Tee square,*
> *But with all I know of trajectory,*
> *They keep hitting homers off me.*

Jay's problem, you see, was not the way the ball curved on the way in but the way it soared on the way out, usually 400 feet or more.

So we accept the idea that a pitcher does make a ball curve, really and truly. But how many ways, and what for? What are the basic pitches?

1. The primary pitch is a fast ball. It is, to all intents and purposes, a pitch with a straight trajectory, although in reality it veers off a little bit. Because it is straight, it is the easiest pitch to throw to any particular spot—and it is the easiest path for a hitter to judge correctly. Its usefulness, then, lies in its speed. In baseball talk, however, any straight pitch is referred to as a "fast ball," even if it isn't especially fast. Almost all other deliveries are lumped under the category of "breaking balls."

If a fast ball is fast enough, it has a "hop" to it. This is almost entirely illusion, but it's a dilly. The pitcher is throwing from a hill, 10 inches above the level of home plate. He releases the ball at some point usually even with his head, so let's estimate this to be about 7 feet above plate level. The top of the strike zone, on the average batter, may be 4½ feet above ground level. Therefore the fast ball, in the course of traveling 60 feet, must drop at least 2½ feet to be a strike.

The faster a ball is thrown—the more force it has behind it—the less it will be affected by gravity during its trip from pitcher to catcher. Gravity, as televised space shots must have taught us all by now, is a constant acceleration: it exerts the same amount of downward pull in the same amount of time regardless of horizontal forces involved.

Now, the batter is accustomed, by experience, to gauging the path of thousands of ordinary fast balls. But the extra-fast ball, being in flight a shorter time, doesn't get pulled down *as much*. It still comes down, or it wouldn't be a strike, but it comes down *less* than the ordinary fast ball. But the hitter makes his decision—remember?—when the ball is still about 20 feet away. At that point, he has no specific landmark to measure its speed against; he *expects* the rest of the path to be that of an ordinary straight fast ball, and swings—but by the time the ball gets to home plate, it is *higher* than the ordinary pitch would have been. This is translated, by the hitter's mind and eye, into a "hop"—a jump.

Whether it jumps or not, a good fast ball "moves" a little bit. It is called "live." A pitch with the same velocity that's absolutely straight is called "flat," and is the reason some men can throw hard and still get clobbered.

2. The second basic pitch is a curve. It would be more accurate to call the curve a family of pitches, because a curve can be thrown with many different degrees of "break"—change of path—and at many different speeds. The main characteristic of the common curve, however, is the downward component of its

break. In giving it the proper spin, the pitcher gives it less forward force, and when it reaches the plate, both spin and spent force (which gives gravity that much more time to operate) work in the same direction—down and away from a hitter of the same-handedness as the pitcher.

3. The third indispensable element of a pitcher's repertoire is some sort of "change of pace"—a pitch that is enough slower than his fast ball to make a strong contrast, but not identifiable as easily and as early as the curve ball is. There are many varieties, often named after the method of grip (like the palm ball), but the one indispensable element is that the motion of delivery must look like a fast ball or regular curve.

Every pitcher must be able to control three pitches of the above type to be effective for any length of time. A man doesn't have to be equally proficient with all: a great fast ball can be supported by a very mediocre curve and rudimentary change-up, and excellent curves can make a moderate fast ball sufficient. But those are the three building blocks—throw it fast, throw it slow, make it bend. Unless a pitcher can get strikes with each of the three types when necessary, he isn't going to be a big leaguer long.

4. The slider is a cross between the fast ball and the curve, and one of the most widely used pitches in baseball today. It's a newcomer, the way things are measured in baseball. The fast ball, curve, and change were thoroughly established weapons before the turn of the century. The slider came into general use only after World War II. The main difference between a curve and a slider is the plane in which it breaks. A slider looks like a fast ball until the last moment, and then veers off to the left or right, not very much, but more than enough to avoid the batter's intended point of contact. It doesn't drop sharply as it bends, however, the way a curve ball does, but stays pretty much in one plane, like a fast ball.

5. The screwball, which is used increasingly but remains a minority pitch, is a reverse curve: thrown left-handed, it breaks

away from a right-handed hitter instead of in. For this reason, it is more popular with lefties, who have so many righties to face. Right-handers have less need to find a pitch that breaks away from left-handed hitters, and they're not looking for one that makes the right-handed hitter's task easier. The main thing, though, is that the screwball puts a tremendous strain on the arm, especially around the elbow, because the wrist is snapped in instead of out when the ball is released. Some men can't use it at all, and many who do pay a physical price if they use it too much.

6. The knuckle ball is thrown with either the fingertips or the knuckles gripping the ball, and it has a minimum of spin. This brings it to the plate with almost all its force spent and extremely susceptible to random effects of air pressure and currents at that moment. Its break, therefore, is unpredictable and as much a problem for the catcher as the hitter. It is, essentially, a slow pitch, although there are some fast (relatively) knucklers, too.

7. Sinkers are varieties of fast balls and sliders, with little horizontal break and a definite downward break at the last minute. Some pitchers have "natural" sinkers. Others have sinkers that are really spitballs.

8. The spitball was outlawed in baseball nearly two generations ago, and, being an illegal pitch, is used by no more than one quarter of the pitchers in the majors. Saliva or some other slippery substance, applied to fingers that hold the ball like a fast ball, will allow the top of the ball to slip out of the hand first, giving it a forward rotation and a tendency to break down.

There is no question that the spitball is an effective pitch, since it seems to be a fast ball until too late, and there is no question that many pitchers learn how to use it, especially in tight spots. Official Baseball, through its umpires and league presidents, prefers to ignore the whole business, which is just as well. Outlawing it in the first place, in the first flush of slugging glamour after World War I, was of questionable wisdom.

Hitters moan and groan about being retired by this illegal delivery—which few pitchers admit using—but, for some strange reason, no one has ever reported hitting a home run off a spitball, and it must happen *sometimes* if pitchers throw so many. In short, it's like any other pitch: used by a good pitcher, it's a wonderful weapon, but a poor pitcher throwing spitballs remains a poor pitcher.

Other "trick" deliveries were outlawed with the spitball, and these, no doubt, still have some unacknowledged practitioners today. In general, anything that can cut, roughen, or slicken the surface of a baseball can give a pitcher a chance to make his pitch behave in an unorthodox manner.

Those are the standard deliveries—fast ball, curve, change-up, slider, screwball, knuckler, sinker, and "trick" pitches, of which the spitball is the most common. Each has its dangers as well as its assets.

The fast ball, if fast enough, is the safest of all deliveries. If not fast enough, it's the easiest for the batter to hit, and is likely to carry farthest, because its own force adds to the force of the rebound off the bat. It is, as stated, the easiest pitch to control.

The curve can be disastrous when it "hangs," that is, doesn't break down sharply enough soon enough. Because it travels slower than a fast ball, it is easier to time, and if the change of direction is too slight, look out! The precept is that curves *must* be low passing the strike zone; a "high curve" is not considered a pitch, but an abomination.

The change-up exists only by comparison with other pitches, and is therefore devastatingly effective when used correctly. The danger is obvious: if the hitter is *not* fooled, it's easy to hit.

Sliders, many people believe (and I among them), are one of the underlying factors in the increased number of homers along with the dip in batting averages. When a slider works right, it is marvelous; but when it doesn't, it's a prime candidate for gopherism. Why is a home-run ball a "gopher"? Because of the self-deprecating expression uttered by pitchers, "It'll go for extra bases or a homer." The "go-fer," especially in country accents, led to the picturesque but unrelated animal image. If a slider doesn't slide, it's just a fast ball with not enough on it; and if it slides into the wrong spot, it can find the hitter's strength instead of his weakness.

The only real disadvantage of the screwball is difficulty—the difficulty of mastering the delivery, and the wear and tear on the arm. Those who can control it have great success with it, because to the automatic advantages of any good curve, it adds the tremendous one of unfamiliarity. It breaks the opposite way from almost all the other breaking pitches hitters see, and they don't see the "scroogie" often enough to become accustomed to it.

The knuckler is the most unhittable of all deliveries—and the most uncontrollable. No one, not even the pitcher, really knows which way it's going to break, and this creates two major problems. One is that it is so hard to throw strikes consistently with a knuckler (and when a man can, like Hoyt Wilhelm, he lasts forever). The other is that it is dangerous to use with men on base, because it gets away from the catcher so often. In fact, plenty of knuckle-ball pitchers have been beaten because a missed third strike put a runner on base (no, *not* Hugh Casey of the Dodgers in the 1941 World Series against Tommy Henrich and the Yankees. That famous pitch that got past Mickey Owen was probably a spitball).

These deliveries are the raw materials of pitching. To succeed in the majors, a man must "have" at least three. "Having" a pitch means absolutely dependable control of it, in tough situations. When a pitcher "adds" a new pitch, he usually works with it for a period of years in practice, and then in a few relatively safe game situations, before feeling that he has acquired it. There are, of course, exceptions (like Wilhelm, whose only worthwhile weapon was the knuckler), but they are rare.

Acquiring the raw materials is the science part of pitching, and so is the constant problem of keeping all deliveries in good working order. Injury, fatigue, carelessness, overeagerness—all the things that can put a hitter into a slump—can afflict a pitcher, causing him to lose his rhythm or pattern or groove or whatever he calls it. Usually, the pitcher or coach can eventually spot some mechanical defect to correct the situation. Pitchers will spend hours analyzing every detail of every movement when a delivery doesn't work right. Only then comes the art, the process of deciding what to throw when, and where. The tactics and the thinking begin here.

Fundamentally, the pitcher wants the reverse of the hitter's coin. The hitter is looking for "his" pitch to hit. The pitcher is trying to make the hitter hit "his"—the pitcher's—pitch.

What does a pitcher think about while on the mound?

First, he is always aware of the count, the number of outs, the score, and the inning. Each of these things will influence the decision on which pitch to throw.

Second, he has his "book" of each hitter's strengths and weaknesses at his mental fingertips, having reviewed each item before the game.

Third, he has firmly in mind the current state of his own equipment—which pitches are working right today and which aren't.

Fourth, he is influenced by the number and location of the men on base.

Let's consider each of the above in more detail.

The first rule of effective pitching is to stay ahead of the hitter most of the time. If the first pitch is a strike, the arithmetic shifts way over in favor of the pitcher. Now he can miss the strike zone three times without issuing a base on balls, and has to hit it only once to give the hitter the problems that come with a two-strike count. In other words, if the first pitch is a strike, the pitcher has plenty of margin for error in trying to get the batter to swing at borderline strikes. Even if only one of the next four pitches finds the mark, he still has an even chance with the count 3-2.

On the other hand, if the first pitch is a ball, things are not so good. If the second pitch is also a ball, the pitcher is in a real hole with a 2-0 count; he *must* come in with three of the next four pitches, and the chances of throwing something the hitter wants are much greater. The psychological pressure of the necessity to come in with the pitch adds to the physical difficulty of throwing to the exact spot hoped for. This is especially true for inexperienced pitchers, but it is a problem for all.

A sure sign, therefore, that a pitcher is flirting with trouble is a pattern in which he is constantly behind the hitters, particularly 2-0 and 3-1. Counts of 1-0 and 2-1 aren't so bad, because the next pitch can even matters, and a pitcher with excellent control (like Warren Spahn) often reaches such a count on purpose.

Don Drysdale expresses a philosophy common to better pitchers. "You don't worry much about a hitter's weakness until you get ahead of him," says Drysdale. "First you concentrate on getting your good pitches over, to put him in a hole. You don't want to get yourself in a hole by missing a spot and falling behind in a count. So you start by making sure he has to hit your best stuff if he's going to hit you. Then, once you're ahead, you can work on his weaknesses."

For their part, many managers consider it an unforgivable sin if their pitcher gives up a damaging hit with the count two strikes, no balls. At that point, they feel, there is no excuse for a pitch that's well within the strike zone, or toward a hitter's strength.

Mel Ott, managing the Giants, once fined Bill Voiselle $500 when a Cardinal hit a home run off an 0-2 pitch. Voiselle, who was earning about $3,500 a year at the time, was impressed as well as appalled.

"Is that the biggest fine anyone ever got?" he asked a writer in hushed, awestruck tones.

"No, Bill," the writer had to tell him, "Babe Ruth once got fined $5,000."

"Whew!" replied Voiselle, whistling. "I couldn't cover *that!*"

But pitchers, of course, and many pitching coaches, object to so narrow a viewpoint on the part of managers. They point to all the times they retire a man on the o-2 pitch by being willing to get it over.

What all this means, really, is that a pitcher won't use the same pitch—necessarily—when he's behind in the count that he would risk when he is ahead. When he is ahead, he can afford to work on the batter's weakness with maximum confidence, and can try pitches that are not his own strength. When he is behind, he may have to reject what would be the toughest pitch for that particular hitter to hit if he can't be absolutely sure of controlling it.

Hitting or missing with a pitch is another aspect of baseball that tends to become overdramatized and misunderstood. Not even the greatest pitcher can, every time, in competition, hit an exact spot in the sense of a dart hitting a target. What he is working with is a dynamic system: it isn't an abstract cross section of a strike zone that he's pitching to, but a living batter. If the direction, momentum, spin, and—for want of a better word—tendency of a pitch are correct, that's enough, even though there may be an inch or two of displacement from the idealized target.

Pitchers are taught, therefore, to make sure that they miss *in the right direction* when they do miss. For example, suppose you are facing a hitter whose weakness is low inside, but who can handle a low pitch pretty well if it is out over the plate. You aim for the inside corner at the knees, but you try to make sure that if you miss it will be *too far* inside, not the other way, which fades into the hitter's strength.

The most common instance of this sort of thing is "jamming" a hitter. If a strong pitch can be made in close, "on the fists," it can be hit only with the thin portion of the bat handle, and therefore hit weakly. A couple of inches farther out, and the fat part of the bat might send the ball out of the park. Jamming is invariably effective, but dangerous if you miss in either direction, because if the pitch hits the batter, he's on.

At any rate, the count on the hitter is a major factor in the pitcher's decision on what the next pitch should be.

The outs, score, and inning have more obvious relevance. It may be easy enough to retire a particularly stubborn free-swinger by letting him hit long, catchable flies—but not with a man on third and less than two out. With a two- or three-run lead, and nobody on base, a pitch that might be hit for a home run if it isn't quite right is a good risk; with the score tied in the bottom of the ninth, it isn't. In other words, there is no such thing as the "right" pitch to a particular hitter: it all depends on the count and the situation in the game.

It also depends on the accumulated analysis of the hitter's strengths and weaknesses. It's not only a matter of which pitches a batter hits better or worse, but also where he is likely to hit any particular pitch. This varies with every pitcher; a hitter may be able to pull one pitcher's curve but not another's. Thus, every pitcher has to work out for himself a table of values, involving his own strengths and each batter's abilities. From this table, he can select the pitch that will tend to make this batter *this time* hit the ball where the pitcher wants—on the ground for a possible double play, to the left or the right, or whatever.

It's hard for the nonprofessional to remember that, in real life, it's not "a" curve that's being thrown, to "a" batter, but some specific pitcher's curve to a specific hitter. What counts is how *his* works to *that* hitter.

Naturally, the pitcher is aware of the state of his equipment at that particular moment. His best pitch, in general, may be a curve—but not that day, so he uses it less and relies more on the fast ball. If he's a regular pitcher, with a well-developed style, the very fact that he is deviating from his normal pattern can be put to use.

In general, pitchers think of "out" pitches—the pitch they hope the batter will swing at—and pitches they "show." For example: Whitey Ford is pitching to Frank Robinson in Yankee Stadium, with one out, a man on first, score tied, sixth inning. Naturally, Whitey would like to get a double play. His fast ball, Whitey feels, isn't the sort that's going to overpower a Robinson, so Whitey will just "show" it to him—he simply will not throw the fast ball into the strike zone. It may still be very useful in at least two ways: as a contrast in speeds, to make a subsequent delivery hard to time, or as an enticement to swing at even if it is just outside the strike zone.

Here we move into the mysterious area of "setting hitters up." Some great pitchers—like Sandy Koufax—scoff at the whole idea, at least as it is often presented. The pitcher, Sandy feels, is always trying to fool the batter anyhow, and it's a two-way guessing game. If the pitcher succeeds in thinking along with the batter and fools him, fine—but the same "setting-up" sequence is meaningless if the hitter isn't thinking in the groove the pitcher assumes.

Others, though, as qualified as Koufax, wax rhapsodic about the artistry with which someone was "set up." Without splitting hairs about just which part of the process is intentional and which isn't, we can see that the sequence of pitches has a great effect on the batter.

Thus, most pitchers are told, don't throw the same thing three times in a row (because obviously the batter will get the range). By the same token, every batter knows that after two identical pitches he is not likely to get a third—and yet, a third one may prove to be the most surprising thing of all. So we're back to the guessing game.

There are, however, some abstract principles that work well in practice: in-and-out, on successive pitches, is a classic pattern; change of speeds is another. In all such instances, the batter's reaction to the previous pitch is still working on him as he responds to this one. Among the refinements are such esoteric practices as saving up a particular pitch, which has been withheld from this batter in previous times at bat, for a dangerous moment.

And finally, in deciding what to use at any particular time, the pitcher gives a lot of consideration to the ball park and the weather. By now, these factors have been touched upon repeatedly. In a large park, where long flies make luscious outs, more high pitches can be risked than in a small one. The same is true if the wind is blowing in rather than out. If the wind is strong out to right field, left-handed hitters must be prevented from pulling the ball, but if the wind is strong blowing in, that may be a good way to get them out. If the day is overcast and dark, or if the lights at a night game aren't the best, speed become more effective. Certain times of day—like twilight anywhere, or when the grandstand shadow passes the mound at Yankee Stadium—create conditions of visibility that can help a pitcher.

One pitching decision is the center of controversy over and over again. It is the practice of throwing close to the batter's head. One common term for this is a "beanball." This implies that the pitcher is trying to hit the batter in the head, which would make the pitcher, morally speaking, an attempted murderer. A term used more often by hitters themselves (and managers, of course) is "knockdown," which has a more accurate connotation: the pitcher is making the batter drop, suddenly and desperately, to avoid being hit. Pitchers themselves invariably refer to it as a "brush-back" pitch, which paints a milder, more strategy-oriented picture of forcing the hitter to get out of the way simply to upset his timing and to prevent him from digging in too securely for subsequent pitches. Whatever you call it, it is a fundamental weapon, universally accepted as a fact of life in professional baseball.

There are all gradations of viciousness involved. When real ill-feeling develops between individual players or whole clubs, beanball wars do develop. As a means of calculated intimidation, throwing close (without intent to hit or hurt) is considered a necessity at times by every single manager I have ever spoken to, although some don't like to admit it while others (like Leo Durocher) use talk about it as psychological warfare. And even the mildest, most idealistic pitcher, who would rather lose than hurt a batter (and there have been plenty of men who feel this way), acknowledges the legitimacy of the almost prehistoric pattern of high-and-tight-then-low-and-away.

Besides, morals should cut both ways, too. Pitchers are hit by batted balls even more often than batters are hit by pitches. The ball comes off the bat faster than it went in, and almost every pitcher, at one time or another, has had to stay in and pitch with a bad bruise on the leg, body, or arm. Cracked kneecaps and other serious injuries have been suffered by pitchers on the mound.

Now, the batter, trying for a hit, really doesn't care where the ball goes. He is trying to hit it as hard as he can, and often aims "back through the box," because that is a good method of keeping eye and stance steady. Whether or not the pitcher succeeds in getting out of the way is something the batter doesn't worry about.

By the same token, pitchers say, it's not their concern how a batter eludes a high inside pitch. The pitcher has as much right to throw it there as the batter does to hit the ball through the box, and it's up to the man in the line of fire to get out of the way. A pitcher throwing high and tight intends to miss—and, if he's any good at all, he wouldn't miss if he were really serious about hitting the batter. Only on the relatively rare occasions when intent to hit the batter comes up is there a real moral question.

The morality of this may be questionable, but since there is no infallible method for distinguishing between lack of control and an intentional high inside pitch, everyone concerned lives with the situation uncomplainingly most of the time. Hitters, no less than pitchers, recognize the inevitability of being thrown at from time to time, especially when they've been hitting well or hurting a particular pitcher too often. Only when there is some additional reason for rancor—personal animosity, or the feeling that a deliberate effort to injure is involved—do bitterness and recriminations arise.

There are two answers: courage and reprisal. The major-league hitter must be able to stand up to the plate just as firmly for the pitch after a knockdown pitch as before. In plain words, if he can prove that it doesn't decrease his ability to hit the next pitch, the knockdown or brush-back simply becomes another ball and therefore of no value to the pitcher. If the hitter can't prove it, he's going to get knocked down over and over in important game situations.

Reprisal is up to the opposing pitcher. You throw at our hitters, I'll throw at yours. In the final analysis, this is the code of loyalty that keeps beanballing in check most of the time. The most direct and effective reprisal—throwing at the opposing pitcher when he comes to bat—occurs infrequently; for an obvious reason all pitchers seem to be reluctant to use it, indicating that "do unto others" is a two-edged sword.

A striking example—it might be called classic—arose in September of 1969, during the hysterical pennant drive of the hitherto hapless Mets. The Chicago Cubs, managed by an aging but not forgetful Durocher, came to New York for a two-game series, leading by two and a half games. The Mets had been winning and closing the gap, but weren't yet universally accepted as a possible winner; the Cubs, who had been losing (but not too badly), were expected to polish them off once and for all.

New York's pitcher was Jerry Koosman, a left-handed fireballer (then), and he got the Cubs out on a fly and two strikeouts.

Chicago's pitcher was Bill Hands, a right-hander who could also throw hard. His first pitch to the first Met batter, Tommie Agee, was a "knockdown," high and tight. Agee went sprawling and the message Durocher habitually preached—intimidation —was presumably delivered.

Agee did bounce out, and the next two Mets went out, and the first batter to face Koosman in the second was Ron Santo, the Cubs' captain and most respected clutch hitter.

Koosman's first pitch cracked Santo on the elbow.

And there was no further trouble. The retaliation was accepted for what it was: a response to the first message, saying "we can play it any way you want." The fact that Gil Hodges, the Mets' manager, had played under and against Durocher for years made it that much more certain that no misunderstanding was possible—or would be permitted. The Mets went on to win that game—as Agee hit a home run the next time up—and the next, and the pennant, and the World Series. But that's another story.

In today's pitching philosophy, the principle of pitching low rules unchallenged. With rare and special exceptions, managers want "out" pitches—the pitches intended to be hit—to be low. The reasons are many. A low pitch is most likely to be hit along the ground, and no matter how hard it's hit, a grounder (or low liner) can't be a homer. In a lively-ball era, home runs are the chief danger. Also, a grounder is more likely to be an out, since there are five infielders (counting the pitcher) defending a narrower area and only three outfielders covering a much wider span. Also, many tactical situations (like needing a double play) call for grounders. Also, almost all high pitches except high fast balls are easier to hit than low pitches; all breaking balls have a downward component as part of the break, so part of the misjudging stimulated in the hitter is to have him swing in a plane above the ball. If a breaking ball starts out too high, and comes down into the top half of the strike zone, the batter may "misjudge" it right on the nose.

Here, a whole new set of variables arises. Not all pitchers are at their best pitching low. Some hitters are low-ball hitters. What happens to the general principle in these cases? Should a pitcher do what is theoretically advantageous when his physical ability is best in another direction? Should he pitch to a hitter's strength because theory dictates that sort of pitch?

The answers, almost always, are in the realm of the pitcher's own strength. If his strong points prove incompatible with most theoretical necessities, he simply won't be around long. Aside from that, a pitcher usually resolves a questionable decision in favor of his own best weapon, and hopes it's good enough.

There is more to pitching, however, than throwing pitches. A pitcher with fine stuff and control can still be beaten if he lets base runners run wild, or if he can't field his position to some degree.

Holding runners on, especially the runner at first base with second base unoccupied, is a major responsibility. If the runner gets too big a lead, he may steal, and thus be in scoring position for a subsequent single. Or, on a single, he may go to third, from where he can score on an out; or he might score from first on a double; or he may break up a potential double play by arriving at second in time to spill the pivotman.

The rules require a different motion (a stretch instead of a full windup) with men on base. All the various types of balks are rules to prevent the pitcher from taking advantage of the base runner. A pitcher must, therefore, acquire complete command of his pitching repertoire from the stretch as well as from the windup, and within the framework of the balk rules. At the same time, he must not let preoccupation with the runner interfere with his concentration on the batter. Striking that balance requires a great deal of experience, and countless young pitchers have suffered defeat because they didn't have it yet.

As a fielder, the pitcher has two big responsibilities: covering first base and bunts. He must—absolutely must—get off the mound and over to first base on grounders hit to the right side. He has to run about 65 feet while the hitter runs 90, and if he doesn't make it, the trouble that follows is his own fault. And he must be agile enough in fielding bunts to prevent this from becoming a surefire weapon against him.

The lefty-righty match-ups, already discussed from the hitter's point of view, have some additional meanings for pitchers.

For one thing, the layout of ball parks makes a big difference. A left-hander has a considerable natural advantage in a place like Yankee Stadium, where left and center fields are virtually boundless, while right field is a tempting home-run target. The right-handed batters, who constitute the southpaw's bigger problem, will have a tough time hitting a homer; the lefty swingers, who have the good home-run target, have a left-handed pitcher to contend with. Boston's Fenway Park is exactly the opposite, with a short left field and a long right, so left-handed pitchers seldom have success there. (One great exception, Boston's Mel Parnell, was a screwball pitcher who could get right-handers out better than left-handers).

For another, the left-handed pitcher has an advantage in keeping a runner close to first. In his stretch motion, he is facing first base. The right-hander, facing third, has to keep an eye on the base runner by peering over his shoulder, and has to throw across his body to throw to first. The lefty's move to first can be much more deceptive, and artists like Ford and Spahn are famous for having picked men off.

For a third—and this is something I've never heard explained satisfactorily—left-handed pitchers seem to have more odd spin on their deliveries, and more trouble with control, than right-handers. This seems to be a fact; if it's a myth, it's one myth that won't be dispelled here.

How to get men out is the main subject on a pitcher's mind. The topic that ranks second is when he will pitch. If he is an established starter, he can usually count on the four-day schedule that seems to be normal in modern baseball. A man can pitch nine innings—between 100 and 150 pitches, not counting warmups—every fourth day without strain. On one of the next two days—it varies with the pitcher—he'll do some throwing, in batting practice or on the sidelines or in the bullpen. On the third day, few pitchers throw at all. In an emergency, a starter can go with two days' rest with good results—Koufax did it in the seventh game of the 1965 World Series, as a prominent example—but he can't do it very often. It is generally considered thoroughly unwise to pitch a starter with only one day of rest, and never on successive days. Nowadays, in fact, perhaps half the major-league managers prefer to use a five-pitcher rotation for much of the season, if their personnel permits it. The pitchers don't like it, because fewer starts mean fewer chances to compile a winning record, but many managers are convinced it pays off in fresher arms late in the season. (On the other hand, Johnny Sain, an independent thinker and a spectacularly successful pitching coach with four different teams, believes that in certain cases some pitchers can do well with only two days off. Under him, Denny McLain won 31 games for Detroit in 1968, and Wilber Wood, a knuckle-baller, pitched regularly on a three-day schedule for the Chicago White Sox in 1972 and 1973.)

If he is a relief pitcher, he must be ready every day—but if he works in a game, or has an extended warm-up without getting into a game, two or three days in a row, he'll probably get a day of idleness.

If he is not fully established as either, as members of the second half of a ten-man staff usually find themselves, he cannot count on regularity of schedule, and this is moan material No. 1 among professional pitchers.

What makes one man a good starter, another a good reliever? Repertoire, physique, outlook.

Other things being equal, the better pitchers are starters. Naturally, you want your best pitcher out there most of the time, and that's the starter.

In the old days, relievers were simply those not good enough to be starters. Today, relievers are specialists, often highly paid, always much appreciated. Many men have certain abilities that can be put to good use in relief.

A reliever, for instance, may have complete command of one outstanding pitch—an overwhelming fast ball, a sinker, a screwball, a knuckler. His other pitches may be mediocre to poor, but his one specialty highly reliable and unhittable. With such an arsenal, he is not a good risk for a full game as a starter—no starter can get by relying only on one good pitch; too many mistakes crop up, and the hitters, facing him a third and fourth time, get too good a chance to lay off his specialty and hit something else. But in relief, one pitch, if it's good enough, is plenty. The relief pitcher's job is to get one or two outs in the middle of an inning with men on base, and to pitch a scoreless inning or two. Rarely will a relief pitcher face more than nine men, which means few batters will see him twice in one game.

At the same time, a reliever needs certain physical and mental attributes that even good starters often lack, at least to a degree. He must be able to get ready quickly, work often, and be at his best in the toughest spots. Because he will be brought in when sudden emergencies arise, he must be able to warm up quickly. Because he will be expected to work only an inning or two—perhaps 20 pitches—he should be able to work two, three, or four days in a row. Some arms can stand that, some can't.

Koufax, with his arthritic elbow, could never have been a relief pitcher, because he needed rest and treatment between starts. Spahn, even in his forties, could never get the right mental approach to relief pitching, because he was too immersed in his own mental processes of preparing for a game, planning how to handle each hitter, and so forth. In fact, some of the best relief pitchers have had devil-may-care personalities.

More specifically, a relief pitcher's specialty must be good enough to get a strikeout or a grounder, since, in almost all the situations he is called upon, it will be necessary to keep runners from scoring or advancing. He must, it goes without saying, be able to pitch with men on base.

Most pitchers are notoriously poor hitters, for two unavoidable reasons. One is lack of opportunity to develop—as pitchers, they get much less opportunity to bat, in practice and in games, from the beginning of their careers. The second is natural selection—not Darwin's, but baseball's. The special reflexes that make a good hitter are totally different from the set that make a good pitcher. When pitchers are scouted and selected, only their pitching abilities are rated and everything else ignored. All other players, at the beginning, are judged on their hitting potential.

But the pitcher who can hit well—Don Drysdale, Spahn, Robin Roberts—has a big edge as a pitcher. In many situations, he may stay in the game when it is his turn to hit in the late innings of a close game, and thus remain to get the victory. The ordinary pitcher, one run behind or even with the score tied sometimes, must be removed for a pinch hitter.

While most fans recognize the necessity for rest, few realize that a pitcher can have too much rest. A starter on the four-day schedule, if held out longer because of rain or blanks in the schedule or other reasons, will often have trouble with his control after four or five days' rest instead of three. Pitchers who work irregularly almost always have control trouble. Regularity seems to be an essential part of efficiency for pitchers. Even relievers can get too much rest.

Relievers, however, are involved in one of the most invisible facets of the proper care and feeding of pitchers: warming up. The box score only shows how much a man pitched in a game. In the bullpen, he may have warmed up three or four different times without being called into the game. It depends on how troublesome the game has been, and how decisive his manager is. The reliever may work the equivalent of three or four innings for several successive days in the bullpen, and never appear in a box score at all.

Finally, after all the mechanical and tactical considerations have been listed, there remain the intangible qualities that lift outstanding pitchers above the mass: applied intelligence, confidence, poise.

Pitchers are the intellectuals of the baseball community. They do much more thinking, in quantity and in depth, about the techniques of baseball than the other 60 percent of the players do. They have to. Even the worst pitcher must have a clear idea of how and where to pitch each hitter, and this automatically requires hours of mental effort. Some pretty good hitters, on the other hand, get by on instinct, paying only superficial attention to the finer points of the game.

Today, hitters help pitchers immensely by being home-run crazy. The harder they swing, the easier they are to fool, since a hard swing commits the batter sooner. Today's pitchers take full advantage of this powermania, which is one reason that the slider is so effective. If hitters concentrated more on just meeting the ball, it would be harder to get outs. As Lew Burdette put it, stating the thoughtful pitcher's case: "I make my living off the hungriness of the hitter."

Confidence, for a pitcher, means confidence in his command of his various deliveries.

"It is better," says Sandy Koufax, echoing a thought many top coaches subscribe to, "to throw a theoretically poorer pitch wholeheartedly, than to throw the so-called right pitch with a feeling of doubt—doubt that it's right, or doubt that you can make it behave well at that moment. You've got to feel sure you're doing the right thing—sure that you *want* to throw the pitch you're going to throw."

For all these reasons, pitchers are the most important and the least predictable people on a ball field. They're good one day, ineffective the next, then brilliant, then helpless. They get sore arms and other ailments that they tend to hide—because everyone is afraid of being labeled physically deficient—and sometimes they can compensate for them, and sometimes they can't.

No one can guarantee, on any one day, that the good pitcher will have his best stuff. They are, in this respect, like opera singers, who can be in good voice or not, regardless of reputation. And the poorer pitcher, every now and then, will have a day when every pitch breaks right.

This is the human factor, again, the unpredictability that makes baseball possible and worthwhile day in and day out. It is also an inescapable inconsistency that drives managers crazy, as we will see when we turn our attention to the genius in the dugout.

3

· **Let him hit it—you've got fielders behind you.**
Alexander Cartwright, June 19, 1846

Playing the Hitters

Fielding is the bread-and-butter activity on the ball field. For every ball he hits, a professional will catch and throw a dozen, both in practice and in games. In a sense, the fielders are the remote-control mechanisms that turn the artistic pitcher's work into put-outs. At major-league levels, fielders are expected to be as efficient as machines, making the routine play every time. They don't, in reality, because they are human, but in the calculations of the manager they are supposed to.

And to most baseball players, fielding is just about as exciting as bread and butter. Hitting is a delight. Without probing, pseudopsychoanalytically, the satisfaction most humans seem to feel when they strike a ball solidly with a stick, the fun element in hitting, is always evident. Even the most experienced players, practicing their profession and apparently blasé about everything else, can be seen enjoying themselves in practice when it's their turn in the batting cage.

But fielding is a chore. Not that there isn't a thrill of accomplishment in making a spectacular catch; any ball player responds to that. But spectacular plays are rare, and many of them are more painful than satisfying (when a tumble or collision results). Most of the time, fielders must handle precisely those routine plays that everyone takes for granted. Therefore, one mistake, after 19 perfectly executed plays, makes a man a villain, while one key hit in 20 tries will make him a hero. In the sphere of ego satisfaction, the fielder has little to gain and a lot to lose.

Furthermore, the public is relatively indifferent to fielding skill. Admiration for the leading hitters and pitchers is unbounded; admiration for a fielder, even misplaced, immediately brands the fan who expresses it as an aficionado. This situation is compounded by the fact that crowds invariably react incorrectly. The plays usually cheered loudest are not nearly so difficult as many others that go unnoticed.

For instance, an infielder will leap high and spear a line drive; an outfielder, running at top speed, will reach up and make a gloved-hand catch a few feet from the fence; a third baseman will smother a vicious smash, and throw the batter out at first; and—absolutely guaranteed to elicit shouts of awe and a trailing murmer of appreciation—an outfielder will throw the ball 300 feet on the fly to third or home, retiring no one and very likely letting someone take an extra base.

But leaping for a line drive is the easiest play of all; there's no danger and nothing complicated to gauge. You leap, and you reach the ball or you don't. The third baseman's play on a smash is dangerous, but it's also in the "you do or you don't" category. An outfielder's long run is not necessarily less routine than a short run, because 99 times out of 100 he knows when he starts whether or not the ball will be within range of his speed, and once the ball is within reach a one-handed catch is no particular strain. And the world-record discus throws some outfielders unfurl are strictly show-off propositions.

Even more realistically, all professional players know that teams choose players for their hitting ability. The two great exceptions are shortstop and catching, but even here, if one shortstop can outhit another by 50 points, he'll get the job unless his fielding skill is downright inadequate.

And here a contradiction arises. All managers, in conversation, stress the importance of defense, the fact that a poor fielder "can't be hidden," the principle that poor fielding will lose many more games than good hitting will win. Yet they seek hitters, and often decide to sacrifice at least some defense for power.

By the same token, the majors are full of players who recognize that their fundamental success or failure depends on their hitting—but who, for that very reason, work hard to keep their fielding skills at the highest level. They will hit as well as they can, and there's not much they can do to improve their batting records; but they can, by practice and concentration, keep their fielding near 100 percent efficiency, and thus save their positions from only slightly better hitters who don't field as well.

This is because fielding skill is teachable and learnable, to a greater degree than either hitting (which is mostly inborn) or pitching (which involves a lot of learning, but only after the special gift of "a good arm" is present).

Naturally, fielders need the basic athletic endowments, and those who can run faster, throw harder, and react quicker have the advantages. However, the differences in endowment are comparatively slight for fielding duties, and the difference made by steady application is considerable.

In fielding, the mental work is paramount. The thinking done by pitchers and batters is primarily concerned with outguessing each other, but a fielder does not have to outguess a moving baseball; he has to anticipate which way it is likely to move before it starts. His mechanical responsibilities—catching and throwing—are coarser and less difficult than the fine-scale reflexes employed in batting or pitching, so that the most important part of the fielder's task is to be properly prepared for what comes up.

Sustained concentration is the key to effective defense in all sports. Anyone (or almost anyone—one can think of exceptions) can manage to extend his attention span through one whole time at bat, or while shooting at the basket or running with the football. The fully effective fielder, though, must focus his thoughts and alert his body about 150 times a game—before every single pitch his pitcher throws, even though the ball will actually be hit to him only a few times. Consistency, not occasional brilliance, is his goal.

And what do fielders concentrate on?

Where to play.

Since individual hitters have discernible characteristics, and hit a certain type of pitch in more or less the same direction, the alignment of the defense must remain flexible. A right fielder may play close to the foul line for one hitter, way over in right-center for another, in close for a third, back deep for a fourth. Every other fielder (except the catcher and pitcher) must also shift his position according to the batter, the type of pitch being thrown, the situation in the inning, and the score of the game.

These refinements are generally lost on the fan, who does have a vague notion that fielders do shift positions. The fan can see "infield in," and outfielders moving very deep, and the extreme shifts employed against hitters like Ted Williams, Willie McCovey, and so forth. But that's about all. The details are seldom realized.

Yet, these details are what make up the chief mental activity of the entire game. Each fielder, if he is paying attention, has an idea of where he should be playing on every batter in every situation, according to that day's pitcher. Managers and coaches, in the dugout, are watching constantly to see if the players are right, and will move them if they are not. Much of the season-long shoptalk concerns where to place the fielders on particular hitters.

The blend of individualism and teamwork peculiar to baseball is seen at its best in the way the defense operates. In clubhouse meetings, the broad strategy of where to play whom is decided. But each individual fielder has to make his own adjustments, according to his knowledge of his own capabilities. An outfielder who is fast, and good at going back, can play shallower than one who is slower; the slower one realizes he is going to let some singles drop in front of him, but he still has to protect against the bigger danger of a ball going over his head. A shortstop with a strong arm can play deeper, but a shortstop who has exceptional quickness in getting rid of the ball (as Phil Rizzuto used to) can make up for lack of throwing power. Clubhouse meetings are not long enough to discuss every possible variation, for every fielder, in detail, so each man must know his own job.

For example, Al Kaline, playing right field for the Tigers, may know that Jim Perry's fast ball will be pulled more sharply, and more often, by left-handed hitters than will Joe Coleman's; yet he may also know that, in Yankee Stadium, Bobby Murcer might pull Coleman more sharply or more often than Perry, or that Roy White (a switch-hitter) may like to pull one and not the other. In addition, Kaline may be aware that the same two hitters hit the same two deliveries differently in Detroit and in New York. He'll also know how time of day, wind conditions, differences in atmosphere, and so forth, may affect his positioning and his "expected" direction of break.

A striking example of what the fan is up against when he tries to penetrate this mysterious area for second-guessing or for just plain fun came up in 1966 in Atlanta. This was mid-June, and the Mets were leading by one run in the last of the ninth. The Braves filled the bases, and Jack Hamilton had to pitch to Henry Aaron with two out. Aaron was leading the league in home runs and runs batted in.

In the press box, I thought I saw something strange. Ed Kranepool, the Met first baseman, was playing close to the right-field foul line, while the second baseman was shaded toward second. In other words, there was a big hole in the right side, and all we experts knew that Aaron frequently hit to right and right-center, much more so than most right-handed sluggers. I couldn't figure out what Kranepool was protecting against, since a single to the outfield would score two runs anyhow and win the game for Atlanta. As it happened, Aaron made the final out by hitting a fly to straightaway center.

After the game, I asked Manager Wes Westrum about Kranepool.

"No, he was just where we wanted him to be," said Wes.

"But doesn't Aaron hit to right and right-center?" I asked.

"Not this year," replied Westrum—and in three words he hammered home the lesson hardest for the fan to absorb: current form is everything; what is a man doing *now?*

"He's been going for homers this year," Wes went on, "trying to pull much more than he ever did. And it's not that easy for a man to adjust his swing back and forth. So we felt that if he hit the ball to the right side, it would more likely be only because he didn't hit it well, swung late, or something like that, and in that case it might be closer to the line. But if he met it well enough, he would be trying to pull it. By keeping the pitch outside, we could make him hit it to center while trying to pull, which is what he did. But even if he had tried deliberately to go the other way, he would be doing it against an outside pitch—so again, the place for Kranepool was way over to the right."

And that's the reality of major-league baseball, once again: think of all the possibilities, anticipate the more likely ones, and trust to fate that the unlikely ones won't pop up to beat you too often.

Positioning the fielder is only the first half, however, of the mental process in defense. The other half is anticipating which play to make.

Assume that I am properly placed and the ball is hit to me. Assume that I handle it flawlessly. What must I do with it?

I'm supposed to know:

1. The speed of the batter, going to first.
2. The speed of all base-runners.
3. The needs of the strategic situation: must a potential tying

run be cut off at home? at third? at second? Is a possible double play more important than the lead runner? Is the chance of throwing out the man going from first to third good enough to risk the batter's reaching second?

4. My own capabilities: where will my best play be if the ball is hit slowly? sharply? to the extremities of my range, right and left? How much can I get on the ball throwing off balance?

5. The capabilities of my teammates.

All this is supposed to be clear in my mind before the pitch is made. Also, I'm supposed to be clear about my alternatives if the ball is not hit to me. Where do I go to back up a play? What base do I cover? What sort of help can I give to some other fielder?

And slight (sometimes not so slight) changes in each of these decisions come up with every new pitch.

Those fielders, therefore, aren't just standing around waiting to be awakened by the sound of the ball hitting the bat. They are thinking all the time—at least they are supposed to be. Being human, they are subject to distraction, most often by brooding over the last time they made out, occasionally by personal worries, now and then by sheer mind-wandering. But such lapses are rare. Most of the time, most players are tending to business quite seriously.

Each position has its own characteristics. Let's go down the list, examining the qualities that go into making a good fielder, and the principal duties involved.

Catcher

Aside from the pitcher, he's the most important player in the game for obvious reasons: he handles the ball all the time, he calls pitches (thinking along the same lines as the pitcher), he quarterbacks the infield (since he is the only player on his team facing all the others), and, when called upon, he must make the most important put-out of all, the one that prevents a run.

A catcher must have a reasonably strong arm, to prevent base-stealing and excessive bunting. Major-league catchers are usually judged first by the quality of the aim.

He must also, not quite so obviously, be a good receiver. That means he must be able to catch low pitches, since good pitching is low pitching. Now, many low pitches will hit the dirt before they reach the catcher, or just as they do, and smothering these is a prime responsibility when there are men on base. He must not only smother them, but catch them, because the runner might be going.

When Chris Cannizzaro was a regular catcher for the New York Mets, Manager Casey Stengel was full of praise for his arm. As time went on, a flaw in Cannizzaro became apparent: while it was true he could really fire the ball to second, it was also true that he had to catch it first—and too often, Chris couldn't hold the pitch on which someone was running.

"I got one that can throw, but can't catch," Stengel complained, "and one that can catch but can't throw. And one who can hit but can't do either."

It was a trying time with the Mets, because they had comparable problems at seven other positions.

A catcher does not have to be able to run fast, because he doesn't have far to run. (He does run down to back up first base on grounders to the right side, but because of the throwing angles involved he doesn't exactly have to keep pace with the batter.) However, he does have to be able to move very quickly for the first few strides, in order to handle bunts, and be quick with his hands. Yogi Berra was outstanding at pouncing on bunts.

And, of course, he must be sure-handed and sure-moving on

all foul pop-ups behind and to the side of home plate. This is a difficult play a large proportion of the time, and the pitcher feels he has earned an out when the batter hits one, so the pressure on the catcher to record the out is considerable.

Foul tips are another story. If you hold one on the third strike, the batter is out—but it is more luck than anything else if you do. The reaction is just too fast to be conscious, in all but a few cases. Usually, a foul tip that is held is simply one that wasn't deflected very much, and the catcher's glove was in the right place to start with.

Then there is the matter of "handling the pitcher." This has nothing to do with fielding skill, but with psychology, rapport, intelligent calling of pitches, pacing, even personality. It's important, but it's largely subjective.

With all these important things for the catcher to do, his weakness in hitting can be borne if he is outstanding at everything else. Nevertheless, the "best" catchers in everyone's opinion are the ones who hit very well and do the other things adequately.

First Base

Many clumsy men have played first base because they were powerful hitters. Traditionally, it is a position that can be used to keep a power hitter who is a poor fielder (like Dick Stuart, Zeke Bonura, Lou Gehrig at the beginning of his career, Bill Skowron) in the lineup. Essentially, he must only catch thrown balls, master some limited footwork, field a few grounders, and some bunts. He doesn't need a good arm, because he seldom makes important throws.

But such situations are merely bowing to necessity. While it may be true that a poor first baseman will do less harm there than in some other positions, it is a certainty that a good first baseman is of great defensive value.

His most important maneuver is the stretch. By stretching far into the infield to take a throw, he can have the ball in his glove a fraction of a second sooner than if he stood up straight and waited for it to cover the additional four feet or so. That split second can be the difference between safe and out, especially at the completion of a double play.

When there is a runner on first and no one on second, the first baseman must "keep the runner on." That is, he must be anchored at first base until the pitcher commits himself to throwing home, so that the runner doesn't get too big a lead. If he did get too big a lead, he might steal, or spoil a double play, or take an extra base on a hit. As the pitcher starts to throw home, the first baseman backpedals, or charges in if it is a bunt situation. All this makes it unlikely that he will be able to field a sharp grounder unless it is right at him, so this situation gives the batter (especially a lefty) a good target for a ground single.

At other times, and even with a man on first in many situations ordered by the manager, the first baseman plays back, some 20 feet behind the bag. Late in a close game, he will tend to protect the foul line, to prevent a double between him and the line even at the risk of giving up the more likely single through the hole to his right.

A left-handed thrower is perfectly at home at first base, since it makes no difference in catching throws, and he has one distinct advantage on the one type of throwing play that comes up—to second base, on a grounder to his normal position, or on a bunt.

On most teams, the first baseman acts as cutoff man for throws home from the outfield. The cutoff man's job is to intercept the throw if it is apparent that the man won't be out at home, and thereby to prevent some other runner from taking an extra base.

Second Base

On a diagram, the second baseman has the same position to the right of second base as the shortstop has to the left of it. In reality, their positions are quite different.

The crucial play for a second baseman is the double-play pivot. To complete a double play, he must take the throw to second with his back or side toward first, and simultaneously turn, avoid the runner, get rid of the ball quickly, and put enough steam on an accurate throw. Second basemen of quality are judged by how well they "can make the double play." In traditional thinking, a second baseman doesn't need a strong arm, because his throws to first are short ones. But many infielders, and managers, challenge this idea. They believe that a strong arm is so helpful in the double-play situation that it is an important factor in judging a man's suitability to play second. A strong arm is also valuable because a second baseman will be the relay man on throws from the outfield when a ball is hit to deep right or center.

Durability and a certain amount of acrobatic talent are needed, too, because the second baseman is often knocked over, from the blind side, by the runner sliding into second.

Naturally, a second baseman must be able to move quickly to either side, since he has a lot of territory to cover laterally. And he has to be able to go back for looping flies in all directions.

Shortstop

The shortstop is the most important player after the pitcher and catcher. He is the key man on the infield, for the simple reason that 75 percent of the batters are right-handed. More grounders will be hit to the shortstop over a period of time, than to any other infielder.

He must have a strong arm, because his throws to first are fairly long—150 feet or more "from the hole" toward third. Because he has to throw farther, he must get rid of the ball quicker and get more on it than the second or third baseman. He, too, is the relay man from the outfield when the ball is hit to center or left.

The greater his range the better, but more than any other infielder, the shortstop covers ground with his head as well as his legs. His knowledge of the hitters, and variation of position, are of maximum importance. He has less chance than the second baseman to recover from a lunging stop to make a throw, so it is more important that he field a ball from a stance that makes a throw possible.

Lou Boudreau, Dick Groat, and Alvin Dark were outstanding examples of shortstops who had no exceptional gift in speed afoot or throwing ability, but whose knowledge of where to play made them exceptionally effective. Of course, all were outstanding hitters, or they wouldn't have been given the opportunity to play short on the basis of their fielding equipment alone.

The shortstop's double-play problem is simpler than the second baseman's, because he comes across the bag facing first, but the shortstop must be a master of timing to start the double play correctly.

 ## Third Base

Outstanding fielders at third are relatively rare, because this is another position where a big hitter can be carried without fatally crippling the defense. But the outstanding ones are or were something to see—Brooks Robinson, Clete Boyer, Pie Traynor, Billy Cox.

The third baseman's most important play is the bunt, or the accidentally topped slow roller toward third. He must be able to come in quickly, field a tricky hopper surely, and fire to first.

The harder-hit grounders, right at him or to either side, are "do-or-don't" plays most of the time.

It is widely believed that a third baseman needs an exceptionally strong arm. Obviously, it's valuable, because every once in a while he must make a long throw from deep behind third—a distance comparable to the shortstop's throw from the hole.

But even on this play, he is closer to the plate than the shortstop, and therefore the ball reaches him sooner, and therefore he has more time to make the throw. On most other plays, when he is lined up even with the bag at third or up to 20 feet behind it and in wide (toward short), a batted ball reaches him in plenty of time for a careful throw, and the distance is seldom more than 130 feet. The *need* for a strong arm at third (as distinct from desirability) can be classified as a myth. Accuracy is far more important than power, and the ability to throw straight while off balance is vital to the coming-in plays.

All the infielders must have "good hands." Sure-handedness in fielding grounders seems to be based on a degree of relaxation. The hands are loose and sort of absorb the ball. Stiff, tense hands are sure to make errors, particularly at important moments. And "good hands" must be quick, because a high proportion of grounders take minute bad hops. Everyone can see the spectacular bad bounce that suddenly goes completely past a fielder with a drastic change in trajectory. But in every game, several apparently routine grounders skip or skid or otherwise shift direction at the last moment, and hands must react reflexively.

The third baseman, because he is closer to the plate and has more time, can succeed more often than other infielders in making the play by blocking the ball and then retrieving. Many a third baseman (like Pepper Martin) made a reputation for "fielding with his chest."

We can summarize infield requirements this way:

The first baseman needs elasticity and a sure glove; the second baseman needs guts and agility; the shortstop needs brains and agility; the third baseman needs reflexes and guts.

⊝ ## Outfield ⊝

The one indispensable quality for a good outfielder is speed. He must be able to run. There's a lot of ground out there and he has to cover it. That's a *good* outfielder. There are lots of mediocre-to-bad outfielders playing regularly because they can hit. You have to have hitters in your lineup somewhere, and if your hitters can't field, they'll do least harm in the outfield—specifically, in left field.

Every professional ball player, it is taken for granted, can judge and catch a routine fly. Outfielders become specialists in four other respects: in how far they can go, in how well they adapt to the special visibility and wind conditions of various parks, in how they handle line drives, and in how they throw.

The center fielder has to be the best man available. He has the most ground to cover, he needs a strong arm, he must be able to come up throwing from either side, he must be able to come in fast to cover the looping-fly territory not quite covered by the second baseman and shortstop, and he must back up right-center and left-center. He will frequently have throws to third and home from right-center, and will have more chances (of every type) than the right or left fielder. In defensive importance, he ranks behind the catcher, pitcher, and shortstop. In fact, some managers maintain he is more important than the shortstop. An infielder's mistake costs one base, an outfielder's three.

The right fielder needs a strong arm, even stronger than the center fielder, because his vital throws will be to third and to home from fairly deep right.

The left fielder can have a moderately weak arm, since the throw to third is a short one, and the throw home (while no shorter than the one from right field) leads to an easier situation for the catcher (who sees both the ball and the runner coming from the same direction, instead of having to catch the ball and turn).

Left-handers are common in right and center, but unusual in left, although that's a convention hard to take too seriously. It has to do with the fact that a left-handed left fielder, if he fields a ball between him and the foul line, has to turn his body before he can throw to second base, so that some possible singles may become doubles.

The main thing for all outfielders is "getting a jump." This is a compound of instinct, reflex, experienced guesswork, and practice. Willie Mays was so exceptional an outfielder in his youth because he got such a fantastic jump—a start in the right direction the moment the ball is hit. Sometimes, knowing the type of pitch being made and the batter's proclivities, Willie would start even as the pitch was on the way to the plate.

In the 1954 World Series, Mays made one of his most famous catches. In the first game, at the Polo Grounds, the Cleveland Indians had two on and nobody out in the eighth inning, with the score tied. Vic Wertz smacked one high and deep to center, toward the bleachers 435 feet away. Willie raced back, caught it over his shoulder a step or two from the wall, and whirled a throw back to the infield. It was hailed subsequently as the "No. 1 sports thrill of 1954" and described as incredible.

And yet, to those of us who had watched Mays all season,

there was no doubt that he had the ball all the way, as soon as he moved. From the press box, when the ball was hit, one couldn't tell whether or not it was going to reach the wall; but, after the first glance at Mays, one *knew* that Willie was going to catch it if it stayed within the playing field.

Now, Willie was exceptional, and the catch was understandably startling to those who weren't familiar with his abilities—but the point is that he "made" the play in the first step, not the last. Once Willie got "the good jump," the ball was his, provided it didn't carry to a barrier.

Every day, in every game, on a more routine scale, the same thing is happening. An outfielder's range is determined more by how soon he can start (in the right direction, of course) than by how fast he can run once he's under way.

A ball that "stays up," however far from home plate it goes, is seldom a problem. It's the line drives that are hard to handle. A liner directly at a fielder is hard to judge correctly, because there is so little apparent trajectory to let the brain's three-dimensional perceptions work on. If it's curving just a little bit, you may find out too late; by the time it reaches the outfielder, 300 feet from home, that slight shift may be a couple of feet. Most liners to right or left have some degree of curve to them (being either sliced or hooked), and when a fielder switches from one field to another, he has some adjusting to do. If a liner is not directly at a fielder, it takes a lot of hustle to get in front of it to keep it from becoming an extra-base hit. The "good jump" really counts in holding such drives to singles.

Throwing to the right base is the outfielder's main mental concern. Here he must make an instantaneous decision about the speed of the runners, his own body position as he gets the ball, the length of the throw, the strategic situation, and his own throwing ability at that moment. He must be sure he has a good chance to get the lead runner out; if not, he is giving the trailing runner an extra base by making a futile throw.

The cardinal sin, then, is overthrowing the cutoff man. High throws look spectacular, but the low throws, even if they bounce, are the better ones, because a cutoff man then has a chance to change the direction of the play. The lead man may get to third, or score, but another runner or the batter may be cut down for a lifesaving out.

The final aspect of fielding is equipment.

Gloves today bear no resemblance to those used before World War II. They are vastly superior, and even different in conception. The old gloves, although they increased in size as they evolved from the 1880s on, were still basically designed to protect the hand from pounding and injury. The ball was still actually caught in the "pocket," which touched the palm, and was gripped by the fingers. Today's gloves are literally traps, and the ball is caught in a snare between the thumb and fore-finger. The fingers are used more to manipulate the glove than actually to grip the ball through it. As a result, today's fielders hold virtually every ball they reach.

Sunglasses have been used for decades, by infielders as well as outfielders. They come with a strap that fits around the back of the head, and the lenses are attached to a hinge at the top of the glasses frame. The fielder doesn't look through them until he has to look up into the sky; then, with a finger, he flicks the lenses down. In most parks, the area around home plate, where the outfielder must look to see the start of the ball's flight, is in shadow, so to have the glasses down all the time would cut out too much light.

Only the catcher wears pads, for protection from foul tips, but sooner or later players will be wearing batting helmets in the field, as they already do while running bases. It's not flattering, but many outfielders look as if they could use batting helmets.

It is possible, after all, to get hit with a batted ball if the sun blinds you—a fairly common occurrence that happened in its most severe form to Willie Davis in the second game of the 1966 World Series. He lost two in a row that way, and made a wild throw off the second one, to give the Baltimore Orioles three runs, breaking up a 0-0 game Sandy Koufax was involved in. It was the turning point of the series and the Orioles went on to beat the Dodgers in four straight.

In the same Baltimore Memorial Stadium in which the Orioles completed their sweep, Yogi Berra was hit by a fly ball in practice in 1962. Yogi's catching career had all but ended, and he was back in the outfield in those days. With the sun low on the rim of the stadium before a night game, Yogi got careless and was conked on the forehead.

The blow opened a gash, and although there was no serious injury, there was a lot of blood. They ran out to right field with towels, and Yogi started to walk to the clubhouse, holding a bloody towel to his head and looking like one of the victims in *The Vikings.* (When Yogi saw that movie, years later, his comment on the graphic swordplay was: "I'm glad I don't live in them days.")

As Yogi passed under the broadcasting booth, en route to the dugout, Phil Rizzuto saw him. Phil was now a Yankee broadcaster, his playing career years behind him, but he was still a "teammate" of Yogi's in several business enterprises the two had in New Jersey, where they lived.

Rizzuto looked down at the apparently mortally wounded Berra, and called: "Yogi, speak to me, it's your partner. You wanna sell?"

Not included in the equipment is sympathy.

4

• **Nice guys finish last.**

Leo Durocher, 1948

• **They say you can't do it, but sometimes it doesn't always work.**

Casey Stengel, 1951

What a Manager
Really Does

Every player, in his secret heart, wants to manage someday. Every fan, in the privacy of his mind, already does. The second guess is the lifeblood of baseball's appeal to the fan, and it is the field manager of a team who is the man to be second-guessed. The actions of individual players, while also susceptible to second-guessing, all hinge on the physical performance of their duties. You can be glad or sorry that your hero struck out, but you can't really second-guess him because he *wanted* the home run just as much as you did.

But the manager—ah, he does nothing but make decisions and issue orders. All his activities are mental. Therefore, he is the ideal object for second-guessing. If things work out right, obviously he must be a genius for having planned it that way; if they don't, he's a stupid idiot who should be fired. Often, he can go from genius to imbecile and back to genius again in the space of one inning.

We will consider the following questions about managers:

Just how important is a manager, as far as affecting the number of victories a team winds up with?

How important is his "handling of men," and just what does this entail?

What are his actual duties, day by day and inning by inning?

What are the qualities a good manager must have?

Let's take these topics in order.

How much difference to a team's record does a manager make? Ten victories over the course of a season? Twenty? Two? None? The best answer I ever heard to this question was given by Bill White, in the spring of 1964 in Florida. He was the first baseman and one of the elder statesmen of the Cardinals then, and Yogi Berra was just beginning his one-year term as manager of the Yankees. Johnny Keane was managing the Cardinals, and no one dreamed at that time that Keane would succeed Yogi as Yankee manager after the Cardinals would defeat the Yankees in the World Series that fall. There was a lot of speculation about how Yogi would do as a manager, and White's opinion was sought in due course.

The question was phrased: "How much difference does a manager make?"

White's answer was: "It depends on the manager."

This wasn't evasiveness, but profundity. Some managers make no difference at all. Others help a team win several games it might not have won. Others can create situations that lead to many lost games. It all depends on how the manager in question operates.

Most managers have little effect on the team's won-lost record, because most clubs reflect their basic talent over the course of a full season. That doesn't mean that most managers make identical decisions, and that everything would turn out the same way whoever managed. It does mean that, given certain material in the form of the accumulated abilities of the players, managers with different styles will get similar results.

Walter Alston might operate in a fashion that would lead to victory in Tuesday's game, but lose Wednesday's; Leo Durocher, in the same circumstances, might lose Tuesday but win Wednesday. On the average, their clubs will finish as high or as low as their material warrants.

This is because baseball's basic tactics and strategy are simply not that complicated. To the professional, who has spent his life playing and studying the game, the alternatives in almost every situation are clearly known from experience. If there is any significant advantage to be gained by a maneuver (like sacrificing after the first man gets on late in the game with the score tied), all baseball people know it with equal thoroughness. If, in many situations, the alternatives are 50-50, it's a guess anyhow.

But it is the *first* guess, and that's the distinguishing characteristic of the manager's craft. He gets the first guess, the only guess that will lead to the tangible result. No one can ever know, afterward, what would have happened if the manager didn't change pitchers, or didn't order the hit-and-run when he did; everybody—including the manager—knows how it turned out when the play is all over. So most qualified people—any experienced player on up through managers—know all the stock situations and would make similar decisions in similar circumstances.

Some managers, however, go beyond the ordinary bounds. They are so sharp at making split-second decisions during a game that their players (and rivals) become convinced that this quickness turns half a dozen imminent defeats into victories. Leo Durocher earned that reputation.

Other managers impress their players as being slow in this respect, or perhaps disruptive in some way. It is generally believed that a bad manager can cause more defeats than a good manager can steal victories. And, as with players, different abilities in managers lead to success in different situations. A manager may be ideal for one group of players, not so good for another. This isn't true nearly as often as most players would like to believe, but it does happen sometimes. By and large, however, the manager has relatively little to do with winning and losing in the short run.

This is contrary to myth, and contrary to the underlying wish of the fan, who gets his kicks out of second-guessing the manager. If the manager's second-guessable decisions don't make that much difference, a lot of the fun goes out of blaming him for mistakes or vicariously sharing his triumphs. And it is also contrary to the interests of the majority of players, who like the emotional comfort of blaming their troubles on the manager, even when they keep the complaint to themselves.

Taken at face value, however, the above remarks can be misleading. The context must be understood: *provided* that the manager is a thoroughly qualified baseball man, and *provided* that he has a fairly free hand in making decisions, *then* almost any manager will get comparable results with given material. Differences in style tend to cancel out.

What is essential is that there *be* a manager.

Only one man can run a ball club. He doesn't have to be the smartest man in the organization, nor the most experienced, certainly not the best liked, and almost certainly in no way unique—but he does have to be the boss.

Someone has to make the final decisions on who will play, who will pitch, what the batting order will be. Someone has to give the order for a bunt, a hit or take, a pinch hitter. That someone is the manager. He can take advice, share his thought processes, delegate some rights, but at bottom the final yes-no decisions are his, just like the President of the United States.

Every team has a manager in fact, even if not in name. The Chicago Cubs tried for several years to operate with a system of several coaches of equal authority. Actually, during games, one of them always performed managing functions. They didn't take a vote on whether to order a hit-and-run play or not. The decisions may have been made by different men at different times, but at any given moment there was only one manager, whatever he was called.

What the Cub system did undermine was the equally important climate of authority a manager creates. Aside from the strategic and tactical decisions, the manager is responsible for *all* decisions—discipline, training habits, practice procedures, and assignments of personnel. He may do a lot or a little in each of these areas, but the players under him consider him the source of all orders and permissions. On the Cubs, this unity of command was lacking. One coach might prefer one player, and ask for one sort of performance, while another had other leanings.

"It's different, all right," said Don Zimmer one day. Zimmer had played for many managers before landing in the Cub system of ten coaches. "Instead of getting into one doghouse, you can get into ten."

Getting into a manager's doghouse, or staying out of one, is a subject that goes right to the heart of the biggest cliché and yet deepest truth about managing: the main task is "handling men." In this case, we are dealing with mythological elements encrusting the carcass of an older, exploded myth. Thanks to increased emphasis on dressing-room coverage, interviews, debunking realism in reporting, and the sheer repetitiveness of radio and television, most fans realize these days that a manager is not simply a glorified chess master, nor a wizard pushing buttons, nor a mastermind outsmarting mere mortals. The image of a supergeneral plotting victory and avoiding defeat, which was part and parcel of John McGraw's public character as "Little Napoleon," is passé.

Instead, everyone talks knowingly of the much more sophisticated notion of "handling men." The manager must "get the most out of his men." Every man is different and has different problems, so each one "must be handled differently." As generalities, such ideas are true enough, but left as generalities they lead to some absurd viewpoints. Pretty soon the second-guessers are absorbed in judging morale instead of ability, psychology instead of strategy, personality instead of performance, the peripheral influences instead of the central events.

Of course a manager must handle men; every boss must. Of course every person is different, and is best treated accordingly. Of course a manager must try to get the best results out of the collection of abilities at his disposal. So does an orchestra conductor. Realizing only this much doesn't lead to much enlightenment.

The real question is, what does "handling men" mean in terms of managing a ball club? Where does it start, and where does it end? Current conceptions about the manager's role tend to cast him as some sort of psychoanalyst, priest, top sergeant, father, brother, and judge, all rolled into one.

With *very* few exceptions, the following propositions apply to every big-league manager:

He cannot change the character of any player. The lazy ones remain lazy, the conscientious ones are conscientious from the beginning. Men may change their own characters, and life can affect them, and a manager can be one of many interrelated influences—but the problem characters under one manager invariably turn out to be problem characters under another.

He cannot change the basic level of ability of any player. There are no "secrets" or miracle-working instructional gimmicks in baseball. Managers and coaches can, and do, recognize what a player does that keeps him from reaching his potential, and can show him how to improve. But only the player himself can make that improvement, by willing application (a reaction rooted in character), and he can only improve so much.

He cannot "inspire" anybody, the way Knute Rockne is supposed to have inspired football teams with half-time harangues. This is a profession, a livelihood, serious business engaged in by adults. All know the stakes involved each day, as well as the manager does. Besides, what must be executed on the ball field isn't helped much by inspiration; in body-contact games like football and hockey, high emotions can bring forth useful extra effort; in baseball, where all vital skills are of the fine-scale, hair-trigger, reflex type, a binge of passion can do more harm than good.

He cannot devise any special, new, surprising strategy, or substantially affect the pattern of offense and defense, as football and basketball coaches can, because all the broad possibilities of baseball strategy were worked out and systematized long ago. All the strategic options in baseball involve "when," not "what." Our friend Yogi Berra, toward the end of his one year as manager of the Yankees, summed it up neatly. His team had lost the first game of the World Series to the Cardinals, and the usual proportion of the 600 or so newspapermen on hand asked Yogi the standard silly question before the second game: "Now that you're down, one game to zero, what do you plan to do?"

"Not much," said Yogi. "It ain't like football. You can't make up no trick plays."

And he can't, in matters of discipline and training, exercise the sort of autocratic control over every detail of off-field behavior that a big-time college football coach takes for granted. He can try, but he can't succeed in imposing it. The nature of both the game (played daily for nearly seven months, counting training) and the players (professionals whose ages range from 20 to 40 and whose salaries may run from $15,000 to $200,000) simply won't permit it.

And finally, perhaps most of all, he cannot, in Charlie Dressen's immortal phrase, "guide that ball." He can tell a pitcher what to throw, but he can't make the ball go there; he can tell a hitter when to swing, but he can't make him hit the ball. He can frequently have the right thought, followed by an unproductive result; very rarely does a wrong thought lead to accidental benefits.

If he cannot do all those things, what *can* he do?

He can, and pretty well must, earn the respect of his players —respect for his technical baseball knowledge, and respect for his integrity in dealing with them as a boss.

He can, and must, maintain sufficient discipline to keep it clear that he is the boss. He may or may not use fines, curfews, little rules or maxims, strict work schedules, and minor punishments to this end, but one way or another he must meet the challenge whenever his authority is flouted.

He can recognize the varying needs of different characters, and treat them accordingly—without creating a group of special, privileged cases. He must know who has to be pushed, to be encouraged, who can take criticism, who can't, who needs help, and who can't be helped—all without turning into a baby-sitter, or a tyrant, or an unapproachable autocrat, or a friendly buttinski.

He can evaluate correctly each player's capacities, and try to use them in ways that bring the team maximum benefit. This is probably the most important single contribution he can make.

And he can run the game—the individual game.

If these are the manager's legitimate responsibilities, our chances to second-guess him become unsatisfyingly meager. About the sort of things mentioned above, the fan in the stands can have practically no knowledge, even if he reads faithfully every word printed in the sports pages and listens to every word uttered on radio and television. The manager might be, in reality, totally wrong, but the fan's opportunity to see that he's wrong is nonexistent.

Am I suggesting, then, that we abandon second-guessing? In a book addressed to intellectual appreciation of baseball, of all places? Not exactly. I merely advocate keeping this undeniably delightful pastime in perspective. Second-guessing

is fun, and that's all it should b
deception. The man making the
times out of 1,000, all the relevant
experience. His reasoning power
baseball, are usually impeccable.
he makes a decision. It may wo
his *reasons* for making it are usu

This is not to say that all man
and that a computer would do
much higher proportion of the time than others—but rarely
because they reason better. The difference lies in the capacity
to notice small things, recognize subtle patterns, remember
applicable situations. Thus a Leo Durocher might—just
might—think of something that Walt Alston wouldn't; but
the chance that a fan (or a writer) has noticed some element
that the professional hasn't is nil. Seeing what he considers a
stupid move, the fan may be aware of a half-dozen elements
in a situation, and may be drawing the right conclusion from
them. If the manager got another answer, however, it is because he is aware of another half-dozen factors that the fan
didn't think of and probably couldn't possibly have known
about.

With this stipulation—that our information is necessarily
limited and that we mustn't come to believe that we're *really*
right when the manager is wrong—let's second-guess to our
heart's content.

Better still, let's first-guess. When watching a game, get on
record—to a friend, or in your own mind—what you think the
manager should do *before* the play happens. Then keep track,
over a period of time, how often the manager's way came out
right when you differed. It requires a little intellectual self-
discipline to do this honestly, and some humility will result,
but a great deal of enlightenment will result also. Soon you'll
feel in the game more than ever, and in return for abandoning dogmatic condemnation of that stupid manager, you will

citement of thinking along with both managers
stically. It's like double-crostics: once you get the
r doing them, plain old crossword puzzles seem one-
ensional and uninteresting.

So, in order to go beyond the old-fashioned "he shoulda
had him bunt!" type of second-guessing, let's break down
the manager's responsibilities and duties. Let's see what he
really thinks about.

There are two totally distinct segments to his job: while the
game is on, and all the rest of the time. Consider the second
segment first.

A manager works all year round. As far as the front office
is concerned, his responsibility lies in getting the best possible
performance on the field from the players supplied. Procure-
ment of players is the province of the general manager, training them to major-league level is the province of the farm
system, finding and evaluating them is the business of the
scouts.

During the winter, the manager divides his time between
public relations work for the club—personal appearances at
dinners, interviews, etc.—and numerous conferences concerning personnel. He is briefed repeatedly on the players in the
minor-league system; he is consulted about possible trades
(but *only* consulted for his opinion of the men involved); he
confers with the general manager about the players already
on the big-league club's roster, about his plans for them in
the coming year, about changes he'd like to make.

He has a voice in choosing the majority, if not all, of his
coaches. He takes a hand in off-season contact with players
who have problems—special conditioning after an operation,
special work for a man who may be asked to change positions,
perhaps a pep talk where needed. If the club has an instructional team operating in late fall–early winter for rookies and
a few convalescing veterans, he keeps an eye on its activities.

He lays out the work schedule for spring training—when

players will report, which players (in addition to roster men) he wants to look at, what sort of calisthenics they'll do, how the pitchers will work, what special practice will be given to selected players.

Back north, as the season is beginning and subsequently, he orders the rules of life around the clubhouse. He is consulted by the grounds keepers on how the field should be tailored, hard or soft. He tells the road secretary which alternatives to choose in making the road trips, whether to leave right after a game, or the next morning, or any other such detail.

There is one subject, though, that the manager steers clear of: player salaries. With few exceptions nowadays, the manager does not get involved in the annual argument over money. That's strictly between the player and the front office. (In the past, managers had much of the authority general managers now have, and they did sign their own players.) Today, a manager tells the general manager who did a good job and why, and who didn't, but he stays out of the negotiations.

While all this is being done, the manager thinks. Almost all his waking hours (which get longer when things go wrong, because sleep becomes elusive), he thinks about one problem or another, one way or another to squeeze out a few more runs, a little better pitching.

He must decide which players to keep when roster limits go into effect. He must plan his pitching rotation, for starters, a couple of weeks ahead and readjust it constantly as one pitcher gets knocked out, another gets arm trouble, another goes bad, and rain interferes. He has to keep his bullpen strong and ready, without killing it by ordering too many warm-ups too soon, and still avoid getting caught in an emergency with no one warmed up.

He has to choose his regulars, platoon his not-quite-regulars, and find ways to give his substitutes enough work to keep them sharp when emergency puts them in action. He has to settle on a batting order, change it when necessary, and decide when to leave it alone.

Through all this, he clings to three recurrent themes, themes that have infinite applications: you can't please everybody, there's always tomorrow, and in the long run the breaks even up.

The conviction that luck cancels out over a period of time is necessary to keep firm the belief in baseball's entire structure of "percentage play." You must choose, over and over, the move that *figures* to be right, even though it just backfired three times in a row on flukes. Baseball men define "panic" as the abandonment of percentage moves in the face of a losing streak. A manager is able to avoid this panic only if he keeps reminding himself that things even up—even if they really don't, in his case.

The awareness that there's always tomorrow, always another game, another season, enters into all the plans of a manager. No game exists in isolation, until and unless it is the last day of the season and his team is tied for first place. Whatever is done to win today's game must be weighed against the price that might be paid. Thus the relief ace, who has already worked three days in a row, may be kept out the fourth day even though he might have made victory possible. Winning today, and then having your relief ace out for a month with arm trouble, is not an intelligent way to proceed. The risks must be measured against the gains, and vice-versa.

Here the handling-of-men facet of managing is prominent. A young player, his confidence fragile, must be brought along gently. Perhaps, in a particular case, he needs to be thrown in over his head, but that's what the manager has to decide. Things must be done with him and for him they may not be, in theory, the best things to do in that particular game. For instance, a potential star may be allowed to bat sometimes for the sake of experience and confidence, rather than removed for a pinch hitter. An older player may be rested in the second half of a double-header, even though it decreases the chances of winning that particular game. And all such cases must be handled with a certain amount of tact, foresight, and calm.

Remembering that there's always tomorrow is important psychologically, too, for both manager and players. Even the best baseball team loses 50 or more games a season. Taking defeat *too* hard will only lead to more defeats. By the same token, thinking the world is your oyster because you won the last six in a row is a sure path to complacency, excessive self-esteem, relaxation of effort, and defeat. Today's hero is tomorrow's bum so often, and the other way around, that all baseball men learn to keep plugging away in defeat and not to "get too gay" in victory.

The most frequent reminder, though, is that you can't please everyone. The manager must learn not to try. There is no way 25 men, whose livelihoods depend on records compiled on the field, can be kept happy in a game that calls for only nine players. Aside from arithmetic, a basic conflict of interest exists: the player, by the very nature of things, is concerned with his own success; the manager must always think of the success of the whole.

Almost all athletes believe that when they play their best, the team benefits most. This sounds like unassailable logic, but it's a whopping oversimplification of reality. In many situations, the conditions that enable one man to do his best interfere with the necessities of others. Every player tends to believe that what's good for him is good for the team; the manager knows that what's good for the team may not be good at all for several players.

This is seen most clearly with pitchers. Here are six men with starting potential. Each is convinced—and correctly so—that he can do his best working every fourth day. But only four of them can be used in such a rotation. Yet the other two are needed, because there will be doubleheaders and injuries. So two men, inevitably, must suffer as far as their personal careers are concerned, for the good of the team.

At other positions, players simply hate to be platooned. In the old days, the universal principle was "find your eight best men and play them every day." Many managers pay lip service to that idea today—but one may be permitted to suspect that they do this more because they know it soothes their players to hear it than because they really intend to do it. Sure, it's great to keep things that simple when every one of your eight men is clearly the best available at his position. But most teams have two or three positions with no one man available to handle all situations reasonably well. They platoon at these positions because they must, to take advantage of the partial skills of two incomplete ball players.

It has been proved, again and again, that intelligent platooning enhances the career and the total income of players who are not solid stars, and that it helps a team win. Yet, players hate it, because most believe privately they could be stars if given the chance. This is a healthy belief, enabling the player to give his best—but it may not be a fact. The manager is the man who must act on the fact when it conflicts with the player's belief.

Under such circumstances, few managers can be liked, or liked for long. As long as the team wins a pennant, everyone may be happy and consider the manager a helluva fella; but 11 out of 12 teams must, by definition, lose the pennant every year. Sooner or later, every team has its bad spell, and then the complaining about the manager begins. If nothing else, he's the handiest excuse for every individual player's failures.

The longer a man manages, the longer he stays with one club, the surer he is to wind up being disliked by a majority of his players. A few years after retirement, these same players may feel real affection and appreciation for him, but not while they are playing. It shouldn't be surprising. In other walks of life, how many men love their bosses? They can respect and even admire them, but liking them is difficult, especially in highly competitive endeavors in which it is the boss's function to drive you to the limits of your ability.

The manager-player relationship goes through various stages. The rookie accepts the manager's authority as a matter of course. To him, the manager represents "Do it my way or you'll get sent back to the minors."

The experienced but marginal player is in a similar position: please the boss or get fired.

The experienced, established player tends to be loyal and conscientious—with secret reservations. In salary and importance, he doesn't rank so far below the manager as to feel overwhelmed. In his own mind, he is storing up the opinions by which he'll try to manage someday, and he has probably worked under several different managers. He obeys all the rules, but he expects to be left alone as much as possible, and he rarely places the manager on a pedestal.

The aging player is the toughest problem of all. The manager is the man who must recognize, and tell him, that he's losing it. The very same fierce competitiveness that made a player outstanding now prevents him, for a while at least, from giving in to the inevitable slowing down. From the human point of view, this is certainly understandable and perhaps gallant; and the emotions of the fans are all on the side of the familiar old-timer's reputation. Yet the manager must tell the star, by actions if not by words, that he's not the man he used to be, before the star can accept this for himself.

No, managers are rarely liked. That's why it's all the more important that they be respected.

What earns them respect?

Baseball judgment and fairness, with a touch of fear thrown in.

By fairness, players mean that a manager treats the whole squad equally—a minimum of privileges for the highly paid stars, a concern for the dignified treatment of the scrubs. Punishment and discipline should be applied impartially, and achievements should earn the same praise and reward whoever makes them. There should be no favoritism. Jobs should be assigned on the basis of ability, not personality. Criticism should be made without adding humiliation to it.

The manager who does these things is considered a fair man by his players (and by the rival players his players talk to). But this objectivity, which makes fair treatment possible, presupposes good baseball judgment. And what is that? Essentially, it's the ability to predict correctly the results that specific actions and tendencies will produce.

First of all, this requires the ability to spot every player's strong and weak points, and to predict reliably the consequences of each. A manager must anticipate how the opposition will take advantage of weakness, and how it will try to counteract strength, and then seek countermeasures accordingly.

Second is the ability to recognize, instantaneously, all or most of the relevant factors in game situations, not just a few: who's the hitter, what does the pitcher have, where are the fielders playing, the count, the score, the inning, the opposing manager's way of thinking and available options, his own available options, and the effect of all this on what may arise a couple of innings later.

As we've already seen, it's not much of a trick, to a professional, to think of the right strategic moves in a given situation; the real trick is to *define* the situation correctly by taking into account all the contingencies.

Third is the ability to maneuver those men available in a way that takes maximum advantage of their assets and minimizes their liabilities. The hitter with an insurmountable weakness can be "rested" against the type of pitching that bothers him most; the good pinch hitter must be used at the right time, not too soon and not too late. There's a well-worn anecdote about this, dating from the 1930s when Casey Stengel was managing in Brooklyn. He had a round catcher named Babe Phelps who was a powerful left-handed hitter. The Dodgers were losing by four runs, 5-1 or some such score, in the fifth inning, and Casey sent Phelps up to pinch-hit with the bases loaded. Babe promptly hit a home run which tied the score. It remained tied until the ninth, when the other team scored and the Dodgers came to bat in the bottom half with no strong pinch hitters left. Sure enough, someone got on, and there was no one to drive him in. "Ya bum ya," one of the few (there were never many in those days) faithful on hand yelled at Stengel, "why didn't ya save Phelps?" Casey, having retold this story a thousand times, once added: "The fella had a point. I shoulda had him hit a five-run homer the first time up."

Liking the manager, then, is a pleasant bonus when it occurs, but neither necessary nor important to the success of a club. Respect is essential, and respect results when most of a manager's decisions prove to be sound. The players are watching like hawks—second-guessing more persistently, more knowledgeably, and more mercilessly than any fan—and they either become convinced or they don't.

Durocher is an outstanding example. Many of the men who played under him and despised him the most on a personal basis remained the most vocal admirers of his managing. Stengel, too, was widely detested by players (who, in retrospect in later years, always spoke highly of him).

Other managers can be well-liked—and unsuccessful. One reason is that "nice guys" often find it difficult to be sufficiently heartless and severe in their judgments, and strict enough to keep control. Give a group of ball players the slightest opening, and they'll take advantage of a manager's leniency in shameless fashion. You don't have to be a rat to be a good manager—but every good manager must do things occasionally that make him seem like a rat to some players.

This was the issue behind Durocher's celebrated quote. Mel Ott, a "nice guy" of the highest degree, had accomplished nothing as manager of the Giants, and Durocher, the archenemy from Brooklyn, replaced him in midseason 1948. It was probably the most startling single happening in baseball history. Whatever else Durocher was, nobody had ever accused him of being a "nice guy," and only the previous year he had been barred from baseball (unjustly, for allegedly consorting with a known gambler, but the mere fact of exile didn't pretty up his image any).

"You're replacing a nice guy," a writer told Durocher.

"Nice guys finish last," Durocher is supposed to have replied. The phrase has become a byword of cynicism, but it can be interpreted in kinder fashion. It doesn't say nice guys *have* to finish last, or that nice guys can't finish first; it does make the point that being nice is certainly irrelevant, and can turn out to be a handicap. Durocher, I am sure, never probed his meaning deeply. If he did say it exactly that way, it was probably because it sounded good.

All right, then. We have an idea of what a manager thinks about and how he operates the year round. What does he actually do with respect to a baseball game?

He begins by choosing his pitcher and making out a batting order. The pitching decision has probably been made several days before, as part of a rotation pattern. The batting order must be thought through every single day, even if it ends up the same as yesterday's.

There are traditions about batting orders, some valid. Pitchers bat ninth, for two reasons: they are the poorest hitters, and therefore you want them to come to bat less often; and, when and if a pinch hitter for the pitcher does something positive late in the game, the top of the batting order—that is, the better hitters—will follow him.

There are other traditions. The lead-off man must be good at getting on base and a good base runner, but doesn't need much power. The second hitter should be adept at bunting, hit-and-run, and other runner-advancing techniques. The third, fourth, and fifth hitters are the long-distance, power hitters, capable of knocking in runs. The sixth, seventh, and eighth hitters are then arranged as well as can be.

The reasons for these traditions are sound. Only in the first inning of a game is the lead-off man guaranteed to lead off, but the first inning is something special, not merely one of nine. If you can get the lead, most subsequent strategy shifts in your favor; your pitcher has a margin for error, the opposition's offense is denied certain risks (primarily on the bases). Besides, in the average game, the batting order will be worked through four times, so the order in which the first few men bat amounts to one-fourth rather than one-ninth of the offensive opportunity.

In addition, the lead-off man leads off a subsequent inning a disproportionate amount of the time. Because the pitcher is so poor a hitter, and because the defense intends to take full advantage of that fact, a pitcher will turn out to be the final out of an inning more often than random numerical distribution would indicate.

Also, if a pitcher happens to lead off an inning, he is likely to make out, so the lead-off man will be in what amounts to a lead-off situation in a curtailed inning (with only two outs coming). Since there are only three possibilities—a lead-off man can come to bat with none out, one out, or two out—the proper batting order has a chance to operate in two-thirds of the possibilities.

So the first man has to get on, by a walk or a hit, and he has to be a good enough base runner to bother the pitcher, perhaps steal second, certainly reach third on a hit to right or right-center, and certainly score from second on an outfield single once he gets that far.

The second man must be able to hit to right field, to bunt well, to control the bat well enough to be reliable on the hit-

and-run play (when he must swing at pitches he'd prefer to pass up), and also to run well. What's more, both these first two men must have pretty good batting averages, or the whole idea is shot.

The No. 3 hitter, traditionally, is the best hitter on the team, the one who combines high average with power. If the first two men have done their jobs, there is someone on base for him to drive in; in any event, he is guaranteed of getting a chance to hit in the first inning, even if the first two men make out.

Behind the top three come the power men, who may have deficiencies in speed or batting average. But, in principle, when they do connect, there will be runners on ahead of them.

The man who bats eighth, often the catcher or the short-stop (since these men are chosen more for their defensive skills than their offensive abilities), is in an unenviable posi-tion. The pitcher will bat next, so the opposing pitcher will make sure the eighth-place hitter doesn't get much good to swing at. Especially with two out, the man on the mound can risk issuing a walk, since the pitcher who bats will probably provide the third out. Our eighth-place hitter isn't the most talented batter to begin with, or he wouldn't be hitting eighth. Now he finds himself teased by ordinary pitchers and mercilessly borne down on by the best ones (who are eager to save the pitcher for an easy first out the next inning). Life is seldom a joy for the eighth-place hitter.

In the American League, starting in 1973, the eighth-place hitter became the ninth-place hitter, and he gained a bit from the shift. With the adoption of the designated hitter rule, which removed pitchers from the batting order, the weakest "regular" hitter was dropped to ninth place and the desig-nated hitter inserted wherever the manager thought best. Now the weakest hitter would be followed by the lead-off man, not by a sure-out pitcher, so it was not advisable to risk walking him. This meant he would get more "good" pitches to hit, while the new No. 8 hitter (now the second-worst regular, as the No. 7 used to be) couldn't be treated so cavalierly because following him was a regular, albeit a less dangerous one.

Getting more good pitches to hit when you are a poor hitter to begin with, however, is only a marginal opportunity. Gene Mauch, always the analyst, put it most directly. "I always know who the weakest hitter on the other team is," he explained, "because the opposing manager tells me by listing him ninth."

All these things are traditions, but not rules. They are idealizations, abstractions of qualities, more than anything. In real life, the manager must adapt the players he actually has to the needs of the day. He may not have a good lead-off man, and his best hitter may lack power, or his whole lineup may lack power, or he may have a bunch of free-swingers who can't run at all. More often, the best fielders are not the best hitters, and the manager has to choose which contribution will mean more to the team.

Here's what can come up: you have two slow-footed outfielders, both poor fielders, both awesome sluggers. They have to play, because their bats are too valuable to do without. Your infield is pretty good defensively and a little weak offensively. Now, you *must* have a center fielder who has exceptional range, to take up the slack for your two sluggers in left and right. Perhaps he can't hit more than .172, but you have to have him out there. You may also have another outfielder, who can hit .280 and do a better-than-average defensive job by one-man standards, who can't possibly cover as much ground as the caddy who hits .172. Very often, you decide to play the poorer all-around player, because he can cover center field and a half, over the other one. And you can guess how lovable that makes you to the pretty good player who is now languishing on the bench.

Getting back to the batting order, you have to take into consideration several other factors, besides the theoretically desirable pattern and the adjustments made to your players' limitations. The lefty-righty business is important. You need some sort of balance. If *all* your hitters are left-handed, a left-handed pitcher would have a terrific edge against you. If your lineup has four left-handed hitters in a row, it might prove to be a sitting duck for a good left-handed relief pitcher. Also, in deciding who is to play, you have to try to hold back at least two pretty good hitters, a lefty and righty, for pinch hitting late in the game. If *all* your good hitters are in the starting lineup, the decisive rally may develop in such a way that you have no sufficiently dangerous batter to take the one crack that can win the game.

So a manager, in devising his batting order, gives a lot of thought to sequences within the order: who will bat after whom, what will happen if there's a change of pitcher at this point, and so on. If you have two slow-footed, heavy-hitting right-handers, you're just asking for rally-killing double plays by batting them consecutively. If you have a good left-handed pull hitter, you can almost eliminate the need for bunting with him by having a good base runner hit right in front of him. If you have a good bunter, he's wasted if the man before him can't run. And so on and so forth.

Stengel, in his glory years with the Yankees, had a wealth of talent and made platooning famous. He would, sometimes, lay out 12 lineup cards on his desk, as in solitaire. He would fill in the two names he was sure of—Mantle and Berra—on each card, and then he'd go to work. He would play out, in his mind, a dozen possible versions of the game coming up, and try to anticipate situations that might arise.

Your final batting order, then, will take account of the opposing pitcher and his equipment; the type of strength the opposition has in the bullpen; the lefty-righty balance and the power-speed balance available in your own club; the optimum offensive-defensive compromises; and the possible pinch-hitting moves you might make.

You sign the lineup card, give it to the umpires, discuss ground rules, take up a favorite position in the dugout, and the game begins.

You have already gone over, in detail, how you expect your pitcher to pitch to every hitter, and where you expect the fielders to play. (This is usually done in a clubhouse meeting before the first game of a series, but it is also a continuing conversation.) Now you quickly check: are they doing it? Are the fielders in the right spots, according to the hitter, the count, and the stuff being thrown? Is your pitcher getting the ball where he wants it?

Most of your attention, during the defensive half of the inning, is on your own pitcher. You watch his motion, and how his pitches behave. You'll be able to tell—amazingly well if you are a qualified manager—when he tires, or loses control, or loses his stuff. Hits may be falling safe against him, but if he's "throwing good," you'll let him weather the storm. Or he may be getting them out, but not showing the control or stuff he should have; in that case, you'll have the bullpen working at the first sign of trouble.

When you have to change pitchers, finally, you make the decision before you leave the dugout. Rarely does a manager let a pitcher talk him into letting him remain, and every manager can cite instances of being sorry when he did.

On the subject of changing pitchers, the second-guessers have a field day. Yet most fans have a completely backward view of the situation. It's not a question of taking a pitcher out, which is the way most fans look at it; it's a question of bringing someone in. The manager must always be thinking about the next play, not the last one. He stakes his judgment on how the *next* batter will be retired. It may be true that his pitcher has been getting hammered, but unless the manager is sure that the *new* pitcher represents a chance to do better, there's no sense changing.

So the moment of decision rests on *who* is in the bullpen, what kind of shape he is in, and who the other team will send to bat to face the relief pitcher. If a team has a great, reliable, healthy reliever, starters will be taken out much sooner than if it doesn't.

This is true of every move a manager makes: in his mind, it's a chance to improve the situation; otherwise, he doesn't make it. And he must always remember to save someone for tomorrow, too.

When the manager's team is at bat, he is much more active. He is calling the plays from the bench, just as so many football coaches do. He flashes the signal to the third-base coach, who flashes it to the batter, to hit or take a given pitch. This is an art in itself. It requires great experience and intuition to use this power constructively. Some hitters can be left pretty much on their own, some can't; what's more, the same hitter may need a tighter rein against one kind of pitching than against another. But it is the manager's unquestioned prerogative to give this order.

It is an order fraught with misunderstanding, even by many players. Batters want to hit; they want to swing at the first pitch they like; they want to avoid getting into a two-strike situation at all costs. Yet the manager, often, wants them to take pitches for tactical reasons. He may see the rival pitcher getting tired. He may want his own pitcher, who just ran the bases, to get a breather. He may, as an intruder into the pitcher-batter battle of wits, recognize a pattern better than his own (less experienced) hitter, and force him to lay off a pitch he knows won't be a good one to swing at.

It's the less intelligent hitter in the first place who gets the most guidance, and he's the one chafing most under a "take" sign. A take sign means, "don't swing, period." If it's a called strike, that's too bad, but don't swing. The hit sign, however, means "you have permission to swing *if you want to.*" There is a regrettable tendency for hitters to interpret, not quite consciously, a hit sign as an *order* to swing, and they proceed to swing at the next pitch even if it isn't a desirable one.

Some take situations used to be considered standard: a 3-0 count, often a 3-1 count. When it's 3-0, the pitcher must throw three consecutive strikes. His chances of missing with one of them are high. He might miss with the first or second, which would be a walk. Swinging at a 3-0 pitch, even though it may look so easy to hit, is doing the pitcher a favor, getting him out of a jam. It's still a round ball and a round bat, and the odds are against any one swing being a base hit. And when the count gets to 3-1 and 3-2, the pitcher still must offer a good pitch to hit. Nevertheless, with more and more emphasis on slugging, today's managers let men "hit" on 3-0 fairly frequently—and pitchers no longer assume the hitter will be taking. A breaking pitch on 3-0, once rare, is common now.

A fascinating instance of the subtleties involved came up in a routine game in 1965. If offered a fine illustration of how managers think.

The Yankees were playing at home. It was the last of the ninth, two out, and the score was tied. Elston Howard was the runner at first base. Ray Barker, a left-handed batter, was pinch hitting. The count went to 3-1.

Johnny Keane, the Yankee manager, made Barker take the next pitch. It was strike two. Then Barker hit a line-drive double to left-center, scoring Howard from first base and winning the game.

"Barker never did understand why we made him take that 3-1 pitch, until we explained it to him afterward," Keane recalls. "Thinking just as a hitter, he'd much rather get a chance to swing at that pitch, since the pitcher had to come in with it.

"But with Howard, who's a slow runner, at first base,

Barker would have had to hit a home run to win the game for us; there was no way he could score Howard from first with a long single or a double.

"However, once the count went to 3-2, Howard could break from first with the pitch, and be halfway to second by the time the ball was hit—and that's exactly what happened. With a running start, Ellie scored and the game was over. But if Barker had hit the ball to the exact same spot on a 3-1 pitch, Ellie wouldn't have started running until the ball was hit, and he would have had to stop at third.

"On the other hand, if the pitch had been ball four, the walk to Barker would have pushed Howard into scoring position automatically, and a single by the next man could have won the game."

Pitch by pitch, through a game, a manager thinks this way. He decides, at the last possible instant, whether to order a bunt or a hit-and-run, responding to what he thinks the defense isn't set for. He tries to do the unexpected, in standard situations, but the unexpected within the context of factors adding up in his favor. That is, *ideally* the manager does that. In practice, most managers are very much aware of the second-guessers—not so much the second-guessers in the stands, but those on his own bench, in the press box, and in his front office.

Most men are not heroes, and there are fewer mental heroes than physical heroes, certainly in athletics. The manager knows all the orthodox moves. If he makes an orthodox move and loses, no one can criticize him; if he goes "against the book" and wins, he's a genius—maybe—but if he goes against it and loses, the second-guessers may never let him up. Too often, too many managers play it safe: they go by the book not out of maximum conviction at that moment that the play is called for, but because it's the safest way to lose in an uncertain situation.

Aggressive, drama-oriented men—like Gene Mauch of the

Expos—would call this a question of "guts." It is debatable, however, whether caution is the exact opposite of courage. Let's say that most managers accept the fact that discretion—at least, some discretion—is the better part of staying a manager.

What's the best single qualification for being a manager?

Being independently wealthy.

Casey Stengel worked in such circumstances, as a Yankee and a Met, and other men have. It is a great liberating force. He might have been right or wrong, but Casey never had to stop to think how it would look. He could act on any crazy, or brilliant, or far-out hunch or idea, and it would work or it wouldn't, but his job would not be at stake—and if his job could be lost on such grounds, he couldn't care less.

If you're not independently wealthy, and have a family, it takes an extraordinary amount of mental discipline to ignore the fact that your decisions are constantly subject to criticism that can cost you your job. The human mind is remarkably efficient at finding sincere justifications for going by the book in such circumstances. And, in all fairness to the cautious ones, "gutsiness" can get just as far out of line. One can get too eager in proving one's contempt for the orthodox, and do things that are not really productive but do look daring. A rebel may acquire a stake in remaining a rebel. Being a brilliant freethinker is fine—if you can guarantee brilliance along with the freedom.

And here we are sliding back into the psychological areas, which remain the most important ones for a manager.

There's a discernible difference between the outlooks of older and younger managers.

The older men, like Stengel, believed that men can frequently be driven to do their best by abuse. They came out of an era that made no bones about employer-employee relationships, and that didn't believe in pampering. There is little to indicate that they were wrong in applying the whip in so combative, aggressive, physical, and essentially primitive activity as professional athletics.

The younger men—Ralph Houk, who succeeded Stengel, Mauch, Al Dark, Sparky Anderson, Chuck Tanner—run the full range of personality differences, but they accept the modern reality that players demand and need gentler treatment. They stress alertness, mental agility, the technical side of baseball, and profess interest in the happiness of their players. They don't live up to all their ideas, but these are their ideas. Their basic tenet seems to be: never criticize a player in public, never embarrass him.

It is thought-provoking, however, that managers seem to change as they grow older. An Al Lopez and a Birdie Tebbetts, who had "good guy" labels when they started, didn't have them ten years later and yet were probably better managers. Perhaps the age of the man, rather than his era, is a big factor: at first, the manager is close to his playing days, surrounded by contemporaries, mindful of his own gripes as a player, eager to do "better"; after a decade or two of managing, he has seen how little difference "happiness" makes, how unchangeable characters are, how inventive alibis can be, how many promises never materialize. He learns that it is never possible to explain everything to everyone, and stops trying. He says, "We'll do it *this* way," and lets it go at that.

And, if he has the players, he'll win. If he doesn't, he won't.

Houk, in three years as Yankee manager, won three pennants. His regime was an era of exceptional good feeling. He was one manager players honestly liked. His credo was "confidence building" and he was a whiz at it. Strategically, he was orthodox and conservative, which worked fine, because he had the best team. But when he returned, two years later, to a weak Yankee team, he finished last.

Another manager who generated deep affection among his men was the late Fred Hutchinson, whom no one regarded as a dazzling tactician. The best way to describe Hutch is to list whatever qualities imply the best meaning of the term "a man," and let it go at that.

Yet Houk and Hutch both produced a little plain, physical fear in the men who respected and liked them so much. They had the physique, and the nature, that convinced you it would not be a good idea to get them mad. They did have a few monumental rages, and after that they were obeyed on trust. Athletes, after all, are bound to be impressed by muscle.

So even the nice guys have to have something going for them. Walter Alston is in the same category: mild, a gentleman, patient, certainly pedestrian in his thinking, strictly by-the-book—but convincingly able to pop you one if it comes to a showdown.

The ultimate difference between managing and playing, then, is this: the player must *do*, and it doesn't really matter what he thinks; the manager must *think*, and he shouldn't really be judged by what players do.

A decision is right or it isn't on the basis of the factors weighed *before* the result takes place. If a manager is thinking right, consistently, things will work out right most of the time, but they'll often go wrong, too.

The sensible question in evaluating a manager is: how good were the grounds for the decisions he made?

If he changes pitchers, he has made a good or a bad move *before* the next batter hits a home run. The question is *why* was a home run hit? Was the pitcher the wrong man for some valid reason, or did he throw the wrong pitch, or was he instructed badly—or did the batter just hit a home run despite the percentages in the pitcher's favor? And did the manager have any real alternative to this particular pitching change?

Great players will make a mediocre manager a genius. Second-rate players will make a genius a losing manager. All the manager can do is get the right ideas; it doesn't follow that his fellas will be able to beat the other fellas in nine innings.

In 1951, the Yankees and Indians had a thrilling pennant

race. Down the stretch, Al Lopez, the Cleveland manager, decided to use his three aces, Bob Lemon, Early Wynn, and Mike Garcia, for the last three weeks of the season, pitching with two days' rest. They did fine. But the Yankees won 20 of their last 24 games and beat out the Indians anyhow. That was when Stengel, a close friend of Lopez, permitted himself a public comment on Lopez's handling of pitchers.

"Well, yes, I see where he's doing that," said Stengel. "They say you can never do that, but he is, and it's a good idea, but sometimes it doesn't always work."

That's managing in a nutshell: the endless search for ideas that always work sometimes.

And that's why there's really a very simple answer to our original question.

What do managers *really* do?

Worry.

Constantly.

For a living.

5

· **Go-go-go!**

Baseball fans' chant

Stealing's Allowed, or, How Maury Wills Brought Back Larceny

To the connoisseur, the most exciting baseball action happens on the bases. It is the one aspect of the game completely free of luck. The base runner who steals or takes an extra base on a hit or an out has no bad bounce to contend with, no infinitesimal physics of spin or ball-against-bat to deal with. Only his mind, his skill, and his speed afoot are involved, and these are constants.

It is also, apparently, the most instinctive part of the game. Great base runners seem to be born, or at least trained in the earliest, formative stages of their baseball experience. The basic ideas of when to run and when not to, of course, can be taught to anyone. But the two things that really count—instantaneous grasp of the situation, and the ability to go from a standstill to top speed in the first step—are rarely acquired and only slightly improved even by years of practice.

Base-stealing was a primary offensive weapon in baseball until Babe Ruth started hitting home runs by the gross in the 1920s. Up to that time, the baseball itself was "deader" than the one used today—it didn't carry as far, because of its construction, and because one battered ball was kept in action longer. Scores were lower, one run meant more, and home runs were few. Standard procedure was for the man on first to try to steal second, so that he could score on a single. Pitcher and catcher developed techniques to prevent this, as one of their main concerns, but even so the risk was worthwhile, because if the runner didn't reach second, the chance of scoring was so small.

All players, then, were expected to be reasonably adept at stealing, even slow ones, just as they were expected to be able to catch the ball and throw it.

Babe Ruth changed all that. By making the home run so glamorous—and proving that is was so possible—he led the owners into introducing a livelier ball, which gave more players the opportunity to be home-run hitters. Once home runs became frequent, base-stealing became comparatively obsolete. Now the risk of being thrown out was too great, since the man at bat might hit a two-run homer. With decreased use, the need for mastering base-stealing skills disappeared. By the middle of the 1930s, only a few specialists in each league practiced the art.

It's not entirely a coincidence that Ty Cobb, who compiled the best batting record in baseball history (a .367 average for 24 seasons starting in 1905), was also the best base stealer. In his day, the two weapons went hand in hand, just as in recent times we expect any really great hitter (Mays, Mantle, Williams, DiMaggio, Aaron, Musial) to have a high home-run output. Since his hits put him on base more often than anyone else, Cobb had more opportunities to steal, and he made the most of them.

And Babe Ruth himself came out of the same era. A little-remembered aspect of a very famous World Series game is worth pondering, because it gives the modern fan a glimpse of how completely different the attitude toward base-stealing used to be.

The seventh game of the 1926 World Series is one of the most frequently retold events of baseball history. The Yankees were playing the St. Louis Cardinals, who had just won their first pennant, in the still new and incomplete Yankee Stadium (which had been opened in 1923). Grover Cleveland Alexander, one of the greatest of all pitchers but now near the end of his career and 39 years old, had beaten the Yankees in the sixth game to bring about this showdown game.

Every baseball fan has heard (and a popular movie has depicted) how Alexander came out of the bullpen and struck out Tony Lazzeri in the seventh game. The Cardinals were leading, 3-2, and the Yankees had the bases loaded with two out when Alexander relieved Jess Haines.

What very few baseball fans know is what happened afterward. It was, after all, only the seventh inning, not the ninth, when Lazzeri fanned. Alex got through the eighth and got the first two outs in the ninth—and then walked Ruth, who had already hit four home runs in that World Series.

The score was still 3-2. A home run would win for the Yankees. The batter was Bob Muesel, a right-handed batter who had led the league in homers the year before.

But Muesel never got a chance. Ruth tried to steal second, on the first pitch, and was thrown out, ending the Series.

Such an attempt today would be inconceivable; then it was the normal way to play baseball. As Ruth told Tom Meany, a young sports writer, in the locker room after the game: "Well, I wasn't doing any blanking good where I was," meaning first base.

Other aspects of base-running didn't decline as much as stealing did after the Ruthian Revolution, but they did to a degree. The hit-and-run play became less important, not so much because of the base runners but because fewer batters could execute their part of it as they concentrated more and more on free-swinging for the fences. (The runners were also important, though, because on a hit-and-run play, the runner has to have a good chance of stealing the base in case the batter misses the ball.)

Attempts to stretch singles into doubles by daring base-running also decreased, because, again, the risk of being thrown out wasn't worth it when a subsequent homer could score the man from first. Least affected was the attempt to go from first to third on a single, but even here there was a shade more willingness to stop at second (in doubtful situations).

In short, the emphasis shifted from maximum *advance* to maximum *men on*. It became more important to have as many men as possible safely on base when the home run did come up, than to risk losing some of them for the sake of an extra base. It would be a double loss: not only would a runner be wiped out, but another out would be recorded, which might keep a home-run hitter from getting another swipe later in the game.

Like most changes, though, this one took effect gradually. Ten years after the lively ball had been installed, the major-league players were men who had been brought up in the old style (like Ruth himself). Only in the mid-1930s did the population of the majors shift to men who never had had to concentrate much on base-running, and by the time World War II ended, stealing was strictly an exciting specialty for such stars as Jackie Robinson.

Then, just as the 1960s began, a skinny little 28-year-old man of exceptional determination revived the moribund art in its full glory. His name was Maurice Morning Wills, and he had spent almost a decade getting nowhere in his chosen profession.

Wills is the man who finally broke Cobb's record (set in 1915) by stealing 104 bases in 1962. If ever a record seemed unassailable, it was Cobb's mark of 96 stolen bases in one season. The game had simply changed too much. Between 1928 and 1959, only three players (one of them twice) had been able to steal even *half* as many as that. Then Luis Aparicio, a slim Venezuelan with the Chicago White Sox, started (in 1959) to steal 50 or more a year.

But Aparicio didn't make the impact on the baseball world that Wills did, because his totals were only high, not undreamed of. When Wills stole 50 bases to lead the National League in 1960, it was the highest total any National Leaguer had posted since 1923—nine years before Wills was born. When, two years later, he stole more than twice as many, it was a far more startling achievement to baseball insiders than the breaking of Ruth's home-run record by Roger Maris the year before.

The story of Maury Wills is interesting enough as a typical success-of-the-underdog biography. But it deserves more thoughtful attention than it gets from many ball players, and it certainly has had an important effect on the attitudes of many players. For managers, Maury has provided an object lesson to be used with certain types of players, and his efforts have revived awareness of base-running among fans and reporters. He has not changed baseball back to what it was before Ruth—nothing could do that—but he has brought about a shift of emphasis. It spread to his teammates and then, after the Dodger World Series victories of 1963 and 1965, to other teams.

Wills was born in Washington, D.C., and went to work in the lowest link of the Dodger chain at Hornell, N.Y., when he was not yet 19. He was a right-handed hitter who played the infield and pitched occasionally, and he didn't do badly. In 1951, however, a black man could not yet take rapid advancement for granted; Robinson had broken the color line with the Dodgers only four years before. To the outstanding talents—like Willie Mays, who reached the Giants that season, and Don Newcombe and Larry Doby—the barriers were down, but the ordinary black player still faced a practical, if unacknowledged, quota. If he were good enough to beat out a white regular, O.K.—but in those days there was little room for the merely equally good black.

And there was nothing outstanding about Maury. He hit well enough at the Class D level—.280 his first year, .300 his second—but he obviously had no power and little special attractiveness to a Dodger organization whose parent club had eight home-run-hitting regulars in cozy Ebbets Field.

Wills moved on to Pueblo, Miami, back to Pueblo, Fort Worth, Pueblo again, and finally Seattle, one step below the majors. His statistics were always respectable, but his power insufficient. He had settled at shortstop by now, where he was a pretty good fielder but not spectacular.

But in 1958, the whole baseball world changed.

The Dodgers moved from Brooklyn to Los Angeles, where they had to play in a football stadium, the Coliseum, which has lopsided dimensions for baseball with no left field and an impossibly deep right field. At the same time, Robinson had retired; Pee Wee Reese was through as the regular shortstop; Roy Campanella had been crippled in an automobile accident; Gil Hodges and Carl Furillo were aging. Suddenly, there were all sorts of new needs and opportunities for the Dodgers.

The chief Dodger farm club was now Spokane, and that's where Wills was. The manager was Bobby Bragan, who had already managed two major-league clubs. The Dodgers were still not terribly interested in Wills, and another club—the Detroit Tigers—had turned him down. Maury was no kid anymore, in an era when $50,000-bonus youngsters were getting more and more attention. He had not yet earned as much as $7,000 in any one year of playing baseball. And not one baseball fan in a million, outside of the Pacific Coast League, would have recognized his name.

Then Bragan made a suggestion.

Maury's main asset was speed. Obviously, he had good bat control and the ability to meet the ball, because his averages were always respectable. What if he became a switch-hitter? Batting lefty three-quarters of the time (against the 75 percent of the pitchers who were right-handed) would put his speed to best use: being closer to first base, he would beat out more infield hits; he could bunt for hits much more effectively; and by reaching first base more often, he would get more opportunities to steal.

Maury tried it.

We can appreciate, after our discussions about batting, what strength of purpose it must take for a man to attempt this kind of change in his eighth year as a professional. Just to accept the fact that he was going nowhere the way he was required a kind of firm-mindedness that many players with poor records don't have.

What Wills had to an exceptional degree was desire to succeed. Given the threshold of physical ability any professional ball player needs, Wills made his career from that point on by his mental discipline, perfectionism, alertness, and willingness to make the utmost demands on himself.

He learned to hit left-handed. Since he didn't have any power anyhow, he didn't have to worry about swinging hard. He could wait to the last moment, smack the ball sharply through the infield, and a good proportion of the time beat it out if he tapped it weakly. By swinging down and smacking the ball so that it would take a high, long first bounce off a hard infield (a technique to which Casey Stengel, a lifelong advocate, gave the immortal name "butcher boy"), Maury could get a hit while the fielder helplessly waited for the ball to come to him.

To do this, however, Maury had to be a leading student of pitching. With his handicaps and his style, he had to hit intelligently, not instinctively. This required, again, mental application in studying all pitchers at all times and a good eye for the strike zone, two things that imply strong mental discipline.

Then Maury applied the same outlook to base-running.

He studied and analyzed every rival pitcher's move to first base just as thoroughly as the most analytic hitters did the pitcher's pitching motion. In his mental "book," Maury came to know exactly when each individual pitcher was going to throw to first, when he was going to bluff, and when—most important of all—he reached a point in his motion that committed him to throwing to the plate.

With this knowledge, and with tireless vigilance for the tiniest deviation from familiar patterns, Maury could take the biggest possible lead without being picked off—and, when stealing, could be on his way to second at the earliest possible moment.

It is an axiom of big-league baseball that a runner steals "on the pitcher," not "on the catcher." At lower levels of competition, this is not true. If the catcher's arm is weak or inaccurate, the base runner will be safe even if he doesn't get the best start imaginable. In the majors, though, while some catchers have better arms than others, all can make the routine play, or they don't get the chance to catch in the majors. The difference, then, lies in how good a "jump" the runner can get—how big a lead, and how soon he can get moving.

It's the pitcher's responsibility to keep the runner under control. Most of his throws to first are not an intention, or even a hope, to get an out; they are a means of making the runner come back if he has taken too big a lead. And to a large extent, a pitcher can keep a runner pinned just by looking at him. If, within the context of the balk rules, the pitcher can keep the possibility of a throw to first open until the last moment, and then make his pitch to the plate with a rapid motion, the runner has very little time in which to make his decision, shift his weight, start his legs moving, and pick up speed.

It's often said, then, that a base is stolen in the first stride, not in the last, unless the catcher makes a bad throw.

Wills perfected these techniques. He did have the gift of a great "first step" (which is also such a great asset to basketball players and football running backs). And he made the most of it. Many, many other men have the same innate ability, but don't develop it; and very few put in the mental effort, the tireless observation, that make such base-running possible. By the middle of 1959, he was a Dodger; by October, he was in the World Series. By 1962, he was a star.

There is a third factor, also deeply involved with spirit and will. Stealing means sliding, and sliding means pain, frequent minor injuries, and always the risk of a more serious injury. To play the type of game Wills did requires stealing whenever possible, keeping on the pressure, establishing a pattern of daring—and this means running when you are already hurt, when the scrapes and bruises and ankle twists are not healed. And the more times you slide into a base, the more times you may collide with or be spiked by the man defending it.

So the steps in stealing are:

1. Get on. "You can't steal first base."
2. Know the pitcher's moves.
3. Be able to spot any lapse in concentration, and take advantage of it.
4. Know the pitching pattern, to find the best pitch to steal on and to avoid pitchouts.
5. Get a good jump.
6. Know how to slide, to avoid a tag even if the ball is there in time.

All these are things that can be learned, or at least improved. Getting on means taking the base on balls by having a good eye, and swinging to meet the ball, not to kill it.

Studying pitchers is just that—study, concentration, dedication, not a gift from heaven. Sliding is practice—hard, unpleasant practice. There are various types of slides, to be used consciously according to the position of the ball and the baseman; the idea is to give the man making the tag the smallest target to touch—a toe or a hand.

Choosing the right pitch on which to steal is a matter that shades into team play, and in this Wills had adept teammates who, in turn, adjusted to or adopted Maury's way of doing things. The manager, too, is fundamentally involved, in giving (in the case of a Wills) the runner free rein to use his judgment. The ordinary player doesn't steal unless he's given permission—a permission similar to the "hit" sign to a batter in that it doesn't *order* the runner to go, but only *allows* him if he thinks he can. The runner is obliged, of course, to try to arrange it so he can, and 99 times out of 100 he will go when given the sign—if he gets it.

The "right" pitch involves the count on the hitter, the type of delivery the pitcher uses, and the psychological battle between runner and pitcher (which includes the catcher, who is thinking with the pitcher).

If the count is 0-2—no balls, two strikes—it is obviously a bad time to steal, since the catcher won't hesitate to call for a pitchout just in case. (A pitchout is thrown deliberately wide of the plate, so that the batter can't reach it and so that the catcher can make a quick, unobstructed throw to second.) With that count, the pitcher can waste a ball, or even two.

By the same token, with the count 2-0—two balls, no strikes—the pitcher is very concerned with making the next pitch a strike, so the runner's opportunity is that much greater. What's more, the batter can even afford to help by swinging at the pitch and missing; it's only one strike on him and he might bother the catcher making the throw.

The type of pitch makes a big difference, too. A knuckle ball is an invitation to steal, because the catcher has his hands full trying to hold it, let alone throw it. *Any* kind of slow pitch is easier to steal on than a fast ball, because it takes the ball longer to reach home plate, and the catcher can't throw the ball until it does. A breaking pitch, especially a low-breaking pitch, also helps the runner by traveling slower and by giving the catcher an extra problem.

If a left-hander is at bat, the runner on first is at least partially blocked out from the catcher (and with a righty, the runner on third). If a pitch is low to the third-base side of the plate, the right-handed catcher (and all catchers are right-handed) will need a fraction of a second more to get into throwing position than if the pitch is to the first-base side. (And why are catchers always right-handed? Because, since most batters are right-handed, there is less chance of the batter getting in the way of the catcher's throwing motion. But this may be more traditional than necessary.)

The base runner, then, by doing the kind of thinking that the man at bat and the pitcher are doing, may find a moment of maximum advantage to steal on.

One quality has been omitted from this whole discussion, and significantly so. A good base stealer, or any good base runner, does *not* have to be exceptionally fast. That's one of the most widespread misconceptions. He can't be slower-than-average, of course, but every team has some men on it (often pitchers) who can beat the best base runner in a foot race. It's not a question of how fast you can run; some sprinters are terrible base runners. It's a matter of deciding exactly when, and starting quickly, and sliding well.

Wills, or any other outstanding base stealer, brings his team many indirect benefits. All are predicated on his percentage of success, however; if he were getting thrown out half the time or more, he would be killing more rallies than he was helping. Most of the good ones run to a percentage of success of .700 or more; they are safe on more than 70 percent of their attempts.

What are these team benefits?

Most of all, a threatening base runner, like Robinson, Wills, Willie Mays, or Aparicio, bothers pitchers. The pitcher worries about him, throws over, looks. All this can interfere with the pitcher's concentration on the hitter. It can spoil his aim. Many a walk has been issued, and many a home-run ball served up, because of a base-runner's harassment. This is much truer today than in the old days, because pitchers aren't as experienced in worrying about base runners. Just as the home-run style bred out the base runners among hitters, so pitchers have not had to master the techniques of constantly keeping runners in check.

Second, the better base runner can keep the first baseman pinned to the bag a trifle longer, thus keeping the right-side hole open a trifle longer. He can force the shortstop or second baseman to play a trifle closer in, since to get the double play they may have to move a little faster. Playing in more, they leave more room for a grounder to go through for a hit. These are small edges, measured in inches, but inches can decide the game.

Third, the good base runner, by his success, increases the efficiency of the offense. The same number of hits can produce more runs.

Fourth, he can upset the entire defense. Fielders may hurry throws and relays, infielders and outfielders may be too hasty trying to pick up a grounder. The catcher, most of all, may be rushed on a bunt play or on an attempted steal or on a pick-off, and may throw the ball away. A small number of such incidents has a large effect on the steadiness of the opposition.

Fifth is the other side of the coin: his alertness and daring can be contagious, can lift the spirit of his own team, can make teammates bear down harder. An air of aggressive excitement can be transmitted to the whole team.

So far, most of our attention has been on stealing, which remains the province of specialists even though the specialty has enjoyed a revival and an expansion. As baseball scoring has decreased, stealing a base has become more important and a more worthwhile risk—for exactly the same reasons that the skill was developed in dead-ball days—and such stars as Lou Brock, Campy Campaneris, Luis Aparicio, Joe Morgan, and Bobby Bonds have compiled base-stealing records unimagined between the retirement of Cobb and the advent of Wills. Nevertheless, just as only a few men are truly suited for hitting homers consistently, only a few have the potential for stealing 40 bases a year.

But the other aspects of base-running apply to everyone.

Coaches at first and third are supposed to help base runners. In most situations, there is little they can do. Most of the time it is up to the runner to see where the ball is hit, estimate how far he can advance, and do so without hesitation. He must take into account the effectiveness of the arm of the fielder involved, the position of the ball with respect to the fielder in terms of how long it will take to retrieve the ball and throw it, and his own established speed (modified by the amount of jump he had).

The base runner must consider the score and the number of outs to determine what sort of risk is worthwhile and what isn't. Trailing by four runs, with one out in the bottom of the ninth, there's not much sense in trying to go from first to third on a marginal hit, because the runs that matter must still get on and score after you; the big thing is to avoid even the remote possibility of an out. Trailing by one run, in the same situation, it's definitely worth a try, because then you can score the tying run, and avert a defeat, on an out.

The most common responsibility faced by every runner—

slow or fast, big or little, bright or dumb—is to try to break up a double play. This is baseball's muscle play. The man from first must try to slide into second hard enough to spill the pivotman and prevent him from making an accurate throw to first. This means, first of all, getting there soon enough, and then being willing to mix it up without too meticulous a concern for the exact location of the bag itself. Games, and pennants, are decided on the success or failure to break up a double play.

The same necessity, but a different means, applies in this situation: men on first and third, none out, the batter bounces to the third baseman or the pitcher. The man on third *must* break for home. If he doesn't, the fielder will start a second-to-first double play and the runner at third will still be there. If he breaks for home, they will have to make a play on him to prevent a run from scoring. He will be a sure out, but only one out, and his team will still be left with men on first and second.

If the man on third is a good and creative base runner, he will manage to get into a chase, and to elude being put out until the other two runners reach second and third. This is hard to do in the specific example given, but it is a general rule: when a runner is caught between bases, he must dodge back and forth long enough to permit the other runners to advance as far as possible.

Always, there is a fine line of judgment: aggressive base-running brings tremendous rewards, in extra bases and runs and in forced errors by the opposition; too much daring results in giving the opposition undeserved outs, gets the opposition out of trouble, and wastes your own hits.

Unfortunately, for the dedicated but truth-seeking second-guesser, those judgments all hinge on the angle of vision of the players on the field, and it is hard to condemn mistakes correctly. It may have been plain enough to me, in the press box, that Joe Pepitone had no chance to score on that hit to left-center, but it may have looked entirely different to both Pepitone, as he left second base, and to the third-base coach, also at ground level.

There is another responsibility every base runner has, and it is remarkable how often he fails to discharge it: he must catch all the signs flashed to him. If the batter is going to sacrifice, or hit-and-run, the runner must be notified; just as the batter is signaled by the third-base coach relaying the manager's instructions, so the runner is signaled, by a coach, or from the bench, or by the batter.

If the runner misreads the sign, it's instant trouble. The batter bunts, the runner is standing flat-footed off first, and an out has been wasted (and possibly a double play made). If the runner thinks the bunt is on and it isn't, there he goes chugging into a sure out at second, or finds himself unable to get back to first.

From the manager's point of view, stealing and hit-and-run merge into a larger concept called "starting." On certain pitches, in certain situations, the manager may want to "start" the runner from first base without the classical hit-and-run play in mind. He may feel that this way he can avoid a double play, or get an extra base. He weighs all the factors—the speed of his man, the pitcher's abilities, the game situation, the position of the fielders, the pitch he thinks is coming up, and so forth.

There is one automatic starting situation known to every baseball fan: two out and a 3-2 count on the hitter. In this case, the runner on first cannot be put out once the pitcher throws: it will be ball four, a foul, or a hit, or the batter will make the third out anyhow.

But on many other occasions in a game, not at all automatic, the manager will "start" the base runner for some purpose. And that's one more reason managers burn at hitters who swing too hard and miss, hanging up a runner.

Almost all the situations we've talked about involve a

runner at first. Most of the action takes place there, because that is where options exist. A runner on second will rarely try to steal third, because the gain—to score on a subsequent out instead of on a hit, which would score the man from second anyhow—is not proportional to the risk. The catcher must throw only 90 feet to third instead of 127 feet to second. And stealing home is strictly a desperation measure or a grandiose gesture.

Wills was criticized for stealing bases "when it isn't necessary," and accused of "showboating"—an accusation discernibly tinged with race prejudice in the baseball world. Maury's reply, aside from self-justification and the emotions he arouses, gives more insight into the real nature of baseball than the views of his critics. "My game is running," he said, "and I have to do it at every opportunity, both to keep myself sharp and to keep the opposition on edge. Besides, when can you have too many runs? Is a home-run hitter criticized for hitting a home run after the score is 10-1? If our team is ahead 10-1—and how often is it?—I'd still like to help make it 11-1 by stealing my way into scoring position. I've got no guarantee the other team won't score nine more runs."

That's the baseball we're talking about: played by humans, with varying abilities, trying to make the winning plays in the situations that exist *at the time*—not in abstract situations after the fact.

On the other hand, some men should *not* try to steal even when they can. The outstanding example was Mickey Mantle. Exceptionally fast most of his career, Mickey also had all the base-running instincts in the highest degree. He could, almost literally, steal a base whenever he put his mind to it; and the relatively few times that it could mean victory, he would. But Mickey's entire career was plagued by leg injuries, and it would have been plain foolishness to allow him to take the pounding and risk the injuries that frequent stealing would entail. He was too valuable in other ways, as a slugger and a fielder, to be lost for two weeks because he was injured when stealing a base.

Besides, Mantle usually played on Yankee teams that had plenty of power, and daring base-running simply never made sense with that sort of lineup. This is illustrated by Willie Mays, perhaps the most innately talented base runner of all, and as blessed with good health as Mantle was crippled. Willie led the National League in base-stealing before Wills arrived—in seasons when the Giants were relatively weak. When the Giant lineup became loaded with sluggers again, like Orlando Cepeda and Willie McCovey, to drive Willie in, the risks of stealing were no longer in the team's interest, and his totals shrank.

With Wills, it was different: he had to take the pounding, because running was his asset. If he got hurt, and couldn't play, his services were lost—but if he didn't run, they were lost anyhow. The Mantles, Mayses, and Henry Aarons have too much hitting ability to run indiscriminately, even though they could.

The revival of "running" baseball—not really a counter-revolution against the home-run era, but a slight shift in values—is not simply the creation of Wills; in fact, he's the creation of it. But he will remain for some time the symbol of the change. Actually, the renewed emphasis on running is the product of an improved level of pitching and an increased number of parks with large playing areas.

After all, the old-fashioned single-bunt-steal-single offense evolved in baseball because the pitcher was supreme. In the dead-ball era, runs came hard. In the lively-ball era, with limitations on trick deliveries, a brand-new white baseball put into play every moment, and lots of short fences, the pitcher was on the defensive. Running could be ignored, because swinging for the fences paid off.

In the last decade, however, the balance has shifted somewhat back toward pitching. Why? Eddie Stanky, a superb baseball analyst who spent years scouting between stints as manager of the Cardinals and White Sox, has a simple answer:

"Pitching can be taught more effectively than hitting can," he says. "Today's youngsters are well-schooled, well-trained, looked after, and advised. We work with hitters as much as with pitchers, but by the nature of things, pitchers get better results. So the day of bad pitching is gone, forever. Outstanding pitchers are still rare, but the level of the second-flight pitchers is way up."

When pitching is better, runs are harder to get. When runs are harder to get, the offense has to try something different. On top of that, Dodger Stadium in Chavez Ravine, Candlestick Park, the Astrodome, Shea Stadium, and the new stadium in St. Louis are far less conducive to homers than Ebbets Field, the Polo Grounds, or old Busch Stadium used to be.

It's not a coincidence that Wills achieved what he did on a team that had some of the greatest pitchers ever assembled on one staff—Sandy Koufax, Don Drysdale, Johnny Podres, Ron Perranoski. They kept pitching shutouts, one-run games, two-run games. With pitchers like that, a couple of runs can be enough to win, and the Wills style of offense is designed to produce a couple of runs a game even if the opposing pitcher is overpowering, too. If, on the other hand, Wills played on a team with poor pitching, so that the other team could feel confident of scoring five or six runs a game, the opposition wouldn't worry about Wills. Let him steal it he's three runs behind; what good will it do, if enough other men are retired? He might still post a fancy statistic, but all the indirect, victory-producing values of his style would evaporate if his own pitchers didn't produce close, low-scoring games all the time.

So even in the most personal of all baseball actions, base-running—where no ball or bat must be controlled, just your own body and will—extensive interrelations and team considerations pop up at every step. That unique blend of individual responsibility and team effect is, as Branch Rickey has pointed out, the combination that makes baseball so distinctive among team games.

6

· **You can't get rich sitting on the bench—but I'm giving it a try.**

Phil Linz, 1965

In the Dugout

According to the rule book, a baseball team is composed of nine men.

According to real life in the major leagues, a team has 25 players, all thoroughly needed.

According to the rule book, no one is allowed in the dugout during a game but active players in uniform, the manager (even if he chooses to wear civies), and trainers in uniform.

According to television networks, their cameras belong in dugouts, too, if that will make an attractive angle to shoot from. And if they can persuade the baseball people to accept the practices pro football accepted some time ago, they'd like to interview the manager and players between pitches, too.

Why shouldn't they? What goes on in the dugout that's so private, anyhow? And why does it take 25 men to play a nine-position game?

These are the topics we'll touch upon as we deal with the fifth and final dimension of a baseball game: the bench.

Originally, substitutes were just that. In the 1880s, when professional baseball was working out its future form by trial and error, a team had only 11 men—eight regulars, two pitchers, and a substitute. (Pitchers could pitch every other day then because overhand pitching was not allowed.) Later the squad became 15 men, as more pitchers had to be added. Before World War II, the active limit in the majors was 23. Since the war, it has been 25. To be more exact, a club is allowed to have 40 men on its roster, some of whom must be farmed out. By opening day, the "active" list must be cut to 25 men, who are eligible to play in official games, and it stays that way until September 1. From September 1 to the end of the season, all 40 may play.

The normal distribution these days is ten pitchers, six or seven infielders, five or six outfielders, and three catchers. This is a very flexible arrangement, fluctuating with the talent available and affected by front-office considerations (when a player can't be farmed out but is too desirable to be abandoned). A team may carry 11 pitchers, or nine; many get by with only two catchers; many utility men can play both infield and outfield. (If the designated hitter rule applies, your proportions may differ, as you may choose to have one less pitcher, or keep a man who can't really play anywhere defensively but can hit well, or keep a defensive specialist because pinch-hitters will be used so seldom).

But there are sound reasons for the standard pattern. Take pitching, for instance: you need four regular starters, who need the full three days of rest; you need at least two others capable of starting, because the schedule will often call for more than four games in four days, and because all four regulars are not likely to get through a whole season without injury; you need at least two capable relief pitchers, a left-hander and a right-hander, for late-game crises, and if they are to be available more or less every day, they can never start. That adds up to eight, which is the minimum. Two more may be young pitchers in the process of development, or older men backstopping the other functions.

Or take catchers. Many catchers are not good hitters, but worth playing because they are good receivers. In the seventh inning, let's say, you might want to pinch-hit for the catcher. Now your second catcher has to go into action in the eighth. But suppose he gets hurt; you can't play the game, especially in extra innings, without an experienced receiver, one who can handle pitchers and keep base runners under control. So you need a third catcher for insurance. (Here we see one of the less noticed benefits of having a first-string catcher who is an outstanding hitter; since you won't pinch-hit for him if he's Yogi Berra or Roy Campanella or Johnny Bench or Gabby Hartnett or Bill Dickey, one extra catcher may be all you need.)

Outfielders are usually chosen for their hitting. If you have a slugger who is a very poor fielder, you probably want a good defensive outfielder on the bench, to put into the game in the late innings if you have the lead. Infielders, especially short-stops, are more often chosen for fielding skill. Occasionally, then, you may want to pinch-hit for a regular infielder, when you are trailing. Then you need another good fielder to put in so that whatever lead your pinch hitter provided won't be frittered away again.

Relief pitchers fall into two categories: "short men," the late-inning crisis specialists, who are supposed to be able to pitch out of the worst sort of trouble; and "long men," the ones who relieve when a starter gets knocked out early in a game. Long men are expected to be able to pitch five or six effective innings, to keep things in hand until your hitters can pull even. Usually, long-man functions are performed by the extra starters, but here, too, it's nice if you can have a lefty-righty balance and some degree of specialization.

When a game starts, most of the extra pitchers and catchers go down to the bullpen. One pitcher who will not be used— yesterday's starter, or tomorrow's, or perhaps one who is nursing an injury—will remain in the dugout and keep a chart of every pitch thrown in the game. It will show, for every opposing batter, what sort of pitch was thrown, what part of the strike zone it found or missed, and where the ball was hit. This is raw material for future analysis.

Every team has some players who develop the knack of stealing signals or "reading" pitchers. Reading a pitcher means spotting some idiosyncrasy or inconsistency in his movements which tips off the type of pitch he's going to throw. The catcher's signals to the pitcher are, of course, invisible from the bench (because the catcher hides his hands between his legs when he crouches). But the coaches' signals, being relayed to the opposing batter, are there for everyone to see. If the other team's intention to bunt or hit-and-run or steal can be intercepted, it can be put to use. This is espionage, pure and simple.

Therefore, at least one player on the bench is busy studying the opposition at all times, trying to crack codes. He may pick up something useful for that game, or for the future, but he works at it. At the same time, the other team is doing likewise, and another player on our team may be studying our own tip-offs as a preventive measure—a sort of counterespionage or internal security check.

Not only the pitcher can give away information. An infielder, by shifting position too soon, or a characteristic gesture, may reveal what's coming. A famous instance happened in the 1920 World Series between the Dodgers and Cleveland. Brooklyn's best pitcher was Burleigh Grimes, a spitball specialist (when this was still legal). His second baseman, Pete Kilduff, developed the habit of grabbing a handful of dirt every time the catcher signaled for a spitball, to counteract the slipperiness of the wet ball if it happened to be hit to him. The Indians spotted this half-conscious habit, and knew when to let the spitball go by to wait for something easier to hit, or to catch it before it broke. Grimes shut them out the first time he faced them, but then they beat him twice.

Sometimes the spy-counterspy activity can get out of hand, with hilarious (from the winner's point of view) results. A delicious incident came up in Washington in 1963. It was August, and the Yankees had a firm grip on first place, but their pitching staff was rocky, and there was still plenty of time for trouble to develop. Whitey Ford pitched the first game of a twi-night doubleheader, and lost. Now Stan Williams was pitching the second game for the Yankees, and pitching his heart out, but it was still 0-0 in the top of the eighth. The idea of losing a doubleheader to the inept Senators made the Yankees distinctly uncomfortable.

Then the Yankees scored. Here's what we saw from the press box: Tony Kubek singled, broke for second, and continued to third when the catcher's throw sailed over second base into center field. Bobby Richardson poked a single through a drawn-in infield and the Yankees had a run. It turned out to be the only run, and Williams had an important 1-0 victory.

And here's what Manager Ralph Houk revealed a few days later:

Before the inning began, while the teams were changing sides, Houk spoke to both Kubek and Richardson in the dugout. "If Tony gets on," Houk told them, "Bobby, you hit and run on the first pitch. I'm not even going to give a signal. Just go up and do it."

Sure enough, Kubek got on.

"My intention," Houk explained to us, "was to make extra sure that no one could miss a sign, or that Washington couldn't read it. Sometimes you can read another team just by the hesitation, by the way the players act, without even actually getting the signal itself. I didn't want anything to go wrong."

Houk overlooked only one thing. He neglected to tell Frank Crosetti, his third-base coach, that he had already talked to Kubek and Richardson. And that was natural enough, because Crosetti was probably on his way to the coaching line before the fielders had returned to the dugout as the teams were changing sides.

So there was Kubek, on first base, nobody out, score 0-0, top of the eighth. Coming to bat was Richardson, one of the best hit-and-run men in the business. The possibility was obvious to both sides. The question was, which pitch?

Crosetti looked into the dugout for a sign. There had to be

one—either hit-and-run, or a take sign so that there could be a hit-and-run on a subsequent pitch. Or perhaps the manager wanted a sacrifice bunt. The coach doesn't make decisions, he transmits them. Crosetti looked.

No sign.

Crosetti looked again.

No sign.

Whatever was happening, it seemed obvious that Houk was not putting on any sort of play, and evidently the hitter was on his own.

So Crosetti decided he might as well distract the Senators with some decoy signs. If there was no play on, it wouldn't matter what motions Crosetti made, but the Senators wouldn't know that.

As Richardson stepped in to hit, Crosetti started giving phantom signals. He put on a magnificent act.

The Washington catcher saw these meaningless contortions, and leaped in the wrong direction to a correct conclusion. He interpreted Crosetti's gyrations as a hit-and-run sign.

So he called for a pitchout.

The pitcher threw. Kubek broke for second. It was a fine pitchout, at least two feet wide of the plate. The Senators had caught the Yankees dead to rights. Kubek would be out by ten feet.

Richardson did the only thing he could do. He flung his bat at the ball, hoping at least to deflect it foul, to save Kubek's running life.

The bat missed the ball.

The catcher made a perfect throw to second.

But the Senator second baseman and shortstop got their own signals mixed. In such situations, they are supposed to have it made up between them, before the play, which one will cover the bag. This time both started, both hesitated, both stopped—and the ball flew right over the base with neither fielder within 15 feet of it.

Kubek, who had stumbled a bit leaving first, just kept running and made third easily.

Houk, having nearly swallowed his cud of tobacco, breathed easier.

Crosetti looked for the next sign.

The Washington catcher (it was Jim Retzer) was so mad he couldn't see straight.

And the Washington manager, Gil Hodges, had no choice. At that stage of the game, he had to bring his infield in for a possible play at the plate.

Then Richardson hit his single and the mighty Yankees had another victory.

Add up the heroes in that play: Houk, Crosetti, and two Washington infielders made mistakes; neither Richardson (unable to hit the ball) nor Kubek (who didn't get the best possible jump) carried out their play well; the only man who was dead right—for the wrong reason—was Retzer, and it was his play that lost the game.

After all, if he had minded his own business, Richardson might have popped up on that first pitch.

That's a good story to relate when someone tells you how incredibly scientific baseball is. It is—sometimes. Mostly, though, it's a game played by fallible men.

In the dugout, then, furious thinking is going on all the time. The manager is watching every pitch, plotting his moves. (He has to think two or three innings ahead about possible pinch hitters and pitching changes on both sides.) The pitcher keeping the chart is writing down every pitch. The sign-stealers and tip-off watchers are plying their trade. In addition, the manager who wants extra security may use another player to flash the signs to the coaches. That is, he tells this player verbally, and it's the player who crosses his legs or touches his cap or rubs his chin, and it's the player the coaches look at.

Three functions are left: shouting encouragement at your own players, insults at the opposition, and complaints at the umpires. The requirements are uncomplicated—a voice that carries, a rudimentary competence at making phrases, and a low level of inhibition.

Taunting the opposition is called "jockeying" (because the bench jockey is "riding" his victim, get it?), and it is a dying art, by and large. The majority of players nowadays are too sophisticated to respond deeply to hackneyed insults. At their salaries, and especially if they started with fancy bonuses, they may still be afraid of sticks and stones but words never hurt them. Since the purpose of jockeying is to distract the man being jockeyed, this lack of response makes it futile. At the same time, much less real animosity exists between players of rival teams than was standard in the old days. Today's players, bound by pension plans and the organization-man outlook on life, feel very much like colleagues in a profession, and channel their antagonism into game actions, not personal remarks. More and more, the jockey's shouts are trying to get a laugh rather than arouse anger.

The physical setup in a dugout deserves mention.

In most of the new parks, dugouts are quite long and spacious. In old ones, they tend to be shallow and crowded. Usually, a tunnel leads to the clubhouse, and just inside the dugout end of this tunnel is a toilet. This is a favorite spot for sneaking a smoke, since it is against policy to be seen smoking on the bench. There is always a water cooler, at one end of the dugout or the other, and I have never seen one that didn't have at least several dents in it: a water cooler is the natural recipient of a violent kick from some player who has just struck out.

Bats, which used to be kept in a tray in front of the dugout, nowadays are stacked in a vertical or horizontal set of cubbyholes. Plastic batting helmets, passed around from player to player as they bat, lie around near the bats.

Most dugouts are equipped with a telephone connection to the bullpen. In most larger parks, the bullpens are located somewhere beyond the outfield fence, but in smaller and older parks, they may be in foul territory beyond the dugouts in left and right fields.

Because the floor of the dugout is two or three steps below ground level, and because the infield has a hump, sloping down gradually in all directions from the pitching mound, a man sitting in the dugout cannot see the entire field. From the dugout on the first-base side, the feet of the third baseman and short-stop, and the whole lower half of the left-fielder's body, will be blocked off; and the right-field corner is completely invisible, blocked by the end of the dugout. Even if one stands in the front of the dugout instead of sitting down, unless one gets up on the top step, parts of the field will not be visible.

This fact, known to all, seriously undermines the position of a manager or a player when he argues with an umpire.

The angle of vision affects the view of pitching, too. Baseball men can tell with great accuracy the variation in speed of a pitch, since they see it from the side. They can tell exactly how high or low a pitch is (unless the batter's body blocks it off too much); but they can't possibly see how far inside or outside a pitch comes. They automatically deduce this from the actions of the batter and catcher, but they can't judge the position of the ball itself.

Batters returning to the dugout, after making out or after scoring, make three types of comment most of the time: self-condemnation, alibis, and sharing of information.

"I'm a stupid so-and-so, I ought to give this game up," a man who popped up might say, bouncing his helmet off the steps.

"That background is terrible," a man who struck out might whine. "All white shirts. Can't see a thing today."

"He's got nothing," a man might say after hitting a 400-foot out to dead center—just as the pitcher wanted him to.

"He's really breaking that curve off today," a victim might report, building up the confidence of his teammates.

"Where was that pitch?" a hitter who had just been called

out on strikes might ask his teammates. (That's one of the good questions: he was at the plate, they were in the dugout, and he's asking *them*.)

"What'd he throw you that time?" a manager might ask a hitter who bounced out—not because the manager doesn't know, but because he wants the hitter to think about it.

From an emotional point of view, one of the hardest things for both dugouts to take is a soft-stuff pitcher having a good day. Both managers die. They can see how easy the slow pitches look, and even though their minds tell them that the timing and various little curves give the batters problems, their instincts still tell them that stuff should be murdered. So the manager whose team is being stifled fumes; he can't see why his hitters don't beat that pitcher's brains out. And the manager whose pitcher is doing it, while gratefully accepting the results, also can't see why the hitters don't beat his pitcher's brains out. It's a nerve-wracking game for everyone but the pitcher.

As a close game progresses, the tension in a dugout mounts. The men who are likely to pinch-hit, or go in for defense, are as aware as the manager of when they are likely to be called upon. They get themselves ready mentally, and perhaps do some knee bends or stretches. (A fielder, if he knows a half inning ahead, may dash down to the bullpen to throw a bit.) Sometimes an established pinch hitter will sneak back into the clubhouse to swing the bat awhile.

The moment of drama comes when the manager says: "Smirkilowicz—go up there and hit." The manager will also give his man reminders or instructions about what the pitcher is likely to do, and how the manager wants his man to hit.

One of the stock Casey Stengel stories stems from his Boston period. In 1939, Casey was managing the Braves (who were called the Bees then). They got involved in an extra-inning game with the Dodgers in Boston. In the 14th inning, the Braves got a man to second base and Casey looked around for a pinch runner. He found a rookie named Otto Huber. Sure enough, Al Lopez singled, and here came Huber around third with the winning run—only to fall flat on his face halfway home. He was tagged out, the game went on through the 20th inning and ended in a tie.

"The next day," Stengel recounts, "I looked at this man's shoes, and the spikes were worn all the way down, almost flat. They buy their own shoes, you know. But in his locker was a brand-new pair.

" 'That the best equipment you got?' I asked him, meanin' the old shoes, of course.

" 'No,' he sez to me, 'but these old ones are more comfortable for my feet, and I had them on because I didn't think you were gonna use me.'

"Can you imagine? For the next three years, whenever I wanted to use a hitter or a runner, I'd call him over first and make him show me his spikes."

A manager, you see, always has to be thinking.

Stengel was always thinking, but sometimes his thinking got mischievous. When he was with the Yankees, his third-base coach was Crosetti—the same Crosetti who had that problem arise with Houk in Washington. With Casey, Crosetti had a different problem. In one-sided games—and the good Yankee teams had quite a few of them—Stengel would hide behind a post when Crosetti would look in for a signal. Why? Just to liven things up.

Another Stengel idea, however, illustrates a shrewder approach. In his years with the Yankees, he had one of the best pinch hitters of all time at his disposal—Johnny Mize, too old to play regularly but a devastating batter. Casey would send Mize out into the on-deck circle, to advertise to the opposing pitcher that he was going to bat next. More than once, this all-too-visible threat bothered the concentration of the pitcher, as much as a brilliant base runner would, and the man at bat got a walk or a good pitch to hit thanks to Mize's presence.

Two aspects of dugout conversation are constants: profanity and a manager's caustic criticism of a player for something that has just happened. Neither is as strong as it used to be. Colorful originality in cursing seems to have been undermined by universally rising levels of education, and growing camaraderie in a prosperous profession has diminished motivation. Plenty of bad language is used, but the vocabulary is contracting and the spirit behind it perfunctory—or simply conformist.

As for the bawling out, modern managers are dedicated to the idea of holding their feelings in and saving their remarks for a more private occasion. They are only partially successful in carrying out this resolve—and the older managers, like Stengel, Dressen, Durocher, never did make such a resolve.

Meanwhile, out in the bullpen—

A fine, detailed, entertaining and authoritative description of bullpen conversation and time-passing exists. A book by Jim Brosnan, called *Pennant Race*, grew out of notes he kept while having a successful year as a relief pitcher in 1961 for the Cincinnati Reds, who won the pennant. It is recommended reading on this subject, a treasure for future anthropological archeologists interested in baseball.

For our purposes, it is enough to note that the chief characteristics of life in the bullpen are:

1. Worry—most of the fellows out there aren't going too well.
2. Moaning and groaning, second-guessing, daydreaming—since most of the fellows out there aren't going too well.
3. Telling lies.
4. Scouting the stands, better known in all walks of American life as girl watching.
5. Freedom of speech—a privilege limited in the dugout by the presence of the manager, who acts stuffy about keeping one's mind on the game. (The experienced manager no longer expects *all* his players to do that, but he does ask, at least, that his own brainwork be free of distraction.)

However, at least one man takes bullpen hours seriously, usually two: the coach and the No. 1 relief pitcher. They concentrate on being ready when the call comes, and follow early developments in batters' patterns for later reference.

And, of course, if a young man *wants* to watch everything that happens and thereby learn and improve, it's allowed.

Why is it called the bullpen? Many explanations exist in baseball lore, all somehow lacking in conviction. But there's no mystery why the name remains appropriate: more bull is thrown there than anywhere else in the ball park except the press box.

So the bench—the dugout and bullpen, but really the men who occupy them—is an integral part of baseball. In a sense, it's the fifth dimension of the game. The first four are tangible and familiar: hitting, pitching, fielding, and base-running. The bench is a less tangible aspect, but inseparably a part of the whole. Strategically, good pinch hitters and reliable relief pitchers are indispensable to a modern pennant winner. In the play of the game, the dugout is central headquarters, source of decisions and orders. In human terms, it's where most players spend most of their time.

It is the manager's own little castle, and few men who have tasted dominion over it ever give it up without regret.

7

· **We'll continue to play baseball rules.**

Chub Feeney, 1973

Something New: "dh"

In A.D. 1973, which was Year 134 of the Abner Doubleday Myth, Year 128 of historically established, recognizable baseball rules, Year 104 of certified professionalism, and Year 98 of the major leagues, the most startling single change in the playing rules was adopted by half the major-league population. The American League installed a "designated hitter," a man who would not play in the field but would come to bat instead of the pitcher, who would not bat.

What made it so startling was that for the first time, the "nine" became a "ten"; and, for the first time, specialized functions of offense and defense were permitted by the rules (as they had been for a long time in football, and had always been inherent for goalies in games like hockey, soccer, and lacrosse).

But, in keeping with baseball's tradition-bound, unchanging, stable-to-the-point-of-rigidity character, this most radical of changes was one that made a remarkably small amount of difference. And even so, only one of the two leagues went along with it.

The designated hitter concept was born of desperation. By 1968 (as we'll see subsequently, in Chapter 23), hitting had fallen to such a deplorable level that even the authorities could see that something had to be done. An endless succession of 2-1, 1-0, and 3-0 games may satisfy managers and other profes-

149

sionals who can appreciate the arcane art of frustrating a hitter, but they bore the customers to death. For the spectator, the action begins when the ball is hit—people running, catching, throwing, sliding; and the competitive excitement comes from the hope or fear that the lead will change hands. In the days when 7-5 was a normal score, the rooters of a team trailing by three runs felt realistic hope right into the ninth inning, even if the rally never materialized. In the late 1960s, as soon as the score became 2-0, the issue seemed decided, even if it didn't turn out that way.

So the need for more hitting was finally accepted, when the level of batting averages and runs scored sank to the levels of 1908, in the deadest of dead-ball eras.

The first response (see Chapter 23) was to lower the mound and restore the strike zone, which had been foolishly enlarged in 1963. But that didn't change the basic trend downward, although it provided temporary relief; and especially in the American League, where things were worse on every level than in the National, the feeling grew that something more was needed.

The designated hitter is a permanent pinch-hitting idea. The vast majority of pitchers, for all the notable exceptions, are pretty sure outs. Even if they hit safely, it's a surprise, and there's no anticipation of a rally with a pitcher at bat. But, under the traditional nine-player concept, if you put up a better hitter, you have to take the pitcher out. Since day-in, day-out baseball success rests on having an effective pitching staff, you simply can't afford to use up pitchers in this way.

So the idea of letting someone bat instead of the pitcher came up, stimulated by the obvious aging of sluggers like Mickey Mantle and Willie Mays, and the shortage of obvious new drawing cards. Perhaps a rule like this might let them linger longer, just as hitters, and sell tickets.

The idea was tried in the minors. It was a rousing success, according to most fans and executives who experienced it.

So, naturally, it was abandoned.

By the end of the 1972 season, however, the American League seemed to be hitting bottom. Once the "superior" league, it was now hitting less than the National, drawing a couple of million fewer customers than the National, and scoring just as little as it was in 1968. Its big campaign for revolution consisted of getting the National to agree to inter-league play; the more prosperous National simply laughed. So the American, determined to do something on its own, adopted the designated hitter. The National laughed at that, too, but at least its participation wasn't necessary.

But note the problem and the nature of the "solution."

The problem was that there weren't enough hitting stars (like Ruth, Williams, DiMaggio, and Mantle in the past) to excite the spectators, and there wasn't enough hitting by ordinary players to make the games attractive. Baseball fans, being as conservative as anyone about their game, still considered a .380 batting average something super and a .320 batting average (for a league leader) unimpressive.

You would think, then, that the kind of change to make, if any, would be one that would help the best hitters improve their records and make the mediocre hitters a little more effective.

Instead, they chose a solution that did nothing at all for the eight "regular" players. And though it did inject some strength into the ninth slot in the batting order, it also allowed a good pitcher—one who gets the good hitters out and prevents them from hitting .380—to stay in the game even if he's losing 2-1.

The new rule did increase offense. It couldn't do otherwise. But it also ducked the true problems. It did remove a weak spot from the batting order, but it did nothing to help the other eight slots.

Nevertheless, it was a success: attendance in the league went up, and for the first time in 10 years the American hit a little more than the National—but only a little. The American's batting average went up from .239 to .259—but the National's, not using the new rule, also went up from .248 to .254; so obviously part of the increase was due to some general cause not related to the designated hitter. (Probably, the baseball was juiced up a little bit.) Even so, the batting levels in both leagues were still lower than what had been considered normal up to about 1950.

That's from the standpoint of the end result. What did the designated hitter mean in terms of "quality"?

Those who oppose it make three principal arguments. One, they say it destroys the "complete player" concept so dear to baseball hearts. Two, they say it reduces the number and kinds of decisions a manager must make (about removing a pitcher for a pinch hitter), and decreases material for second-guessing, a basic delight of the fans. Three, they say it doesn't do enough good (if you admit that more scoring is good) to make the first two losses worthwhile.

Those who like the designated hitter start at the other end: they say that any increase in offense is better than none; they say the opportunity for the good pitcher to keep pitching in a close game, or the ability to leave a good relief pitcher in for several innings even if his team is trailing, is a plus in itself; they scoff at the "strategy" involved, since 90 percent of the pinch-hitting decisions are as painfully obvious as the "strategy" of having the weak-hitting pitchers bunt whenever possible; and they simply don't see the relevance, in an age of specialization, of the "myth" of the complete ball player, since clever managers manipulate their personnel anyway to use special skills (as in the new use of relief pitchers during the last 20 years). To the loss of "pinch-hit strategy," they offer the increase in "hit-and-run" strategy possible with a nine-hitter lineup.

"One thing I've noticed," says Ralph Houk, who favors the system, "is that every inning is a potential scoring inning. You used to have two or three innings in a game in which you felt, just by seeing where the pitcher was going to come up, that it was unlikely anything would get started or keep going. Now you have a potential sequence of hitters every time anyone gets on."

Billy Martin, who used the system while managing the Tigers in 1973, didn't like it as well. "I think it does cut down on the strategy," he said. "What it does do is help a mediocre team. On the Tigers, we had lots of good hitters, and we couldn't get the full benefit of having better pinch hitters than the other team. It's the team that doesn't have many pinch hitters that benefits."

Well, then, it's good or it's bad, but how does it work?

Many varieties of a "permanent pinch hitter" are possible. The version the American League chose was liberal and complicated. It was liberal in the sense that it permitted the man who started the game as a designated hitter to move into a fielding position later, thus eliminating the problem of keeping a catcher (or any other player) in reserve for emergencies. A "never in the field" type of rule would have confronted a manager with more values to weigh when deciding whether or not to use a designated hitter that day. Under the rule that was adopted, it became automatic to use one every day.

The "dh" can be placed anywhere in the batting order, not necessarily ninth. At the start of the game, the manager hands in a nine-man batting order. One of the nine is the designated hitter. None of the nine is the pitcher. The pitcher is the tenth name on the list.

The designated hitter *may not* be used in place of another player (the shortstop or catcher, for instance) with the pitcher also batting. He may be used only for the pitcher.

Once the game starts, the regular nine-man batting order (with the designated hitter and without the pitcher) is followed in the normal way. The pitcher, then, never has to be removed from the game unless the manager wants to remove him for pitching reasons.

Suppose the manager wants to use a pinch hitter for the designated hitter. He can, in the normal way. Then the pinch hitter becomes the designated hitter for the rest of the game, taking his proper turn in the batting order but never playing in the field. This kind of substitution can be made as often as one likes, just as it can with any other position in the batting order.

Now suppose the manager wants the designated hitter to play some position in the field. For example, Frank Robinson of the California Angels is today's designated hitter, and Lee Stanton is playing right field. In the fifth inning, Stanton injures his leg and Manager Bobby Winkles wants Robinson to become the right fielder. At that point, the designated hitter evaporates. Robinson becomes the regular right fielder, keeping his same spot in the batting order. And the pitcher, whoever he is at the moment, must now come to bat in the spot vacated by Stanton when he left the game.

From that point on, either the pitcher bats for himself, or he must be removed from the game entirely if another pinch hitter hits for him, just as under traditional rules.

In 1973, in the American League, fewer than half a dozen pitchers ever came to bat. But the following statistical comparison is provocative:

In 1972, all the American League pitchers batted .146. All other players hit .246.

In 1973, the designated hitters hit .259. And all the other players hit .259.

It's easy to see why the designated hitters—established professionals like Orlando Cepeda, Tony Oliva, Tommy Davis, and others who would have been unable to play regularly in the field because of chronic leg injuries—would hit better than pitchers. It's not so easy to see why everyone else's average went up 13 points. The inspiration of being in the same lineup as a designated hitter hardly accounts for it.

Whether or not the designated hitter will become a permanent feature of the baseball scene is not yet clear. The National League, at the end of 1973, remained adamantly against it. ("We will continue to play by baseball rules," said

Chub Feeney, the league president, with a certain amount of hauteur.) The American was not about to give it up. But it would seem hard to maintain, in the long run, separate playing rules for the two leagues. Just what sort of compromise might be possible wasn't even being discussed.

On the other hand, the wedge toward true two-platoon baseball has been made, and it would be rash to shrug off the significance. By acknowledging that pitchers are "unqualified" batters, one is accepting the principle that the game should be played by the nine best possible hitters and the nine best possible defensive players, without demanding that they be the same individuals. If a designated hitter works well for the pitcher over a period of years, why not another one for the shortstop? Whatever justifies his use for the pitcher will justify it just as well for another important defensive player. And then why not for the catcher? Or for the center fielder? Separate units for offense and defense are the logical end-result of this process. (Not that you would need completely separate units, as you have in football, since a Mays or an Aparicio has obviously superior talents in both respects, and there is no terrible fatigue factor in playing both ways; but a lineup of three or four men going both ways and the rest specialists would become standard.)

There's another objection to the designated hitter, voiced only by batters. Because the pitcher never has to come to bat, he is free of the risk of suffering retaliation if he throws at batters. In 1973, no serious issue arose along those lines, but that's not to say it couldn't. No one supposes that the majority of pitchers will turn into "head hunters," but even two or three around the league, secure that they can never be thrown at themselves, could create a lot of trouble.

All in all, though, the overriding significance of the rule is that it represents a willingness to experiment, perhaps the surest sign that not even baseball is immune to the pressure for change.

8

· **Take two and hit to right.**

Anonymous

Communication Theory and Practice, or, Signs, Signals, Simplicity

Signals—giving them, taking them, missing them, and understanding them—constitute the greatest gulf between the experience of the professional and the fan. To the ball player, they are second nature and a subject of greatest awareness while a game is on. To the fan, they remain a dimly perceived activity, despite periodic explanations.

The need for signals is inescapable. The pitcher and catcher must be in agreement on what's to be thrown, while the hitter must be kept in the dark. The bunt and hit-and-run must be agreed upon by hitter and runner, without tipping off the defense.

Signals, then, must be simple, in order to be reliably received, yet complicated enough to keep the opposition from cracking the code. That, at least, is the theory.

Pitcher-catcher signals are traditional—with variations. The ordinary vocabulary is: one finger for a fast ball, two fingers for a curve, three for a change-up. All the special pitches can be covered by these general categories, according to the particular pitcher's equipment.

In order to keep one of the coaches on the coaching lines, or a runner on first, from seeing the signal, the catcher places his hand along the inside of his right thigh while crouching, thus shielding his fingers. But when there is a runner on second base, he can see the signal as plainly as the pitcher.

That's when the complications come in.

The answer is sequences. The catcher flashes one finger, then two, then two. Which is the meaningful sign? Perhaps the first sign, one finger, meant "throw the first of the next two signs"— that is, two fingers, or a curve. Perhaps it has been decided beforehand that the third signal, or the first, will be the "key" to a second set of signals to be given.

All that matters, really, is to keep the pattern complicated enough to keep the man on second from deducing the code by watching half a dozen pitches and correlating them with their signs.

The pitcher often helps. He may have a prearranged plan with the catcher for shaking off signs—as a decoy. This is often directed more at the hitter, as psychological warfare, than at signal-stealers. When a pitcher indicates he's dissatisfied with what the catcher called for, the batter may start thinking— while he's thinking, he may be a trifle off balance mentally. In that case, there never was any real disagreement between pitcher and catcher; it's all an act.

Every couple of years, a big fuss arises about more elaborate signal-stealing, by means of an agent with binoculars in center field. There has never been a specific rule against this, but it is generally considered unethical, because the home team can arrange it while the visiting team cannot. (A favorite hiding place was the scoreboard, before these million-dollar electronic marvels replaced the human-occupied types located in center field.)

Still, there is an element of self-protection that is considered proper in baseball, and the simple defense against sign-stealers, however placed or equipped, is to use deceptive signals. The same attitude is taken by most baseball men concerning throwing at hitters: judicious retaliation will keep that situation under control better than rules or admonishments.

And here we have one of the basic limitations on sign-stealing: it can be awfully dangerous if it backfires. If the batter is told that a fast ball is coming, and it turns out to be a curve, he may wind up looking foolish; but if he is told curve and it turns out to be an inside fast ball, he may wind up unconscious.

If a pitcher gets the idea that his signals are being intercepted, and the hitters seem a little too sure of what's coming, all he has to do is reverse matters for a couple of deliveries: throw one good fast ball off a curve signal, and the reliability of the other team's cryptanalysis is destroyed.

Signals can be reversed at any time—every day, every inning, between pitches. It's even possible to make the other side think you are changing your signs when you're not, so don't assume every time you see a catcher go out to talk to a pitcher that they are changing their signs. It may be a decoy, or a misunderstanding between them, or a plan to set up several pitches in sequence, or a discussion of something about the hitter.

But who really decides what pitch is to be thrown? The catcher? The pitcher? The manager?

There are no simple and unambiguous answers to this question. It is analogous to the quarterback's play-calling in football. In the final analysis, the manager or coach is always the boss, but there are also great advantages to having an experienced player, actually in combat, making the decisions.

Some managers do call the pitches from the bench, signaling the catcher what to signal the pitcher; all managers do it at some point. The main consideration is the experience of the pitcher and catcher, and confidence in their judgment. An older, established pitcher working with a young catcher will obviously take the lead; if the opposite is true, it will be the other way around.

Most of the time, however, the catcher and pitcher are simply thinking along the same channels. The same knowledge—of hit-

ter, of situation, of the pitcher's equipment and its behavior that
d? —lead them to the same conclusions. In a showdown,
the pitcher always has the last word: he's the one who
꞉w the ball, and if he is not convinced that he's throw-
꞉ght thing, he's asking for trouble.

Garagiola, who was a pretty good major league catcher
e he turned to the banquet circuit and radio-television for
uch better living, stresses the inanity of some pseudo-expert
꞉ctions. Talk that a catcher "called a great game" is just as
silly as blaming "a bad call" for the home run that was hit. The
pitcher is doing the throwing, and the responsibility is his. Great
pitchers make brilliant catchers, and poor pitchers make dumb
ones.

Sandy Koufax relates an incident that shows the degree of
rapport achieved by pitchers and catchers who have worked together a lot. In the 1963 World Series, Sandy struck out 15
Yankees in winning the first game, and now, in Chavez Ravine,
he was one out away from winning the fourth game for a Series
sweep. He was leading 2-1 with two out in the ninth, and the
batter was Mickey Mantle. The only Yankee run had been
scored on Mantle's home run his last time up.

The count went to two strikes. The catcher was John Rose-
boro.

"I could see John put down two fingers, for the curve," says
Sandy, "and I could see him just start, as if he were uncertain,
to wiggle them. That would mean, take something off the pitch.
A change curve at a time like that was some idea—but I was
sort of thinking the same thing. If it didn't work, if Mantle hit
it out and tied the score, we would turn out to be dead wrong
in theory. And yet I had the feeling that it would be the right
thing. So even as John was still sort of hesitantly suggesting it,
I gave him a quick nod. Well, now everything was great. We
were in it together. Understand, what was worrying John was
that I might feel uncertain about *throwing* that pitch; he had
no doubt it was the pitch he wanted. But once I showed him

that I was thinking the same way, he had every confidence in it."

What Sandy threw wouldn't have been a "change curve" for any other pitcher, because it still had so much on it. But it was something softer than the most explosive curves Sandy had been throwing the whole Series.

It was strike three.

Now, one of the oldest supposedly unforgivable acts in baseball is to let a man get a hit when the count is two strikes, no balls. The idea is that the pitcher then has three balls to work with, and shouldn't throw a pitch the batter can get hold of. Remember Bill Voiselle?

Where this shades into myth—and a myth shared by some professionals unconsciously—is that with an 0-2 count you're not supposed to throw a strike. Of course you are. In fact, if 0-2 is such an advantage (which it is), it's the ideal pitch on which to get a man out—and every now and then, the pitch intended to get him out may be hit safely.

But many managers, older ones in particular, consider it a sin if a pitcher gets hurt in that situation. Actually, it's a completely one-sided and unfair criticism: they say nothing if the man makes out, but blame the pitcher if the man gets a hit.

Criticism would be legitimate, of course, when the pitcher threw the wrong *kind* of pitch 0-2. He has maximum opportunity to work on the batter's weakness, or use his own strength. If he fails to do that and *then* gets hit, he's in the doghouse for fair.

The pitcher-catcher signals are a subject in themselves. Things go wrong, inevitably, but very rarely. When a pitcher "crosses up" a catcher, a wild pitch is often the result, but it happens an insignificant proportion of the time.

The other signals—to batter and runner—have a much, much higher mortality rate. For the average player, the hardest thing in the world to achieve is a high level of concentration, and it is lack of concentration that leads to missed signals.

Most signs are body movement signs, and since most situations are yes-no two-valued—bunt or don't bunt, hit or take, run or stay—a simple enough gesture will serve. For example, skin touching skin may mean "take": if the coach rubs his chin, or claps his hands, that's the sign. A sign may be more specific: hand brushing the letters across the chest.

Again, if the signs were given too simply, in a discoverable pattern, they would be worthless. So all the many motions a coach makes are intended to camouflage the real sign. Once again, there is some key: let's say, only if his feet are wide apart is the skin-on-skin sign in force.

Now and then, teams will devise ways of giving the sign *before* the usual time, so that all the subsequent arm-waving is nonsense. This is the principle Houk was trying to follow in the incident in Washington, in Chapter 6.

A good player, then, *always* looks at the coach for a sign, even if he knows there isn't any; that's part of the long-range protection of the code. And a good player knows how to pick up the sign quickly, reliably, unobtrusively. After all, if he stares long enough at the coach, the opposition will see plainly that *something* is being ordered, and it's often easy enough to figure out what.

Since all the crucial strategic decisions depend on *when* rather than *what*—which pitch to bunt on, when is the defense deployed best for a hit-and-run—managers often wait until the last moment to decide. Then a sign must be given and received quickly.

Equally important are the signals that take a play *off*. Suppose something changes. Suppose the defense shifts before the pitcher has even begun his stretch. It must be possible to change the sign, to cancel the original signal. Missing the off sign causes as much trouble as missing original signs.

Here the human factors run rampant. One of Garagiola's stock stories—true or not—involves Dick Hall, who was a rookie outfielder on the last-place Pittsburgh Pirates of the early

1950s. Garagiola was on this team, Fred Haney was the manager, Branch Rickey the boss. Hall, a bright young man out of Swarthmore, eventually became an outstanding relief pitcher with Baltimore (in the 1960s), but at this point he was just a kid and fair game for a Garagiola anecdote in the making.

According to Joe, here's what took place:

Before Hall went to bat, Haney said to him: "If you get on, I'll want you to steal. Now this is the steal sign: I touch the bill of my cap, like this. Got it? Bill of my cap means steal. You see me do that, you run. Right?"

"Right," said the Phi Beta Kappa.

Sure enough, Hall singled. On the first pitch, Haney gave him the steal sign.

Hall didn't run.

On the second pitch, Haney gave the steal sign.

Hall didn't run.

The same thing happened on the next two pitches.

Finally the next batter grounded into a double play that Hall could do nothing about, since he was slow leaving first base.

After the inning, Haney called Hall aside. Calmly and patiently, Haney said, "Did you see me touch the bill of my cap?"

"Yes, sir."

"Do you know what that meant?"

"Yes, sir."

"You know that's the steal sign?"

"Yes, sir."

"You saw me give it?"

"Yes, sir."

"Well, whyinhell didn't you run?"

"I didn't think you meant it."

Just as intellect can be an obstacle in some situations, physical problems can arise in others. Ryne Duren, whose blazing fast ball made him an outstanding relief pitcher for several years, was almost unbelievably nearsighted, and he did all he could to exaggerate the impression of semiblindness he created. (It was a great asset to have batters wondering whether the launcher of this lethal fast ball could see the man at the plate.) Ryne wore lenses so thick they looked like "sawed-off ends of Coke bottles," and his poor vision was common knowledge and a standing gag.

With all this, you can imagine how bad a hitter Duren was: not only was he a pitcher with natural lack of hitting talent and no chance to practice, but he couldn't see the ball.

In 1964, Ryne was with the Phillies. In spring training, he was pitching in a B-squad game against some Met rookies, and everything was very informal. Gene Mauch, the Philadelphia manager, was talking to sports writers as much as he was paying attention to the game.

Now it came up to the top of the ninth inning, with the score tied. The first Philadelphia batter got on, and Duren was due to be the third hitter in the inning. If the second man got on, Mauch would want a bunt.

"Hey, Ryne," called out Mauch, as Duren headed for the on-deck circle. "You know the bunt sign?"

"I *know* it," replied Duren, "but I can't guarantee I'll *see* it."

There is also the danger of giving unintended signs inadvertently. A manager or a coach must be careful at all times. If skin-on-skin is a signal, a thoughtless scratch of the cheek at the wrong moment can have unexpected consequences.

One of the more bizarre instances of this occurred in Pittsburgh when Leo Durocher was managing the Giants in the early 1950s. Leo had managed to get himself thrown out of the game by some thin-skinned umpire, and had gone up to the press box for the remainder of the game. There he chose a seat next to Barney Kremenko, a tall red-headed man who worked for the then *New York Journal-American* and just happened to be the most clearly identifiable New York writer sitting in full view of the Giant dugout. Every now and then Leo would ask Barney to make a certain movement, and Barney would oblige.

The game reached its exciting stages with the Giants at bat. Barney, innocently enough, started to take off his glasses to wipe them.

"Hey, stop that!" yelled Durocher. "You just gave the steal sign!"

Fortunately, the Giants won the pennant anyhow.

Almost as important is the nonsecret communication that goes on all the time, sometimes not as much as it should: plain talk. Teamwork involves a good deal of talk between players, and between a player and a coach.

Most of it is devoted to reminders. Alertness in a game calls for endless repetition of the obvious—just in case someone's mind is wandering. The catcher will usually remind the infield how many men are out, after every out. At the same time, the coach will remind the base runner of the same thing, and perhaps something about the right fielder's strong arm. Infielders may remind each other about how they intend to make a possible play, although they've made the same play with each other hundreds of times. Catchers will remind pitchers, again and again, how they intend to work on the next batter. The pitcher knows perfectly well—but one more repetition can't hurt.

Whenever you see men on the same team talk to each other, chances are it's some sort of reminder.

The other main topic is calling plays. On a high pop-up, one infielder can act as traffic cop for others as all converge. On bunt plays, the catcher must always tell the pitcher which base to throw to, because the catcher is facing the bases and the pitcher isn't.

In a crowded, noisy park, the cry "I got it" may not be heard, or it may be misunderstood as "you got it." A collision can result. A standard practice on balls hit to the outfield is: the man who is going to take it is the man who calls; if you don't intend to catch it, keep still; if you yell, keep going for the ball, no matter how far. That way, comprehending words is unnecessary; if you hear *anything*, veer off. If you don't, keep going.

Talk can also be used, especially by catchers, to try to distract hitters. Sometimes that works remarkably well. Garagiola was good at it, and his boyhood friend Yogi Berra was one of the best. But then, Yogi was a remarkably garrulous, gregarious, gossipy sort who just couldn't keep still on a ball field no matter where he was. Late in his career, when he wound up playing left field, he kept chatting with fans in the stands and occupants of the nearest bullpen.

Yogi's talkativeness once produced an unforeseen problem, and this story illustrates how inexhaustible is the ball player's ability to pick up any trait at all and use it to advantage. During Stengel's first five years with the Yankees—all pennant-winning years—Casey had exceptional success with hit-and-run plays in unorthodox situations. Yogi, although he was a catcher, was a pretty fast runner, and Casey liked to hit-and-run with Yogi on first.

Then, inexplicably, the play started backfiring. Several times in succession, when Yogi would take off from first, there would be a pitchout and he would be thrown out. Signals were changed, security was checked, but still the opposition was spotting the play. Stengel would have decided that his methods were simply being figured out, except for one thing—it was happening mostly with Yogi on first.

After much thought, the Yankees finally realized what was happening. As a rule, Yogi would always be deep in conversation with the first baseman: how was the wife, what sort of football team would Notre Dame have this year, and so forth. Given the hit-and-run sign, Yogi would begin to concentrate on getting a good lead—and shut up. The opposition had noticed that when Yogi became still, he was preparing to run.

The solution was to tell Yogi to keep quiet all the time; and when that quickly proved impossible, to keep talking all the time.

Even silence, therefore, can be eloquent on a ball field. And this is the answer to those who say baseball is such a "slow" game. It is, in terms of physical activity, compared to football or basketball or hockey—but that doesn't mean nothing is happening. Most of the apparently purposeless action between pitches isn't purposeless at all. The fan who has the opportunity to watch every day and become familiar with the idiosyncrasies and motives of his home team's players is fortunate, because then he can get a type of pleasure from baseball that the more active, several-things-happening-at-once games can't provide.

9

· You're blind, ump, you're blind, ump/You must be out
of your mind, ump!

From the song "Six Months Out of
Every Year" in <u>Damn</u> <u>Yankees,</u> 1955

Everybody's Enemies:
The Men in Blue

And now—the bad guys. The umpires. No game can take place
without them, so they are at once the most essential and the
most neglected element of the game on the field.

"Kill the Umpire" is regarded as an expression of some
underlying mystique in American culture. We seem to take
pride in our irrational response to the one impartial element of
the contest, as if it somehow relates to our love of freedom,
independence of thought, and individuality. The contradiction
that Europeans and South Americans, supposedly more willing
to accept authority, actually get far more violent and often try
literally to "kill a referee" in a disputed soccer match is just
ignored. Hating the umpire is as American as the hot dog that
drips mustard on your neighbor while you shout your opinion
at the object of that hatred.

This attitude is shared, by and large, by players and club
officials, even though they really know better. More today than
in the past, participants accept the idea that an umpire is doing
his objective best; but on the emotional level, it's hard to resist

blaming the umpire for a play that turns out wrong—especially if the umpire really is wrong, which does happen.

As far as the fan is concerned—the fan rooting in a given direction, that is—the umpire cannot be right. If a play happens in favor of your team, the umpire has merely done his job by calling it correctly and he, as a person, is nonexistent. If the play goes against you, the umpire is suddenly the center of attention and obviously at fault.

Let's try to consider them realistically.

Umpires are human, just as human as the ball players. This means that they do make mistakes occasionally, that they have varying degrees of skill in different directions, and that they have feelings and ideas. In major-league baseball, the umpire has attained a position of unquestioned impartiality, much more than in any other major spectator sport. His integrity is beyond question, and no one has seriously questioned a big-league umpire's honesty in at least 40 years.

Competence is another question. Umpiring a baseball game is a much easier task, in some respects, than refereeing football, hockey, or basketball. There is not, in baseball, the simultaneous movement of many bodies in a confined space; whatever comes up for decision comes up alone, usually at a predictable location. With almost no exceptions, the baseball umpire can make his call while standing still, able to get a good look.

In one respect, however, the baseball umpire has a tougher job: absolutely everything he calls is in the open, subject to second-guessing. In the other games, it is taken for granted that the official can call only a certain proportion of all the technical violations that actually occur; in baseball, there is no such thing. *Everything* that calls for an umpire's decision is called, right or wrong.

As a result, umpires can display distinct personalities, and it is a shame that today's charcoal-gray approach to baseball has all but eliminated the personal flair from major-league umpiring. The umpires of a generation or more ago were fewer in number but much more present in the fan's awareness.

Bill Klem, of course, was famous and unignorable as a tyrant in the National League between the World Wars. Small, strong-willed, combative, he expressed an important principle: "I never called one wrong." An umpire *should* feel that way, at the time he makes a call. Another version, ascribed to many umpires, has the impatient player asking, "What was it, safe or out?" and the umpire answering, "It ain't nothing until I call it." This exaggerated definiteness, in Klem's case, was accompanied by personal sensitivity. The nickname "Catfish," used in his presence, would send him into a rage (and send the player who uttered it to the showers), because Bill's face did, in all fairness, resemble a catfish.

Leo Durocher tells of being at bat in St. Louis with Klem umpiring. Leo was young and new to the league. In a box near first base, someone was giving Klem the business, and Klem couldn't catch who it was out of the corner of his eye. Naturally, he wouldn't turn to look.

"Take a pitch, kid," he ordered Leo, "and see if you can spot the guy who's yelling at me."

"Sure, Mr. Klem," said Leo, as obliging a fellow then as always (in his own stories).

Klem called a ball, and Leo started to point with his bat at the offending voice.

"Don't point, you dumb blankety-blank fresh busher," Klem yelled, seeing his air of aloofness thus given away. "And that was a strike."

Then there was Art Passarella, who used to umpire in the American League in the 1940s. Talkative and friendly, he was one of the best umpires to be stuck in a club car with. But players would accuse him of showboating, of putting on an act. They might have been right—because Passarella went to Hollywood and became an actor. The last time he was seen umpiring, by a large number of people, was in a movie with

Cary Grant and Doris Day, in a scene which included (as guest extras) Mickey Mantle, Roger Maris, and Yogi Berra.

And talking of Yogi as an actor, another scene comes to mind. One of the ball players who made out well as a television actor was Johnny Berardino, once an American League infielder. Johnny became a leading character on a soap opera about a hospital, playing the role of a doctor. Once he arranged the following scene: he comes into a cafeteria, and Yogi, in a white gown, is seated at the next table. Yogi never says anything, but Berardino keeps giving him funny looks, as if recognizing the face but being unable to place the name. Finally, Yogi leaves, after a long close-up of his unmistakable features. "Who is that?" Berardino says to the nurse with him. "That's the famous brain surgeon," is the reply.

However, getting back to umpiring: they're much more anonymous than they used to be.

The universal theme of good officiating—consistency—applies most of all in baseball. Calling balls and strikes is strictly a matter of judgment, built on conventions. Unless the umpire has a very firm strike zone, both pitcher and hitter are at a loss. He must call the same pitches the same way all the time.

The strike zone itself is flexible. It changes with every hitter (since the rule says "armpits to knees in a natural stance"). Two men may be the same size, but one may have a smaller strike zone because of a habitual (but it must be habitual) crouch.

In addition, it is well established that National League umpires have had a "lower" strike zone in the last 20 years than American League umpires. That is, they are more likely to call a border-line low pitch (at the knees) a strike, and less likely to call the border-line high pitch (above the letters) a strike. Sometimes, the difference between conceptions in the two leagues has been called as much as two inches. That's why some hitters and pitchers, by the way, have better success in one league than the other. A low-ball hitter, for example, will suffer less in the National League than a man who can't hit the low pitch; a low-ball pitcher may have trouble adjusting to the American League, because he may not get as many low strikes, and then get clobbered when he comes up with the ball in an attempt to compensate.

National League umpires work from a position between the catcher and the batter, looking at the plate a trifle off-center. American League umpires stand directly in back of the catcher, looking over his shoulder and head. Perhaps this accounts for the difference in viewpoint, perhaps not.

In any case, the actual strike zone is not the same as the theoretical one. Ideally, the strike zone would be three-dimensional, covering not only height and the width of the plate (17 inches) but its depth as well. The plate is a pentagon in shape, fitting into the junction of the foul lines. It is 12 inches on each side along the lines, and about 8½ inches on the sides extending into the field toward the pitcher. A curving pitch that catches the back edge of the plate, or a high pitch that is too high at the front edge of the plate but low enough before it passes the back point, *should* be a strike. In real life, such gradations are a little too fine to handle. The umpire draws an imaginary rectangle that is two-dimensional at the front of the plate, and judges pitches by that. Pitchers know that he does, and accept it.

Less capable umpires aren't entirely reliable even in those terms. They may be influenced by where a catcher catches the ball. If he gets it at his shoe tops, the pitcher's contention that it was high enough at the front of the plate may not be honored.

Aside from balls and strikes, almost all umpire decisions fall into two categories: safe or out on the bases (including home), or the position of the ball (fair or foul, in the stands or out, caught or trapped).

At first base, the umpire glues his eyes on the bag and listens for the ball hitting the first-baseman's mitt. This two-sense measurement is the surest way to determine whether the runner is safe or not. (A tie, says the rule book, is resolved in favor of the runner.)

At second base, the two frequent plays are double-play pivots and steals. On the double play, the umpire must decide whether the pivotman had the ball in his possession while his foot was in contact with the base, not before or after. Here there is a tremendous leeway, by convention: the fielder is trying to avoid being hit by the base runner, and the umpire is not there to promote collisions by being a stickler for mathematical accuracy. Any reasonably well-executed pivot is allowed unless the umpire feels that wandering off the bag is the thing that made the play possible. On steals, the umpire must look at two things: when the runner actually reaches the base, and when the tag is made. The tag may be late, or it may miss, or the runner's feet may pass over the bag before contact is made.

On such plays, umpires are almost always right. They are right on top of the action, and have the best angle. When stop-action replays came into television, there was much fuss about such electronic second-guessing of umpires' decisions; if you watch a lot of replays, however, you'll come away impressed that the umpire is right in the vast majority of cases.

Among themselves, umpires talk shop about two subjects: rules and position. Naturally, they must know the rule book inside out. But the technique of their craft consists of anticipating plays and getting planted in the right spot to call them, close enough to see everything, but out of the way, and in the proper direction, so that the view won't be obstructed at the crucial moment by one of the players.

What can umpires be blamed for legitimately?

Lack of hustle—failure to stay alert at all times and to move into the proper position to call a play.

Inconsistency—in calling balls and strikes.

Arrogance—refusing to listen to a reasonable complaint about an unusual play, or refusing to get help from another umpire on a play he didn't see.

Umpires do help each other. They have signals. For instance, on a half swing, the plate umpire may be uncertain whether or not the batter actually broke his wrists. A glance at the first-base or third-base umpire, and a gesture, can settle it. The plate umpire makes the call. The trouble is, no umpire wants to overrule another, so that even if one of them is dead wrong about a ruling, the others won't make him change it unless the umpire in question asks for their help.

I once saw a game in the Coliseum in Los Angeles. Bob Skinner, a left-handed batter for Pittsburgh, sliced a high drive along that short left-field foul line. There were five umpires working the game, the fifth one at the base of the left-field wall. The umpire at third base, spinning around to watch the ball, stepped on the base, or on the third baseman's foot, and fell into fair territory.

The ball went into the stands foul by at least 20 feet. The umpire who would normally make the call was lying on the ground, making no gesture at all. Skinner, and the runner in front of him, circled the bases for a two-run homer. The third-base umpire couldn't possibly have followed the flight of the ball—yet none of the others would overrule him, and he was too embarrassed to admit he couldn't make the call. There was a 20-minute argument, which the Dodgers lost. The two-run homer stood, and Pittsburgh won the game, 4-2.

On the other hand, umpires take so much abuse from players and managers that much of their refusal to listen is justified. If players weren't such wolf-criers, their few legitimate complaints might get attention. Although, they might not; a large school of thought exists that advocates constant harassment of umpires. "If you let them alone, they'll walk all over you," this school says. "You have to stay on them to make them give you an even break. You complain long enough and at least they'll pay attention; if you don't and the other side does, the other team will get the best of it." It's a moot point—undoubtedly true of some umpires and not others.

At bottom is personality. It takes a certain kind of personality to want to be an umpire, and a good deal of thick skin to stay one. Constantly under pressure and repeatedly insulted, umpires demand one thing above all: outward respect. A player will be thrown out of a game not on the merits of an argument, but for a word that shows up the umpire in front of other players, or a gesture that shows him up to the crowd. It's summed up by the comment attributed to many umpires: a batter is called out on strikes, he flings the bat high into the air as a public demonstration of his disgust, and the umpire says: "If that bat comes down, you're out of the game."

A pugnacious personality, needed to do the job, is going to lead a man into the types of trouble pugnacious personalities get into. An umpire must establish his authority. Then, when he does miss a call or two, these mistakes will be accepted in remarkably good grace by players who have come to respect his effort, his fairness, and his competence.

In no circumstances, however, must an umpire permit himself to carry a grudge, if he is to remain a decent umpire.

Much used to be made of the isolation and loneliness of an umpire's life. This was part of the myth promoted in the Judge Landis era. Landis had been made commissioner to counteract the damage done to public confidence by the Black Sox Scandal. Landis exuded stern morality, and even racetracks were supposed to be off limits for baseball people. An owner who had racetrack interests was vetoed by Landis, in the guise of keeping baseball pure. In this context, umpires had to make special travel arrangements to avoid spending the night on the same train as a ball club, to live in separate hotels, frequent different restaurants, and so forth.

Today, all this is ignored. Some of baseball's most powerful and distinguished owners—John Galbreath and Mrs. Joan Payson, for instance—are racetrack people. And umpires get around as best they can, often getting a ride on some club's chartered plane, because no comparable convenient public transportation is available. And baseball's integrity has survived such social contact very nicely.

From a professional point of view, baseball's treatment of the umpire can be summed up by one word: disgraceful. They are underpaid, inefficiently supervised, and often insufficiently backed by their bosses, the league presidents. They do exert absolute authority during a game, but are not made important enough the rest of the time. They have been left behind in pension arrangements, paid as little as possible, and fired on whim.

"As little as possible" meant, if you can believe it, between $9,000 and $17,000, with a few rare exceptions above $20,000, as late as 1970. By that time even umpires had learned the lesson that if they wanted more money, they had better organize. They did, and they actually called a strike of sorts at the start of the 1970 playoffs. It lasted one day and did get them higher rates of pay for playoff and World Series games, and eventually a better overall contract. But they remain essentially underpaid, under-pensioned, under-respected, and under-supervised.

Millions of dollars ride on the winning or losing of a pennant. Crucial decisions are left daily to umpires being paid $17,000 a year. The ones with longest service might attain $30,000.

That's an example of how baseball runs its business.

SECTION

2

Behind the Scenes

10

> · Rooting for the Yankees is like rooting for U.S. Steel.
> Red Smith, 1951

Where the Money Is

The difference between baseball, small *b*, and Baseball, capital *B*, is money. Small *b* baseball is a game "that even children can play," indulged in by millions of people in all sorts of circumstances. Capital *B* Baseball is a business, a profession, an occupation; it was created and developed to make money, and it takes money to keep it going.

And money must come from somewhere.

The source of money in baseball, and the details of its acquisition and use, interests baseball fans in a unique way. It is hard to find a counterpart in other entertainment fields of public concern with finances. The most rabid theater lover is unlikely to become fascinated with box-office receipts, income from movie rights, amounts spent on scenery and so forth; in worshipping stars and thrilling to the content of a play, in pursuing autographs and biographical details, in second-guessing the work of playwright, director, and actor, the theater buff behaves in ways analogous to the baseball fan's reactions. But fiscal items, even so personalized as a star's salary, stir at most an occasional curiosity.

Not so in baseball. The star's salary is an extremely personal concern of the fan; the amount of money involved in a player trade is a vital bit of information to any hot stove discussion; the paid attendance is a part of the box score, and large crowds invariably applaud themselves when their numbers are announced ("Tonight's crowd—a high for the season on a Tuesday night—is 26,486. We thank you." . . . "Yaaaaay!").

When Red Smith made his celebrated observation that "Rooting for the Yankees is like rooting for U.S. Steel," he meant to call attention to the impersonality and air of invincibility with which the Yankees marched to pennant after pennant; he considered his image an unflattering one. In another sense, though, his meaning has been perverted into an accurate, acceptable vision. Some fans react as if they are rooting for the stock, as well as for the team, of the club involved.

Others don't root, but take just as lively an interest, siding with the players. When a player holds out for more money (and he really has had, until now, no bargaining position whatever), fans get quite worked up over what they consider the merits of the case.

A few years ago, we did a sketch in the annual New York Baseball Writers Show that dealt with this point. There had been stories of a modest salary dispute between Yogi Berra and the Yankees (this was still January). In the sketch, the scene was the bleachers in Yankee Stadium. Two fans of obviously anarchistic sympathies were playing cards and discussing the world. Everything, in their view, stank: the subway fare had gone up to 15 cents, the hot dogs were terrible and overpriced, they were out of work and not likely to find any, the seats were uncomfortable and they were convinced that the Yankee management consisted of greedy, venal capitalists. But the thing that really incensed them was the treatment being given Yogi. "Imagine not giving him the extra $5,000 to $55,000," was the punch line. "Those cheap rats. Yogi desoives it."

These days, after a player strike and other forces for social change, including million-dollar deals for athletes in many sports, the thrust of such a sketch would be in the opposite direction. In the 1970s, there is much more resentment of high salaries, rather than envious identification with the recipient.

But the vicarious involvement in some stranger's income and his negotiations with his boss remains strong.

This by-product interest in business affairs is one of the things that makes baseball so unusual a business. Perhaps it stems from the underlying nature of baseball interest: rooting and second-guessing. Perhaps the habit of rooting for the team's success on the field carries over into rooting for its success in all ways. No doubt, deep personal identification is involved in the matter of high salaries for favorite players, and civic pride is touched by attendance figures.

And yet, for all this interest, not one fan in a thousand has any clear idea of baseball's financial structure. He knows the rudimentary formula that high home attendance means profit, and that 1,000,000 is a sort of dividing line for good and not so good home attendance in a major-league season. But that's about all.

This is not accidental.

Baseball clubs have always been extremely secretive about the details of their income. They plead the necessity for secrecy as a facet of business competition—although it is hard to see how this applies in a completely monopolistic enterprise. As owners have stated in court and before Congress, clubs are "competitors on the field but partners in many other ways." Just how one club's business would suffer if another club knew the exact details of its television deal is not clear. There is only one legitimate area for secrecy, and that's player salaries, because of the potential jealousies that may be aroused—and yet, when a high salary is involved, the club boasts about it through its publicity machinery.

The truth is that all clubs have an excellent idea of each other's business arrangements. It is not from their partner-competitors that they want to hide the facts, but from the public. And in this, they have been more effective for nearly a century than the Central Intelligence Agency, the Japanese Imperial Command, and Agent 007 all put together. After all, the Japanese code *was* broken during World War II; but from 1876 through 1965, baseball people succeeded in keeping any detailed, meaningful scrutiny of their figures from reaching the public—despite numerous court cases, nosy reporters, and even a long series of investigations by the Congress of the United States.

Why?

The answer is typical of the baseball business: because an originally sound policy has been maintained by tradition beyond all contemporary relevance.

At first—through the end of the nineteenth century—baseball *was* truly competitive in a business sense, because it was still in the process of establishing its monopolistic, monolithic structure. Secrecy then served the same purpose as in any business.

Moreover, in the early years, many of baseball's troubles were rooted in the precarious level of public confidence in the "integrity" of the game, and many of the financial arrangements of that time worked against such confidence (especially "syndicate baseball," the practice of one owner controlling more than one club in a league and shifting players around to suit his needs).

And, more fundamentally still, it was a wise principle to play down *all* business aspects. In the nineteenth century, and really down to relatively recent times, people's attitude about "sport" was much more idealistic than it is today, and "professionalism" still carried a tinge of unworthiness. It was certainly sensible to try to keep the fan's attention focused on the noble, "sporting," emotion-generating aspects of the game on the field—and it would still be sensible today. Unfortunately, time and events have destroyed this possibility. The practice of keeping the business side private was made impossible, if not deliberately abandoned, when franchise moves, lawsuits, Congressional hearings, pension plans, television negotiations, and other front-office activities became the daily diet in sports pages and on the airwaves. Since the business image of baseball has been so publicized anyhow, and since the public is more tolerant toward professionalism as well, accurate revelations would do no harm and might even help by reducing speculation.

Nevertheless, obfuscation remains the rule on this subject. One striking example will serve as an illustration:

After one set of Congressional hearings, a fairly thorough set of balance-sheet statements was issued by the House Judiciary Committee. It covered the years 1952–1956 for all of the 16 major-league clubs then in existence.

In 1965, the *Sporting News* (the weekly that has served traditionally as an exceptionally complete trade paper for baseball) ran a story about Tom Yawkey's investments in the Boston Red Sox. Accompanying the story was a table of figures, showing profit, loss, and other items concerning the Red Sox from 1933 through 1959.

Now, let's compare the Red Sox figures given Congress with the figures given (by the club) in the news story. Remember, this is the *same* team in the *same* years:

YEAR	CONGRESS	SPORTING NEWS	DISCREPANCY
1952	$342,014 loss	$183,651 loss	$158,363
1953	$421,276 loss	$286,749 loss	$134,527
1954	$3,086 *profit*	$151,728 *profit*	$148,642
1955	$242,901 *profit*	$148,379 *profit*	$94,522
1956	$122,032 *profit*	$616,640 loss	$738,672
Cumulative Totals	$395,271 loss	$786,753 loss	$391,482

Let's be fair.

Let's stipulate that bookkeeping methods are mysterious, infinitely variable, and malleable, and that such things as before-and-after-taxes, fiscal years, and other technicalities may confuse the layman. Let's assume that a competent accountant, examining all the pertinent data, would explain away all the apparent discrepancies (although I must confess throbbing curiosity about any money-counting system that produces a $122,000 profit and a $616,000 loss simultaneously, as the Red Sox seem to have done in 1956).

The point is that *these* are the sort of figures one finds being released to the public. They prove one thing conclusively: any search for hard-and-fast, reliable, complete, relevant, and comprehensible dollars-and-cents figures on the baseball business are not available. It is true that more of such material is available now than used to be, thanks to antitrust trials, Congressional hearings, a new generation of serious historians who have researched baseball's past, some current work by trained economists, and, perhaps most of all, the attempts by Marvin Miller, executive director of the Players Association, to educate his players and the public. With all this, however, the confidentiality of actual, official financial figures has been maintained; and even in the Curt Flood antitrust trial in 1970, the court honored requests to keep such figures secret.

Nevertheless, the general outline of baseball finances can be understood, and it is worth keeping in mind if one wants to form a picture of what the business is really like.

The basic factor is paid attendance at home, but it is by no means the only important one. In fact, profit or loss is usually determined by the other factors. Attendance is basic, though, because many of the peripheral items, like concessions and parking, vary with it.

Here are some representative figures, not for any particular club but just as an idea:

Gross annual income from all sources: $6,000,000.

From paid home attendance: $3,300,000 or 55 percent.

From share of attendance on the road; $600,000 or 10 percent.

From radio-TV rights to home games, and share of any nation-wide television package: $900,000 or 15 percent.

From concessions (food, beer, and souvenirs sold in the park, any restaurants or stadium clubs, parking, etc.): $600,000 or 10 percent.

From miscellaneous items (including interest, marketing rights to club emblems, rent from other users of the stadium, etc.): $600,000 or 10 percent.

Such figures would represent a fairly successful club in a large city, like New York, Chicago, or Los Angeles.

Clubs in smaller cities—like Cleveland—have a considerably smaller gross, and a larger proportion of it comes from paid admissions, because the radio-TV cut tends to be less. Radio-TV rights have a value directly proportional to the population of the area being reached; thus, New York, with a 15,000,000 potential reaching into southern New England, is the prime TV area; Houston, which has constructed a radio network, with relatively little television, over an area of hundreds of miles, because no other major-league team is geographically close, commands a million-dollar fee; but Kansas City, with St. Louis to the east, Minnesota to the north, Houston to the southeast, and sparsely settled plains and mountains to the west, can get only a couple of hundred thousand. The Los Angeles Dodgers, in car-bound California, get as much for radio as Eastern teams do for television, and escape the self-inflicted competition of home-game telecasts.

Now let's examine some of the refinements in connection with attendance. Fans are familiar with turnstile counts, but that's only the beginning.

First of all, there's the split. For decades, major-league teams gave the visiting team its share in so many cents *per admission*— in other words, 29 cents for every paying customer, whether that customer bought a bleacher seat for 75 cents, a box seat for $3.50, or anything in between. Obviously, it made a difference whether the 20,000 customers on a particular night occupied 10,000 box seats or 2,000 box seats. Let's say the remainder of the seats average out at $1.00 per seat. In the case of 10,000 box seats, the gross is $45,000; with only 2,000 box seats, it's

$25,000; but in both cases, the visiting team's share is $5,800. In the first case, the home team has kept $39,200, in the second $19,200. (In the illustration, we have ignored taxes.)

Only in 1965 did the American League get around to changing the visiting team's share to a flat percentage—20 percent of the gross. According to this system, in the above illustration, the visiting team would get either $9,000 (with 10,000 box seats) or $5,000 (with 2,000 box seats), obviously a fairer shake.

But this tends to cancel out. Usually, the teams that are drawing well at home are up in the race, and therefore drawing better on the road. But even the weak club, when it visits a strong team, gets a bigger visiting share—and when that same strong team repays the visit, either the weak team benefits from a bigger crowd, or the strong team suffers from a small visiting share.

A more important angle is advance sales.

The New York Yankees pioneered large-scale season-box sales right after World War II. The advantages are self-multiplying.

Suppose you can sell 10,000 season box seats before the season starts, at $250 per seat. (Counting doubleheaders, there are about 70 home dates.) That means you have $2,500,000 in hand by March 31. Just six months' bank interest on this amount comes to $150,000—which is $150,000 you wouldn't have if you sold the same number of tickets at the gate. (Actually, you *save* rather than get the interest; you use cash for current bills and avoid borrowing.)

But there is another advantage: many of these tickets will not be used. The ordinary fan does not shell out $250; almost all such tickets are bought by business firms (as a tax-deductible expense) for goodwill use for customers or employees. On anything except the best attraction, one-half to three-quarters of these seats will be empty.

Remember what the visiting team gets? A percentage of the *turnstile count*—the people actually in the park. Our 10,000 season box seats, sold in advance, represents 700,000 individual tickets at $3.50 each. If that many had been sold one by one, as people came into the park, the visiting teams would have taken out 20 percent, $500,000 (and even under the other system, of 29 cents a head, the visiting share would come to about $200,000). But if half the seats are unused, the home team keeps the *whole* $3.50 on them.

So let's do the arithmetic again: 700,000 box seats sold before the season started equals (roughly) $2,500,000 in the till; only 350,000 actually attending means only $250,000 to the visiting team (on a 20 percent basis); that means $250,000 sheer profit on unused tickets.

And that brings us to television.

It cannot be denied that free home television of every game cuts down paid attendance. The home team is willing to do this because the money paid by television sponsors exceeds (it thinks) the difference in gate receipts. But the visiting team gets *nothing* from the local television money even though it provides half the show. Theoretically, the visiting team has the same right; it keeps all the money from the television rights when it is at home.

But if one team is the New York Mets, collecting more than $1,000,000 a year for its television rights, and the other is San Diego, getting less than $200,000, the theory doesn't stand up so well. Whatever ticket-buyers are kept away from the games in New York by free television are a dead loss to the visiting team, while the home team is compensated by television income that it doesn't have to share with the visitor.

In the past, sale of players could be an important factor in profit and loss. When Branch Rickey ran the St. Louis Cardinals and the Brooklyn Dodgers, with extensive farm systems, he made fancy profits by selling minor leaguers in quantity and an aging star just soon enough. Today, however, such deals tend to cancel out. Major-league teams all have farm systems, of approximately the same size, and the day of selling an outstanding player for money (rather than trading him for another outstanding player) is gone. Unlike a generation or two ago, it is money that is plentiful and playing talent that is in short supply, instead of the other way around.

Today's big factor is television—and it is a factor changing at breakneck speed.

In 1952, the total television-radio income of the major leagues (16 teams) was about $4,000,000.

By 1956, it was up to about $7,000,000.

By 1966, it was up to $27,500,000.

And by 1971, it was $42,000,000. Of this, $18,000,000 came from a National Broadcasting Company package that included the World Series, the All-Star Game, the divisional playoffs, and regular-season Saturday afternoon and Monday night games televised nationally. This sum was divided equally—$750,000 a club. The other $24,000,000 came from deals made individually by each team for its own radio-television rights—as much as $2,000,000 for the Los Angeles Dodgers, as little as $350,000 for the Washington Senators (who then became the Texas Rangers, largely for that reason).

Since total attendance for 1971 was about 29,000,000, the income from ticket sales (averaging $2.50) was about $73,-000,000—so the income from television and radio was more than half as much as actual gate receipts.

The question in the 1970s became, how much longer can this spectacular upward trend continue? Where are the limits? Actually, baseball's live attendance, despite the hypos of a dozen new parks, has not kept up with the growth of population. From 1921 to 1971, the population of the cities in which major-league teams are located increased from 15 million to 65 million, or 4.3 times, while attendance went up only 3.4 times (from 8.5 million to 29 million). Another way to put it is that 50 years ago baseball was drawing considerably more than half its potential customer area, while now it draws considerably less. Even more striking is the fact that in 1948, at the peak of the 16-team era, the average per club was about 1.3

million customers a year, while the 1971 average was 1.2 million, with a much larger base and greater seating capacity. But broadcasting income, which didn't exist at all in 1921 and was still a minor factor in 1951, provided 10 times as much money in 1971 as it had 20 years earlier.

Sooner or later, in one form or another, pay television will come into the picture. It is possible that before long television will provide more than half of baseball's dollar income—and if that happens, it will be a danger sign, because when gate appeal decreases, television in turn loses interest. It takes a crowd in the ball park to help make the game exciting and attractive for the television audience.

So much for *income*. What about *profit?*

It's high.

Bookkeeping may not bear this out, but the reality is not always in ledgers. The hidden elements are taxes and prestige.

Taxes are used in two ways: depreciation and losses. The only real assets of a baseball club (if it doesn't own its own ball park) are player contracts. The value to be set on a star is quite flexible—how much is a Mickey Mantle worth?—and the depreciation is very rapid (the average life of a player in the majors is about five years). This is a book loss—no actual dollars are being spent; but the money that is being spent on developing replacements (bonuses, minor-league operations, scouts) is also a business expense, and therefore deductible.

At the same time, few men in today's world own a ball club outright, with no other sources of income. In most cases, it is possible to tie enterprises together in some fashion so that the "losses" in one division can be deducted from profits in another. (This is the reason for many theatrical investments.) The "loss," then, actually is merely a means of reducing taxes on some other profitable enterprise, and therefore costs the owner nothing.

Prestige can't be measured in dollars and cents—but it has very real dollars-and-cents consequences. Owners, as we've just noted, usually have another business. The daily attention and publicity that stem from connection with this glorious, glamorous, noble, patriotic, wholesome, and exciting "national game" enhance the standing of an owner in all his other affairs. In his other business connections, people know who he is, are eager to hobnob with his stars, to bask in baseball's reflected glory.

Finally, there is the matter of executive salaries. Very often, owners of a club are officers of the organization, active or titular. Their salaries—earned and deserved and legitimate—are an "expense" to the club as a corporation, and help make a negative total in the profit-loss column. It is not, however, a "loss" to the owner who is taking money out of one pocket and putting it into another. Besides, he can all but live off the expense account, quite legitimately.

In 1950, for instance (a Congressional report showed), the 16 major-league clubs declared dividends totaling only $192,000 —but paid $775,000 in salaries to officers who were also stockholders.

Just how indeterminate the profit-loss situation can be is well illustrated by a few isolated figures:

In 1955—their second season—the Baltimore Orioles took in $1,280,782 in home attendance; the next year, they took in $3,169 *less*; in both years, concessions, radio-TV, away games, and "other" income were virtually identical. Yet, they showed an $86,000 loss in 1955 and a $69,000 profit in 1956, a swing of more than $150,000.

The Pittsburgh Pirates, in 1956, took in more than $1,-250,000 in home attendance—and lost money. At the same time the Washington Senators, who never reached $650,000 home attendance in the five years 1952–1956, made a profit each year.

In 1956, the year Walter O'Malley decided that the Brooklyn Dodgers would have to move to Los Angeles, the Dodgers made a profit of $487,462—20 percent of their gross income and the highest profit in dollars of any major-league club. Yet O'Malley felt "forced" to move.

In short, the frequent claims of philanthropy and attitudes of "sportsmen" assumed by owners of major-league baseball teams should be viewed with suspicion. Many owners sincerely love the game, and have real emotional responses to the fortunes of their teams on the field—but if baseball were not an effective way to make money, it would long since have passed out of existence. Some clubs, of course, handle their affairs better than others, but major-league baseball, as a whole, never fails to come out way, way over in the black.

Monopolies always do.

11

· **If it ain't, you got a helluva story.**

Grantland Rice, 1925

· **How could you call that a hit?**

Cap Anson, 1876

In the Press Box

The envy of most baseball fans, and particularly young boys, seems to be directed at the occupants of the press box. There they are, these baseball writers, getting into the park for free, sitting in the best location, constantly informed by a private little public-address system (which the nearer paying customers can overhear), privy to secrets, able to talk to Mickey Mantle in person, with presumably unlimited opportunities to collect autographs.

They also write stories, which appear in the daily papers. The writers themselves achieve almost perfect anonymity, because there is no way to connect their names (even if noted by the reader) with their appearance (they do not yet wear uniform numbers), and because newspaper photos that sometimes accompany columns are (by careful scientific test) four and half degrees less identifiable than old passport photos. The stories, however, are alternately brilliant (when they confirm the reader's belief) and stupid (when they don't).

It's all pretty soft. The better-informed fan also has a vague idea that the writers are provided with foodstuffs and libations, free of charge, and sumptuous hotel suites (in which champagne parties are constantly in progress) while traveling.

Then, if the fan is well-grounded in myth, he knows that the typical writer is a drunkard who talks in short, dramatic clichés; that he is either the bitter enemy or the closest friend of the best player or manager, either endlessly sarcastic or loyally all-boosting. He is the *confidant* of the star's harassed family, or tireless uncoverer of scandal (which threatens the integrity of the game), or the one who gives the friendless rookie the one bit of advice that opens the door to success.

How does the fan know all these things? Well, he goes to movies, doesn't he? And watches television?

And yet, the most frequent question asked of a sports writer in real life is: how do you get your story to the paper?

Now, if all these characteristics of baseball writers are so well known, and yet their most basic function remains a mystery, something must be wrong.

To get a more realistic picture of what goes on in the press box and of who the occupants are, perhaps it's better to start from scratch, with the obvious.

Physically, the press box is usually located behind home plate, at the front of some upper deck. This vantage point—well up into the air and in line with the pitcher and catcher—is best suited to providing a clear picture of the largest number of plays that may come up. It is not, necessarily, the most interesting or even the most informative angle from which to watch a base-ball game; other locations (near first and third) are often closer to the action; from ground level (to either side of the plate) more can be seen about certain details of pitching (as from the dugouts). My own idea of the best seat in a ball park was the upper-stand box right above first base in Ebbets Field.

But a reporter's need is not the best possible view of *some* plays and a poor view of others. He needs a reasonably good look at *all*, and, for this, the traditional position is ideal.

In most of the older parks, press boxes were afterthoughts and are generally uncomfortable: narrow aisles, narrow desks, hard metal chairs, little protection from wind and rain. In most of the new parks, the physical accommodations are fine. Not all parks, new or old, have elevators from ground level to the press box (which may be the equivalent of five or more storeys up), but most do—and that's important for men in their fifties who go through life carrying a ten-pound typewriter in one hand and a bulging briefcase in the other.

However, what do the press box occupants really *do?*

They (1) converse, (2) keep score, (3) watch the game, (4) make notes, (5) write stories, (6) interview players and managers (before and after the game), (7) travel with the team when it goes on the road, (8) keep records, and (9) argue.

Record-keeping is an essential part of baseball coverage these days. All the standard statistics—batting averages and so forth—are supplied daily, in mimeographed form, by the club publicity man on most clubs (but not all). However, all sorts of more interesting and useful items must be kept by individual writers. It is customary to keep a "pitcher's book," usually a small ledger, in which one can note the results and the participating pitchers of each day's games throughout the league (or both leagues). The purpose is twofold: such a book makes possible reference to dates, scores, and other details of the current season (who has a winning streak, when did this pitcher last beat that club); and it is an automatic method of paying attention to the results of all other games—much like writing down words repeatedly to learn vocabulary in a foreign language. This sort of activity takes up to an hour a day, but most of the time it can be done while watching the game.

Travel is a subject in itself, which will be dealt with in a later chapter. However, two points must be made here: the paper, not the ball club, usually pays the expenses; but the ball club, in most cases, makes the arrangements for the writer by simply listing him on the room list and the ticket list of the squad. The paper is then billed by the club, a bookkeeping transaction that makes no difference whatever to the writer involved.

Interviewing is a much misunderstood craft, often misunderstood by younger writers as well as by the public. In the context of baseball life, with its continuing, day-to-day contact with people, interviewing *does not* consist of question-and-answer interrogation, pencil and notebook in hand. This has to be done sometimes, but rarely, and only when major stories are involved. Almost all worthwhile interviewing is accomplished by informal conversation, the bulk of it idle and repetitious. In this field, unlike so many other journalistic assignments, the personal familiarity of interviewee with writer is an essential element in gathering worthwhile information.

Thus most writers come to the ball park an hour or two before game time, and spend their time during practice gossiping and visiting with players and managers of both teams, with club officials and with newspapermen from the other city.

This seems pleasant, which it is, and idle, which it is not. It is impossible to pinpoint how a writer's knowledge, and therefore his judgment, is developed. "Hustle," for a writer, consists of the hours spent hanging around, talking, listening, absorbing; the amount of informal time he puts in is in direct proportion to the quality and quantity of the information he acquires—and that's the reporter's basic job: gathering information. You can't transmit to your readers what you have not gathered.

The gathering process goes on all the time, for an hour or so after a game as well as before, and, when traveling, in hotel lobbies, over breakfast, on buses to the ball park, on plane rides, in clubhouses, dugouts, and pressrooms. The good reporter's mental receiver is never turned off, although his transmitter—what he writes—is sensibly selective.

Writing a story is primarily a process of selection. Skill with words is entirely secondary. A newspaper story is seldom as long as 1,000 words, often as short as 400. What matters is not cleverness of imagery or expression, but choice and ordering of material. The writer must decide *what* he wants to tell, and must have the point of what he wants to tell about clear in his mind, before he can find an amusing or interesting way to say it. Writing under a deadline, the technique one must develop is the quick, clear ordering of thought; the words take care of themselves.

At this point, we must separate writers into two entirely distinct categories: "morning" and "afternoon."

The "morning" men, that is, those who write for a morning paper, face deadline pressure. A Tuesday morning paper has a first edition that goes to press sometime between 6 and 9 P.M. Monday, depending on the paper. If a day game is being played, and if it ends early enough, the writer can write one story when it's over and that's that.

Most of the time, however, he will be covering a night game, or a day game that might run close to his deadline, or a double-header in which the second game certainly will run late. In those circumstances, he must write an "early" story (on some angle found prior to the game), and also a "running" (some form of play-by-play account while the game is on). That way, whatever editions are published during the course of the game will have at least a partial result. Then, when the game is over, he "subs" (substitutes) a complete new story.

This is much more labor than an "afternoon" man must do. Afternoon papers go to press in the early-morning hours of the same day as the date on the masthead, and afternoon writers file their "overnight" stories any time during the evening or night. The afternoon man, therefore, waits until the game is over, gets his postgame interviewing done, and then writes his story.

On the other hand, when it comes to the content of the story, the morning man has the easier job. His subject matter is pretty well defined for him by the event: he must describe what happened, presumably to readers who don't know, and however he embellishes it, and no matter what comment he adds, the central story line is always in front of him, always automatically provided: who won, how, and why.

The afternoon man, however, is always confronted with a multiplicity of choices: he needs an "angle." The assumption is that the afternoon paper's reader already knows the result; he wants something additional *about* the result—personal reaction of the players, explanation of strategy, humor, human interest, revelation, or interpretation about some situation in the club. The afternoon writer, who has far more freedom in the means of expression he chooses, must constantly seek the most attractive and pertinent aspect of yesterday's events. His mind is "on duty" 24 hours; he must always "find" a story, or at least select the best one. As soon as he finishes today's story, he starts to wonder about what he'll get tomorrow, and he is always subject to second-guessing (by his bosses and by himself) on whether or not he found the best angle today. The morning man, in contrast, can relax once his final story is written, with the knowledge that tomorrow's game will provide its own built-in news story.

The time element is important too. Whatever happens during the day, the morning writer need worry only about his first-edition deadline early in the evening. But the afternoon man has editions of his paper "alive" all day, and must be on the lookout for the infrequent but important occasions when a story of some sort breaks during the day. The morning man does his worrying about possible newsbreaks during the evening, up until about 1 A.M. local time in his home city, by which time the bulk of the final edition has gone to press.

All the above applies to the "beat" men, the men whose beat is covering the ball club day after day. Columnists are a different class. They are one step higher in the newspaper hierarchy, and have a free choice of subjects. Few columnists attend many baseball games. They are present basically at the World Series, All-Star Game, opening days, Old-Timer celebrations, and other special or newsworthy occasions, and are not concerned with reporting the game as such. They deal much more in opinion and interpretation—although the writer on the beat also expresses his views in a much more subjective way than straight news reporters do.

And how does the story, when written, get to the paper?

In the case of a morning paper, by telegraph most of the time. For afternoon papers, telegraph or telephone may be used, and, in some cities, the writer actually brings his story to the office even if he doesn't write it there. A new device started gaining popularity in the early 1970s: a photo-facsimile machine that can be hooked up to any telephone and transmit copy just as it comes out of the typewriter.

In the press box (or in an adjoining room in the newer parks) Western Union has telegraph facilities—teletype machines and operators (the days of the hand-operated Morse-code "bug" are gone). The writer, who uses his own portable typewriter, hands over his copy, one page (or, if it is necessary to rush, one paragraph) at a time. The telegrapher copies it on his keyboard printer, and almost simultaneously the result appears on a receiver-printer in the newspaper office. This copy (with built-in carbons) is immediately handed to a copyreader, who makes necessary corrections (and, according to all writers, various unnecessary ones) and sends it to the composing room. In the composing room, the story is set on linotype machines, the type is assembled and placed in the proper portion of the page. Meanwhile, the copyreader has written a headline and that has been set, too.

The whole process, from typewriter at the scene to metal type in place ready to be processed for printing, can be handled within 10 minutes if sufficiently important. Ordinarily, a writer figures on a lag of 15 to 30 minutes between the time he hands his copy to the telegrapher and the time his copy clears the sports desk.

Afternoon writers, by and large, have no need for on-the-spot transmission. (If an afternoon paper prints play-by-play of that day's afternoon game, it usually does so without bothering the writer on the scene; we'll come back to that in a minute.) So they simply write their stories, however late at night, at home or before they leave the park, and file them at any Western Union office. Most of the time, they write at the park and file there because that's most convenient; but, on the road, many will tend to return to the hotel with the team (gathering more material with less haste) and to write there.

Some papers have efficient phone-recording devices. A writer can read his story at almost normal speed, and a transcriber in the office can play it back at a slower speed while typing the copy. This method is as fast as, and cheaper than, using a wire (in newspaper talk, a "wire" is always a telegraph wire, never a telephone)—provided one has a completed story to read. It is an inefficient method for a running story, or any other story that's involved with a deadline. When morning men write "early" stories the day of a night game, they usually phone them in.

Meanwhile, there are three standard services in operation, common to all papers. The Associated Press and United Press International, to which almost all major newspapers subscribe, take care of the box scores. In each park, the AP and UPI have either a staff man or a local newspaperman who acts as correspondent. He compiles the box score as the game goes on and transmits it immediately after the game. Thus, reporters from individual papers don't have to bother with sending a box; the office just picks it off the wire.

Another standard service, purchased by some papers but not by others, is a play-by-play wire run by the AP. Every play of every major-league game is sent, as it happens, on special teletype circuits to the central office of the AP at Rockefeller Center in New York. All or any of these games may be plugged in by an individual paper. The afternoon paper that wants to run a play-by-play of the home team's game, for instance, can get it most easily this way, without forcing its reporter on the scene to send a comparable account on a leased wire. The general lead can then be written in the office by a rewrite man.

Both the AP and UPI send fairly brief game stories as soon as the game is over. These are the stories you read about all out-of-town games, and the stories people see in cities that don't have major-league baseball.

The third service is run by Western Union, the Commercial News Division or CND. This is the well-known "ticker"—the same machine that sends stock-market reports. It prints on a thin roll of paper, about one inch wide—the ticker tape of ticker-tape parades—scores and other information about games all over the country. Newspaper offices, radio stations, and radio broadcasters depend on this service for the quickest reception of all the out-of-town results. When you hear a radio or television announcer give you the other scores between innings, he is getting them from the "ticker"—and so is the scoreboard in the ball park, when it posts out-of-town scores.

The ticker used to be more glamorous before radio became so widespread. It gives the score by innings after each half inning; the batteries at the start of the game; all pitching and catching changes; and all home runs as they are hit, with the number of men on base. Special messages (like "N. Chi. Time called. Player hurt.") are sent from time to time, and at the end of each game a final summary gives hit and error totals and winning and losing pitchers.

Hanging around the ticker, waiting for the next half inning, noting home runs ("Colavito just hit one with a man on, so they got at least two runs . . . and now they're changing pitchers . . . they're changing pitchers again, it must be a big inning"), can get pretty exciting when you care about an out-of-town game, but before radio it was also the only source of information for the more intensely felt local game.

Keeping score is a pleasure every true fan indulges in, but a writer must do it more carefully. There are several standard shorthand systems in use (see Appendix IV), but every individual develops his own refinements. The point is, anything you may want to refer to when it comes time to write the story must be noted in some way.

Between keeping score, writing a running story, looking up statistics, and keeping his records, a writer has his eyes off the field a good proportion of the time. To some extent, this is just a wandering of attention, but, to a very real degree, it's simply impossible to keep one's eye on every single play. Thus, by all odds the most frequently uttered remark in the press boxes of America is: "How'd that last man go out?" The companion piece, used after two or more batters have done something that you didn't mark down, is "bring me up," which means, fill me in on the plays I've missed.

Kenny Smith, a pixie of a man who fought deadlines most of his life for the *New York Daily Mirror* and then became curator of the Hall of Fame at Cooperstown when the *Mirror* folded in 1964, suffered more than most from the head-down problem. (The *Mirror* had the earliest deadlines in the world—about 4 P.M. for the next morning's paper—and Kenny would be kidded about "sending running" as soon as he arrived at the park.) Like the rest of us, Kenny developed a Pavlovian reaction to the sound of ball hitting bat, and usually managed to look up in time to see the play. The only trouble was that when a batter walked or struck out, there was no such sound, and, not realizing a man had been disposed of, the writer would enter the next man's hit or out in the wrong box—causing confusion and aggravation when the error would finally be discovered. So Kenny Smith, for many years, advocated a solution to this difficulty: "They ought to ring a bell whenever a man walks or strikes out," he would say. But, like the weather, nobody ever did anything about it.

By far the biggest distraction, however—despite all the legitimate mechanical tasks—is conversation. And press box conversation is of a very special kind. It is, basically, a defense against boredom, since most of the time nothing very exciting is happening on the field. Its form, for the most part, is a running fire of sarcastic comment on whatever is happening, spiced by shameless exaggeration and literary license bordering on anarchy. It is seldom scintillating, but it usually tries to be cynical.

It is, also, an exchange of information and an endless "bringing up." Baseball writers aren't much concerned with scooping one another, since the details they deal with are too petty and the day-to-day contact too intimate to make such mock heroics worthwhile. Only on the rare occasions that something really important occurs does competition enter the picture—and the job of the publicity man is to see that important announcements are made to everyone simultaneously. So, much of the conversation is devoted to swapping anecdotes, gossip, statistical tidbits, and opinions gleaned earlier and elsewhere.

The language used is uninhibited, and one lamentable fact of life must be accepted by intellectuals: when writers and ball players spend a good deal of time together, it is the writers who begin to talk like ball players, not the other way around.

This automatic use of barracks patois was one excuse offered —ingenuously—for a tradition only recently abandoned: no women in the press box. In the context of Women's Lib, civil rights acts, new life styles, and general enlightenment, it is hard to realize that this could have been a volatile issue only a few years ago. As recently as 1967, when this very chapter was first written, it was possible to say: "The principle is still upheld as far as lady reporters are concerned; and since there are no full-time lady baseball writers for one obvious and inescapable reason, there is always a fuss when some editor gets the idea that a girl reporter assigned to a one-day feature (invariably some 'women's angle') is going to crash the sacrosanct barrier."

The "one obvious and inescapable reason" is access to dressing rooms, which just shows how misguided a male chauvinist can be. The fact is, there are plenty of women acting as sports news commentators on television; and the *New York Post*, for one, sent a woman reporter to cover the New York Yankees' spring training in 1973. The stuff she wrote (doing her interviewing outside the disrobing room) was absolutely indistinguishable from what everybody else wrote, proving that a woman can do the job every bit as well as a man but not, alas, necessarily better.

Actually, "women in the press box" ceased to be an issue in practice long ago, when Western Union began assigning women teletype operators to the box. And despite local curmudgeons, no one tries to bar from the press box someone on a legitimate "baseball" assignment. The question is much more one of proper function than of gender (or, in the face of occasional accusations, of race). The press box, during a game, is a jealously guarded sanctuary for those who are working as daily newspaper reporters or columnists, and for those few guests— a former player, a club official, a statistician—who help them get stories. If the reporter happens to be a woman who really is covering a game, needing the special facilities provided, there should be no problem.

Psychologically, there was another reason for prohibiting women as long as the men could get away with it: some women are wives. Rare is the man who can tell his wife he doesn't want her around while he's working, and get away with it, if she decides she does want to be around—especially at a most attractive, and therefore most crowded, game. But if there is a general rule against women, the individual husband is off the hook. In unity there seemed to be strength.

And unity is one thing the baseball writers have. The Baseball Writers Association of America is an organization of unique prestige and power on the sports scene. It is organized by local chapters—one in each city that has major-league baseball—and it is the BBWAA, through its chapters, that polices each press box. The Association issues credentials to qualified members, and Baseball has delegated to the writers complete authority for conduct in and admission to the press box. This is a precious privilege for practical reasons as well as for prestige.

All press facilities are limited, and, while the atmosphere is relaxed, the wrong kind of distraction really can interfere with a man's work. By keeping the press box clear of family (children would be harder to deny than wives), friends, "umpty-six" varieties of hangers-on or self-appointed guests, work remains possible. As individuals, baseball writers could never achieve that much privacy. A club, in the business of selling tickets, can't tell an important politician (for instance) that he's not welcome in the press box; the writers, with an independent and national organization, can—and do.

The BBWAA plays an important role in several other aspects of major-league baseball:

It sets up committees to vote on official baseball awards (Most Valuable Player, Cy Young Award for the oustanding pitcher, membership in the Hall of Fame, and so forth).

It takes on the responsibility to provide official scorers for all games.

It handles the press-seating arrangements for the World Series and All-Star Games.

And it takes part in the formulation of scoring rules.

The controversial part is scoring. The idea evolved, early in this century, that, of all the available alternatives, the most conscientious and impartial scoring—at the least cost—could be done by experienced baseball writers.

Contrary to the belief of most players, the writers who act as scorers take their job very seriously. Two tasks are involved: during the game, the scorer calls the plays—that is, whether it is a hit or an error, a wild pitch or a passed ball, and how that complicated run-down play went; after the game, he fills out an intricate game report, a sort of super box score, that is sent to the league for its official records and for the compilation of official statistics.

The job requires complete concentration on the game while it is on, and about an hour's work filling out the form afterward. The fee, in the course of 60 years, has climbed from $10 to

$40 a game. Scoring assignments are rotated, within each chapter, among the qualified writers—a writer must have covered at least 100 games a year for three years before becoming eligible to score. In a city with only one or two newspapers, individuals score more often, but on the average, between three and five men will take turns during a season.

The big fight, of course, is over hits and errors. Players want hits—except pitchers, who want hits to be errors to keep their earned-run averages down. The average player's capacity for objectivity (according to recent measurements at the Objectivity Evaluation Institute of the University of Caramba) is .00000000023, plus-or-minus .00000000001. While the figure may be disputed, it is, in any case, a very small quantity.

This basic conflict in motivation—the player wants his record, while the scorer wants to call the play correctly—is complicated by several exceedingly human conditions: some scorers are less competent than others, some do not manage to give 100 percent attention, and some do permit themselves to favor the home player a wee bit. For the latter service, incidentally, no scorer has ever been thanked; he has merely put a scorer in another city on the spot, since now all the players in other cities yell at *their* scorers, "In every other town they give the home team a break, but not here, you no-good, little four-eyed——."

Fans, naturally enough, side with their favorites. If a game is hitless for four innings, and in the fifth inning a visiting player gets a scratch hit, the reaction is predictable: wholehearted boos for the scorer, whether his decision was questionable or not. But the idea, from the scorer's point of view, is neither to preserve nor make difficult a no-hitter: it is to get the play right. In this function, a scorer is just like an umpire.

There are "tough" scorers (who tend to call more errors) and "lenient" ones (who tend to call more hits), but the important thing is consistency. Reasonable men may disagree about a particular play, but a good scorer should call similar plays the same way, and he should have a defendable reason for every decision.

The basic principle of scoring is easy to state, although not always easy to apply: unless *ordinary effort* by a fielder would have produced an out, it is not an error. The most common misconception (especially among players) that it makes some sort of difference whether a ball was "touched" or not has nothing to do with it.

But the disputes generated by scoring decisions are unavoidable, and not necessarily bad as long as they stop short of violence. Many a player has threatened, and some have actually managed, to punch a scorer whose decision seemed sufficiently objectionable.

Fellow writers, also, are not above criticizing a scorer, and this is one source of some of the pretty good arguments that erupt in the press box. Another source is opinion of some player or team —or of someone's story. Another is just plain accumulated cantankerousness. Between the salty language and the high decibel level, a press-box conversation is not something you would enjoy in your living room.

Through it all, though, runs one theme: "bring me up." Writers, especially those who have worked together for many years, develop the habit of simply calling out a question as they write, expecting and getting an answer from anyone within earshot.

"Did you say 11 left on base?"

"No, 12."

"How many out of how many is that for the Yankees?"

"Nine out of 11."

"What did he say that injury was? A sprain?"

"No, a strain—a strained ligament."

"Who's that coming in to pitch? What was the second out in the fourth inning? Who's pitching for them tomorrow?"

We have here reciprocal cooperation at its best.

My own favorite example, for some reason, comes from football, but it remains a summary of the attitude, atmosphere, and content of most press-box conversation. The game had just ended, and the sun was sinking behind the rim of the stadium, and the young reporter was obviously intent on combining accurate fact with his poetic thought.

"Is that west?" he called out, pointing to the far side of the stands, where the sun was setting.

"Son," replied Grantland Rice, "if it ain't, you got a helluva story."

· **How about that!**

Mel Allen, 1938–1964

Behind the Mike, or,
Government Radio

Only a few feet away from the press box is the radio-television booth. It's a different world.

While writers, with very few exceptions, are anonymous, broadcasters are celebrities. Their voices, and since television their faces, are instantly recognizable to thousands of fans; and listeners develop a much more personal feeling for them than for any writer, even a famous columnist. Autograph seekers converge on announcers almost as often as on ball players; never on writers.

This difference is a reflection of the nature of the jobs. A writer, to take the most flattering self-image possible, is a creator; the broadcaster is a performer. The writer composes his story in the privacy of his mind, and upon setting it to paper can correct or modify his language before exposing it to public view; the broadcaster is "on" at all times while working, and must get it right instantly; he reacts to events without the opportunity for reflection.

A writer may produce, in the course of a day's work for several editions, 2,000 words; the play-by-play announcer will speak 20,000 words or more as his share of a single game.

The broadcaster, then, is a "personality," in a very real sense.

The impact he makes upon the listener is the direct result of his whole personality—voice, accent, manner, appearance (on television), known identity (if a former player), expression, and mood, as well as the result of the things he says. A writer's personality is largely irrelevant and unknown. The reader has contact only with disembodied words (although, of course, there is an indirect effect of a man's personality on what he writes).

These factors would be enough to make writing and broadcasting different worlds. But there are others, still more important.

The broadcaster is a salesman first, a reporter second; the writer is never a salesman.

And the broadcaster is an employee of the business he is describing; the writer is not.

As a result, the degree of objectivity that a good writer maintains cannot be expressed consistently by a broadcaster. This is a very touchy subject to broadcasters. Many like to consider themselves "reporters," and pride themselves on "impartiality" —a rather inappropriate synonym for "objectivity" that reveals the underlying pressure they feel to be partial.

There is also a difference is backgrounds. The vast majority of baseball writers have been sports writers most of their professional lives, but only a handful of broadcasters have grown up in their craft. About half, nowadays, are former ball players, hired for their name value; they become skillful in time, and are great assets to the program—but they certainly have neither training nor inclination for objective reporting, and most of them don't pretend that they do. Most other announcers were announcers first, and successful to some degree in that field—on the basis of voice, diction, convincing reading of commercial messages—and came into sports later. They, too, have only rudimentary journalistic conditioning, although they pursue it.

Now, no one denies that a good announcer is more objective than a biased writer—and there *are* biased writers. The point is that no announcer, regardless of his personal inclinations, can afford to be as objective as a *good* writer. The announcer may—and usually does—describe the event in front of him with complete accuracy of detail; but beyond that, comment and value judgments are needed, and it is simply impossible for a broadcaster to go on expressing opinions that his employer objects to.

This doesn't mean, naturally, that a writer is more virtuous; he is merely, by the conditions of his employment, more independent. The writer's employer is just as concerned as the broadcaster's with selling something—but what he is selling is a newspaper, and the only thing that will contribute to selling a newspaper in the long run is lively, objective reporting; the broadcaster's coemployers (the club and the sponsors) are selling a very different sort of product—tickets to the games, and whatever commodity the sponsor makes—and the only thing that contributes to that kind of selling is repetition.

The primary skill, then, that a broadcaster must develop is the ability to deliver commercial messages convincingly. He must also, it goes without saying, be able to describe the game—but the people who can do that far outnumber those who can read a good commercial. The announcer's career is made or broken on this point, from the employer's point of view, and even the big-name retired ball player must learn to perform this chore reasonably well in order to keep trading on his identity.

Once this position of the broadcaster is understood, he can be properly appreciated on his own terms. The former professional player, of course, has advantages in knowledge that no lifelong writer can have; but even nonplaying announcers, in my experience, often rank far ahead of newspapermen in their ability to notice accurately all the relevant details of a complicated situation. As eyewitnesses, they are remarkably reliable and thorough. And they achieve, through the nature of their work, a level of sustained concentration on the game that writers approach only at an intensely dramatic or peculiarly important moment.

The one thing they cannot do is knock the product. In their world, every action is positive: it is always a great pitcher striking out a fine hitter, never a poor batter failing to hit a mediocre pitcher. (This is an exaggeration for the sake of example, of course, but only a little exaggeration.) The last-place team coming in next week is always "interesting" and usually "improving." Every player is always trying his hardest. Every game (almost—they can't quite make it in baseball) is exciting, full of thrills and superlatives. Their short suit is the bright writer's long suit: irreverence.

Strangely enough, the charge broadcasters are most sensitive to—rooting for the home team—is the least justifiable one. It is true that in some cities, it is the conscious policy to have the broadcaster throw in "let's go gang's" and "we win's" and other provincially chauvinistic remarks—but so do writers in some towns. As a general rule, the less metropolitan (or perhaps cosmopolitan) a city is, the more likely rooting will be widely practiced—by newspapermen and broadcasters alike. So even in this little corner of the baseball world, we find a minor myth flourishing unchallenged.

How do announcers work?

The usual team has two announcers, or three if a great many games are televised as well as broadcast. The airwaves group has two other permanent members, as a rule: an engineer, who hooks up and monitors the radio broadcast, and a statistician. The statistician is provided by the club and doubles up in publicity functions for the press, but during the game he works in the radio booth, supplying up-to-the-minute averages and other items of interest. The newspapermen, after all, will need only one or two significant statistics for their stories; but the announcers, with their 20,000 words to spiel and plenty of dead air to fill while pitchers rub up baseballs and batters fidget, need immense amounts of such material.

Before a game, the broadcasters do exactly the same things the writers do: come to the park early, circulate, gossip, ask questions, and gather background. All the rest of the time, particularly while traveling, they keep their antennae tuned just the way the writers do.

During a game, they work much harder. Two men, obviously, do half a game each on the mike. If a three-man team is handling television as well as radio, each man is performing for two-thirds of the game.

Some commercials are prerecorded inserts, but others are read live. These are supplied by ad agencies in the form of script. Commercial references—like "Ballantine blast" for a home run—are interspersed at the wisdom of the announcer (and the wiser he is, the more he intersperses them, unless he has some other career in mind real soon).

More numerous than product commercials are house announcements for the ball club. Most general managers insist that the broadcasters repeat, at frequent intervals each day, the "upcoming" home schedule, the special promotion days, and the location of ticket offices. Some general managers, in fact, harass their broadcasters on this point beyond belief.

The final distinction between broadcasters and writers is financial. Broadcasters make much more money—perhaps five times as much and more.

There are several legitimate reasons for this. Since the real job is selling, and since huge sums of money are involved in commercial radio and television, the effective salesman gets his share. Besides, the broadcaster is a show-business personality, and, as he becomes successful, is in demand for other broadcasting assignments (apart from baseball coverage) and personal appearances—all at fancy fees. Whereas a reporter working for top minimum salary in New York is earning $18,000 a year from his paper and perhaps another $4,000 from outside writing, a top broadcaster can reach the $100,000-a-year level.

On the other hand, the writer, working in a unionized industry, has great job security. The broadcaster (although he also may be a union member) has no security whatever in the baseball field: he can be hired and fired at a moment's notice by the whim of a sponsor or top club executive—and whims come thick and fast in that business.

Finally, the on-the-air broadcaster carries far more responsibility than any writer: remember, he can't cross out, he must maintain interest, and his job is to sell tickets and beer. All a writer has to do is write his own story.

All these legitimate bases for a difference in pay don't prevent most writers from feeling intensely jealous and, in some cases, bitter. From the writer's point of view, the broadcaster is doing "the same job"—reporting the game—with less background, knowledge, wit, and objectivity than the writer possesses (ask any writer). The plain fact that it is *not* "the same job," and most writers would no more be qualified to do it than most broadcasters to write daily newspaper stories, is blithely ignored by much of the fourth estate. However, a more enlightened view is gaining ground in this area, too, just as on the woman-in-the-press-box question.

Being show-business people essentially (if not former ball players), announcers often tend to flamboyance and personal trademarks. Bob Prince of Pittsburgh, for example, is famous for wearing kaleidoscopic jackets with Bermuda shorts. Lindsay Nelson, of the Mets, wears even brighter jackets, but keeps his knees concealed. Mel Allen's highly individual intonation of the words "How about that!" became a part of American speech. In Brooklyn, young Vince Scully was merely a talented kid from Fordham who was an admirer of, and apprentice to, Red Barber, the dean of all modern and literate baseball announcers; since moving to Los Angeles with the Dodgers, however, Scully has achieved a status among Southern California baseball fans roughly analogous to the position Moses held among the Hebrews.

In recent years, there has been a welcome trend toward greater informality, less pompousness, and more explanation of baseball subtleties. The influx of articulate ex-players has contributed greatly to this, since they know both what they're talking about and express themselves in authentic dugout language. The best conversations, though, don't always deal with technical baseball, and the following example will illustrate two points: that a relaxed atmosphere is preferable to gee-whizziness; and that an announcer—unlike the writer who can cross out—should *always* be thinking ahead, before he gets in too deep.

This one came up during spring training in 1966. At Fort Lauderdale, the Yankees were playing the Pirates. It was a night game, and the Mafia of the Yankee broadcasting department, Phil Rizzuto and Joe Garagiola, was on the air. Rizzuto had just returned from a few days off, and Garagiola had made a remark about how nice it must be to be able to stay home with the dog, and Rizzuto had said he didn't have a dog.

Now the fourth inning was starting, and the word "dog" was in their minds. Willie Stargell was coming up to hit for the Pirates, and it went like this:

GARAGIOLA: Hey, Phil did you read about the trouble Stargell got into last week?

RIZZUTO: No, Joe, what trouble?

GARAGIOLA: About his dog.

RIZZUTO: His dog?

GARAGIOLA: It seems he has a dog back home, and he decided that if he were away from it for six weeks in spring training, the dog would forget him. So he had the dog flown down to Florida. Only when he went to pick it up at the airport, the plane was late, so he was late gettin' back to practice, and the manager fined him. So he wound up in the doghouse, him and the dog both.

RIZZUTO: No kiddin'! There's ball one, low outside. . . . Did this really happen, Joe, or are you makin' it up?

GARAGIOLA: Naw, I'm not makin' it up—there's a story about it in the *Sporting News.*

RIZZUTO: Holy Cow, imagine that. . . . There's a strike. . . . [Now,

Rizzuto could have dropped the subject right there, right?
Oh, no.]

RIZZUTO: Joe, was it a big dog or a little dog?

GARAGIOLA *(laughing)*: I don't know, Phil, it didn't say—but pardon me for asking, but does it make any difference?

RIZZUTO: Well, I just thought that if it's a little dog, like a Chihuahua, it wouldn't be so bad if he did forget, because he wouldn't bite you anyhow, but if it was a real big dog—well, I wouldn't want to come home either if he didn't know me.

[And here, certainly, Rizzuto didn't have to go any further, eh? Uh-uh.]

RIZZUTO: You know, we've never had any luck in our house with dogs. . . . There's strike two. . . . I mean, we could never train 'em right. . . . We had two of 'em.

[A sputtering sound from Garagiola, off-mike; silent hysterics from Joe Cooper, the engineer, Bill Kane, the statistician, and Joe Ripley, the ad agency man; but Rizzuto is just getting started.]

RIZZUTO: We never had any luck with cats, either. . . . We had two of *them*. . . . You should see our garage. . . . I guess we just don't know how to train 'em.

[By now the other occupants of the booth are rolling on the floor, stamping around or trying to hide, and Rizzuto feels he ought to say something to reassure them.]

RIZZUTO: Well, for that matter, we don't train our kids so well either. . . . I mean, in my house, the only one who's housebroken is me. . . . Well, I don't mean housebroken exactly, but I mean, at least I *obey*. . . .

At that point, perhaps, Garagiola could have helped him out —but he was too busy gasping for breath to help anyone. Phil did the only thing he could: he paused.

Stargell struck out.

"And there's strike three," said Rizzuto. Neither the game nor the broadcast remotely approached such a peak again.

On televised games, the situation is quite different. The camera does the work words have to do on radio, and explanations can be much more effective when tied to something the home viewer saw (especially since instantaneous replays came into use). The working procedure is far more complicated, too.

For radio, the announcer simply watches the game and talks into a mike. For television, he must watch both the field and the monitor screen; his comments must be geared to what the home screen is showing, not to what his own roving eyes may light upon.

And how does that picture get there?

There may be as few as three or as many as eight cameras scattered around the park. In a room under the stands, or in a mobile unit outside, sits the television director; facing him is a separate screen for each camera. He has intercom communication with each cameraman, with other technicians in the same room, and with the announcers. It is the director, scanning all the various camera shots, who decides which shot is going out over the air at any particular moment. There are few more specialized jobs in the whole world, and the quality of a baseball telecast depends on how the director does his job; he has to know both the game and the pictorial possibilities of a TV screen intimately to be able to anticipate plays and to make instantaneous choices, to supply the best possible views of all the plays that come up, and still to provide variety and human interest with close-ups and odd angles.

The monitor that the announcer watches, up in the booth, shows the selected picture actually going out over the air.

One final difference between broadcasters and writers should be mentioned—the different response they arouse in players, managers, and club officials.

Writers are, automatically, the natural enemies of athletes (except for certain enlightened athletes). Writers dig up "dirt," ask "stupid" (i.e., embarrassing) questions, and have no loyalty to the ball club. A player must be always on his guard in talking to reporters (players think), because he is sure to be misquoted (or, much worse, accurately quoted).

Broadcasters are employees of the same organization as the players. If there is "dirt," they can be counted upon to suppress it, not broadcast it (both literally and figuratively). They can be trusted, their loyalty is clear—and they usually give nice gifts for pregame and postgame interviews. Besides, half of them are ex-ball players, members of the lodge. For sympathetic shoulders, broadcasters can't be beaten.

As I said, it's a different world.

13

- **The incidence of immorality among itinerant workers is highest.**

Harold Rosenthal, 1952

- **This trip is beginning to drag.**

Traditional

On the Road

In one category, those who live the major-league baseball life far outstrip those who are concerned with any other team spectator sport: days away from home.

A baseball season begins in mid- or late February, when spring training begins. It ends in early October for all but World Series participants, who have another week or two of business to transact. It lasts, then, seven and a half to eight months, and 60 percent of it will be spent on the road.

For most players, it is 100 percent on the road. Their "home" cities are not their real homes, just the location of the team they play for. If they have children of school age, it is not easy to bring them to Florida or to the "home city" until school lets out in June, and they have to be back in school in September. Even during July and August, the player will be away from the "home city" half the time. If he can have a few weeks with his family between February and October, he's lucky.

In addition, there is the matter of expense. The real home, wherever it is, must be maintained all year. Temporary homes in large cities (and only large cities have major-league teams) are not easy to find, and rarely inexpensive. Plane or train fares back and forth, for a wife and two or three or four children, can run to a considerable sum (after all, there are plenty of players from California playing for New York or Philadelphia, and vice versa). And a wife with small children, in a strange city, is likely to need some sort of domestic help.

And it is precisely the player who has the least money who is least stable, least sure of not being sent back to the minors or traded to another team. The minimum salary, which was as low as $7,000 as recently as 1967, has come up to $16,500, but the increase over the 20 years from 1950 to 1970 has hardly kept pace with inflation. Most rookies get the minimum, and another large group makes less than $20,000. The majority make under $35,000. Since such men have a career expectancy of less than five years (it's the stars who bring up the average in years played as well as in dollars), the cost of living in large cities is a perpetual problem, and most of them solve it by leaving their families at home.

The better-established players have it easier. They are better off financially, as their salaries cross the $40,000 level and (in a few cases) climb skyward, and they are sure enough of playing out the season to think of moving their families, permanently or temporarily, to the "home city." They usually do bring their families to Florida for spring training, or at least for part of it.

Once the actual season begins, however, in the second week of April, all players, regardless of status, are on the road half the time—that is, away from even the "home city." The way baseball schedules are made, that means (taking as an example the Atlanta Braves' pattern of 1973): home five days, away 12, home nine, away seven, home three, away four, home six, away 14, home 10, away 10, home eight, away six, home 10; then a two-day All-Star Game break for all but those who make the All-Star team; then away five, home seven, away 13, home 10, away eight, home six, away four, home two, away five, and finally home seven.

If you think that's tiring, you are dead right.

The two main hazards of being away from home that much are loneliness and worry. Your companions, by and large, are not of your own choice, and by the end of the year, constant contact with them may be more irritation than companionship. And meanwhile, the wife is somewhere trying to cope with both the mother and father functions of raising a family, and kids have accidents and illnesses. For anyone with strong family feelings, peace of mind is not easy to maintain when one has to travel that much.

Some men, of course, are perfectly happy in this situation. Some don't have families; some have families they don't care too much about; some care but also prize the "freedom" being away from home represents.

But most are not like this. Most respond to the glamor of new places and new people for the first couple of years, but then begin to feel an increasing sense of alienation from the people they really love. They accept the traveling as a necessary evil, an unavoidable element in earning their livelihoods, but they don't enjoy it. It can be argued that the accumulated weight of constant separation—especially as children grow older and the father's absence becomes more of an issue from all sides—is a major factor in ending a player's career. The old saying is that "the legs go first," but this is not true—it's the *desire* that goes first, and in many cases the desire to go on playing is undermined by the desire to lead a more normal life.

So far, we have mentioned only the emotional problem of separation from family. But the practical aspects of ceaseless traveling also wear men down. Irregularity causes physical fatigue, and monotony promotes mental fatigue.

The irregularity is much worse than it used to be. Since baseball went on a coast-to-coast basis, time-zone changes are involved in many trips, a three-hour change between the East and California. Going westward, that means a 27-hour day for your body, no matter how you manipulate the hands of your watch; going eastward, it's a 21-hour day which really means an abbreviated night, since most trips are made at night. It takes a couple of days to get one's mealtimes and sleep straightened out—but within a couple of days, you're off to another time zone.

Besides time-zone changes, there is the crazy-quilt baseball schedule to contend with. Most of the time, the jump to the next city is made after a night game, which means arrival in the next city's hotel between 2 and 4 A.M. Within a city, there is often a day game after a night game (at least once each weekend). After a while, your stomach and your mind have totally different ideas about when it is time for breakfast or dinner; and usually, in wee-hour arrivals, no decent meal is available anyhow.

A player tries to eat a substantial meal four to five hours before game-time, and another big meal after the game. Imagine what that means when the schedule runs like this (again, we'll take an actual example, this time from the Yankees): Thursday, 6 P.M. game at Minneapolis, so the pregame meal is around 2 P.M. The game ends around 8:30, and the team is flying by charter to Kansas City. You can have a sandwich or cold cuts in the clubhouse, or an airline dinner in flight, but neither is likely to afford the type or quantity of food a hungry ball player craves. If he waits until the team gets to Kansas City, it is 1 A.M. (actually 2 A.M. where he started out, because Kansas City is on Standard Time while Minneapolis is on Daylight Saving Time), and a neat 12 hours since his pregame meal. Besides, all that's open at 1 A.M. in Kansas City is the 24-hour coffee shop in the hotel, and that isn't going to be much better than the plane food.

In any case, it's hard to get right to sleep after the trip, so on Friday morning the player will tend to sleep late. But if he has a late breakfast, he'll be crowding in on his next pregame meal, which must be about 3 P.M. for a 7:30 night game. He'll be back at the hotel about 11 P.M., which isn't too late for a heavy meal with respect to the time gap since the pregame meal—but it is pretty late if you expect to go to sleep before 2 A.M. And you don't want to sleep too late Saturday morning, because the Saturday game is at 6 P.M., which means a pregame meal about 1:30.

The answer to that one is to skip breakfast Saturday morning. But Sunday is coming up, and the doubleheader starts at 1:30 P.M., so even if you eat well after the game Saturday (at about 10 P.M.) you've got to be up in time to have your bag packed and in the lobby (to be picked up by a truck) before you leave for the ball park (at 11 A.M.). So Sunday you have breakfast, but no real pregame meal—and a doubleheader means you'll be in the ball park for at least eight hours.

Immediately after the game (in this case in real life, a violent rainstorm interrupted the second game for half an hour, so it was about 8:30 when the team bus left the ball park), the team goes to the airport, gets on another charter, with another airline-meal tray, and flies two and a half hours to Detroit—where it takes nearly an hour to get into town from the airport. On Sunday night at 2 A.M. in Detroit, good food is out of the question, unless you like Chinese food (Victor Lim's is excellent and open); but by now (we're back on Eastern Standard Time, the same as Minneapolis's Central Daylight), it is about 15 hours since that solid breakfast in Kansas City.

However, there is no game Monday, so you can catch up on sleep and skip a meal to get straightened out. Tuesday and Wednesday night games start at 8 P.M., and immediately after the Wednesday night game, there's a charter back to New York (you're lucky this time, it's a jet), and by the time the bus takes you to Yankee Stadium, where your car is parked or where a loving wife might meet you, you have a fighting chance to be home by 3:30 A.M., Eastern Daylight Saving Time.

The result of all this has to be, sooner or later, insomnia and indigestion.

You'll notice, in the above itinerary, that all the jumps were made in chartered planes. This is the standard method of travel these days. A still-little-realized fact, by those who have not done a lot of it, is that plane travel tires you out. For one thing, because airports are so far out of town in most places, the realistic travel time is often double (or more) the actual flying time. You get on a bus outside the ball park, ride half an hour or more, get on the plane, sit in the same kind of bus-type seat for a half hour before takeoff, fly two hours, then sit in another bus for half an hour. By this time—if you are 6 feet 2 inches tall and have just played a tough ball game—your legs are pretty stiff and all sorts of back muscles are protesting. It's true that plane seats do tilt back, but most fellows can't sleep anyhow.

And then there is tension. The fact remains that the majority of players feel at least some apprehension about flying, rational or not. They make, after all, 35 to 40 flights a year. Veteran players have taken off and landed several hundred times, and have been through various near-accidents or alarms, or at the very least delays. Some people can take this in stride, but most can't.

It was much more relaxing in the old days. A Pullman berth may not be the best place to sleep, but, in general, train travel was more relaxing even though it took longer. Until expansion —that is, through the 1940s—most trips were overnight train rides: New York to Cleveland, Detroit to Chicago, Philadelphia to Boston, and so forth. Ball clubs had private cars, there were few night games, and one could either eat dinner before boarding (if the train left late in the evening) or have dinner in a special dining car. One could relax with a couple of drinks in a club car as the evening wore on, play cards, stretch one's legs, and at least lie down if not actually sleep. And at both ends of the trip, the station was within five minutes of the hotel and the ball park.

But progress is progress, and Dick Young, of the *New York Daily News*, summed it up better than any man I know. In 1959, the Los Angeles Dodgers and Milwaukee Braves tied for the pennant, and the first play-off game was in Milwaukee. The second had to be played in Los Angeles the next day, and a special bus was acquired to take the flower of American journalism from Milwaukee's County Stadium to Chicago's O'Hare Airport, where a connection to a jet flight to Los Angeles could be made.

Young, doing his usual thorough job, wrote and wrote and wrote and happened to be the last man finished. We (writers from a dozen cities) were sitting on the bus, impatient to start, worrying about missing the plane, when Young finally appeared at the gate and ran across the parking lot to the bus—ran carrying a heavy typewriter, field glasses, an overcoat, and a small bag. He was panting as he climbed aboard and the bus started.

"I'll be a son of a bitch," he declared. "There's something wrong when you have to run yourself into a heart attack to catch a jet to save time."

Amen.

So much for the physical problems. The mental effect is bad, too.

When day games were prevalent, life on the road wasn't so bad. One could make friends in each city, visit, meet for dinner, go to a show, and keep fairly regular hours. Now, with more cities and shorter visits to each, made less frequently, this sort of social life is rarely possible. Although the number of hours spent in the ball park is the same as it used to be, the free hours are less useful. The late morning and afternoon hours are unproductive—one can go to the movies, or watch guessing games on television, or hang around the lobby, but that's about it. And if one does try to see friends after a game, it is both late and inconvenient, with few places to go in most cities.

What one finds, then, is a numbing succession of bus rides, airports (all the new ones look alike), hotel lobbies (all the new ones look alike), coffee shops and bars, small hotel rooms, ball parks (all the news ones look alike), and a few nice restaurants. It is all immensely unstimulating.

But wait! What about sex? Doesn't everyone play around on

the road? Isn't every man a wolf away from home? And aren't glamorous major leaguers, above all, afforded the most marvelous opportunities simply to snap their fingers and have the most luscious females compete eagerly for their attentions?

Not quite.

There are, without doubt, some astonishingly successful Lotharios in the baseball set. There are others, just as willing, who are much less successful. There are those who think, and even look, but never really try, and there are those who don't even look.

In this area, as in so many others, reality puts a damper on some favorite fantasies. A cross section of the baseball population would reveal, I'm sure, the same proportion of woman-chasing (and woman-catching) as any other group matched for age, economic status, and appearance.

It is undoubtedly true that casual infidelity is more frequent among men who travel a good deal with some money in their pockets—traveling salesmen, sailors (and soldiers), expense-account executives and actors, for instance. It is no accident that so many stock jokes involve these characters in such situations.

It was Harold Rosenthal, of the former *New York Herald Tribune*, who came across, and was delighted by, the line in a sociological abstract: "The incidence of immorality among itinerant workers is highest."

"What that means," chortled Harold, a bookish man always ready to translate, "is that the road'll make a bum outa the best of 'em."

And it's not surprising: loneliness and boredom, added to the natural urges of healthy young men, would tend to promote what might be termed temporary, even fleeting, liaisons.

And yet, in action instead of in talk, there is comparatively little of it. The bulk of the activity is concentrated in the small number of men who devote themselves to it. It remains, in baseball as in all other walks of life, an intensely personal, private decision rooted in character, not circumstance. Some do, most don't, and no more meaningful general picture can be drawn.

A far greater habit pattern, which used to be considered a vice, is drinking. Baseball players, as a group, contain a sizable number of heavy drinkers and a large majority of occasional drinkers. The conditions of baseball life increase whatever tendency a man has in this direction—terrific tension, continued over many months, about his performance, combined with the boredom and loneliness of the road.

Now, baseball happens to be a game in which it is perfectly possible to drink a moderate amount of liquor and still be in condition to play. To a greater degree than in other sports, just the right degree of *relaxation* is as important as tense effort. In fact, many great baseball players consumed great quantities of liquor regularly, with no noticeable effect on their performance.

What is harmful to a ball player is not liquor by itself, nor sex (licit or illicit) by itself, but the prolonged pursuit of either or both. It's the night spent pub-crawling, or woman-hunting, at the expense of some decent amount of rest, that really does the damage. That's why many managers have a curfew, formal or informal. The idea is not to force grown men to be teetotalers or to act like celibates; it is to get them to bed at a decent hour, whatever they did before.

"Staying in shape," in the sense that a track man fine-tunes his body, is out of the question for baseball players. The season is too long, the games too many; a man simply couldn't stay that sharp that long without developing a nervous condition that would nullify his muscular efficiency.

But staying in shape within the context of baseball life is something most players are conscientious about. In any case, it is especially difficult, in this sport, to draw direct comparisons between off-field behavior and on-field effectiveness. It seems to boil down to this: some really wild high livers remain great ball players, while many pure and dedicated physical culturists don't make it; but the man who doesn't take care of himself shortens his career, even if he doesn't necessarily damage his performance while still fairly young.

Now we can begin to piece together some of the factors that make playing on the road a disadvantage:

1. Physical fatigue.
2. Boredom, loneliness, and other mental states that can take something away from full concentration and alertness.
3. The unfettering of those individuals who do play around; at home they are, at the very least, more discreet.
4. The tangible baseball factors: last lick for the home team, unfamiliarity with the ball park and various sight lines, less practice time.

That's why teams expect to win more at home than on the road.

Let's summarize some of the routines:

On the road, the ball club pays all the expenses (travel, hotel) and either gives meal money ($19 a day) or permits signing of meal checks in the hotel. The player pays his own "incidentals" (phone calls, laundry, etc.).

Players are housed in pairs, except for elder statesmen and superstars who earn the right to a private room. Roommates are selected by the manager, or by the road secretary, if the manager leaves that to him. The manager gets a two-room suite. Newspapermen and broadcasters who travel with the club (but whose bills are forwarded to their own employers) get single rooms.

In most cities, the club has a bus that goes from the hotel to the ball park (two and a half hours before game time), and back (about 45 minutes after the game). Players are not required to make the bus, but if they don't, they pay for their own cab.

On "getaway day," bags are packed and left in the lobby before the bus goes to the park. A truck picks them up, then proceeds to the ball park where the team's equipment (bats, uniforms, etc.) is loaded on at the end of the game. Then both truck and bus go directly from the ball park to the airport.

Most of the time, a team likes to move on to the next city as soon as possible after the last game of a series, even though it means traveling late at night. It is considered more restful to be on the scene of the next series—and, of course, the risk of bad weather holding up a flight at the last minute is eliminated.

The writers and broadcasters on a trip face a special hazard: calories, as well as alcohol. With so much unusable time on their hands, writers tend to socialize over meals and drinks; a typical situation arises at breakfast, when one man straggles in before another has finished, and then a third comes along, while the extra cups of coffee and extra pieces of pastry mount up. Then there's the manager sitting across the way, and some time must be spent talking to him. Or one joins a player at his pre-game meal when it is only an hour or so after the writer's own lunch.

Once at the park, the writer is exposed to the pressroom, or press lounge. It is customary to serve a hot meal, and the drinks are free. On the one hand, this sounds like shameless freeloading, but while it is certainly freeloading, it isn't exactly shameless. A writer, on assignment, is required to be inside a ball park for five to nine hours, always encompassing at least one regular mealtime and often two. A hot dog may be a treat to a fan, but it's not much as a regular diet for those who have to be in a ball park every day. So the ball clubs try to make the cuisine in the pressroom attractive, and this public relations gesture is much appreciated. At the same time, the club uses the same facilities as a "hospitality room" for its own employees, visiting dignitaries, ad agency people, and so forth, very likely under the expense umbrella of "entertaining the press," so it isn't being entirely selfless.

Pressrooms usually open a couple of hours before a game, and stay open for an hour or two afterward. Many have working space where afternoon writers can do their stories after visiting the locker rooms.

Writers tend to spend more time in pressrooms on the road than at home. On the road, they come to the park a little earlier (why not?), and stay later. Also, on the road, they have much more need, and opportunity, to talk to the baseball officials in that city, informally and for background; their own team is pretty well known to them and accessible, so they don't need to spend as much time on this sort of gossip when home.

The morning-paper man gets on an accelerating treadmill as the team goes farther west. By the time he gets to California, the New York morning writer is almost on round-the-clock duty. He should have an early story in by 4 P.M. New York time —which is 1 P.M. in California. That means where he is he has to start finding people to talk to around 10 A.M. Once he files, he kills a couple of hours and goes to the park with the team. The game doesn't start until eight o'clock—which is 11 P.M. in New York. He pieces together a running story, slams a quick lead on it in time to make only those papers that go to press at 2 A.M. or later. And if he's wise, he won't stay out too late after the game, because he has to be looking for another early story at 10 A.M. the next morning.

One final hazard should be mentioned: colds. In April and May, games are played in 40-degree temperature, with high wind, and you can go, in a space of four days, from Boston (freezing) to Los Angeles (hot) to Minneapolis (brrr). In midsummer, places like Kansas City, St. Louis, Los Angeles, Houston, and Washington—not to mention New York and Cincinnati—can be model infernos; but nowadays, all hotels and restaurants, all planes and some buses, are air-conditioned. Going in and out of those places a few times is guaranteed to bring on sneezes and sore throats.

Is it all really so terrible, then? Is baseball travel a form of torture?

No, not really; but remember, we're trying to deal with realities as contrasted with long-accepted illusions, and one of the most cherished dreams of the home-tied fan is the opportunity to make one of those glamorous road trips.

Well, one trip *is* glamorous; even two, or three. But, week after week, month after month, year after year, the glamor wears off, and the repetitious details pile up—pack, unpack; get up early enough to send laundry that will be returned the same day; what time does the bus leave? Have they brought the bags from the airport yet? Fasten seat belts. How'd the last man go out? Operator, I want to call long distance, collect. . . .

A baseball writer, we all agree, is the lion of the sports-writing profession. But along about late July or mid-August, he starts to feel a lot more like one of those little hamsters in a revolving cage.

And the ball players feel it right along with him. That's one time they are in complete agreement.

14

· **Ouch.**

Traditional

· **Ooowwww!!**

ibid.

On the Rubbing Table, or, Through Whirlpool to Diathermy

The most intimate place on any ball club, the inner sanctum sanctorum, is the rubbing table, and the trainer is its high priest.

To the outside world, a trainer is perhaps the least noticed and certainly the least-thought-about person in the ball park. Even the batboys get more attention, because they are more frequently visible. What most fans see is a figure in long white pants, running out to administer first aid whenever a player gets hurt during the game, and they pay no more attention to him, once he disappears again, than to a grounds keeper.

To ball players, it's entirely different. The trainer is the man who takes care of their most important asset: their bodies. He is also, if he is a good trainer, a potential father confessor. If a player has any brains at all—and there are players who don't— he will be completely honest with any trainer he trusts, and will reveal and discuss many a minor ailment he wants to hide even from his manager. Proper care for a small injury soon enough can often prevent more serious trouble, without forcing the player out of action; neglect, or failure to follow prescribed treatment, can have crippling consequences.

The wise manager, too, relies completely on a trainer's good judgment. He lets the private player-trainer relationship exist without prying, and yet can be sure of accurate and pertinent information when he seeks it.

In other circumstances, however, a trainer can take on the aspects of a house detective. When he does, the ball club may or may not win, but life is a lot less fun—and in the long run, unhealthy.

A trainer's duties are more than applying Band-aids and listening to moans. They form the focus of two of the major activities of a modern major-league organization: physical condition and logistics.

A trainer is the first line of diagnosis and therapy. Every team has a doctor, often an orthopedic specialist, because so many athletic injuries call for one. But the official club physician rarely travels with the team, and may not be in the ball park at home at all games. Therefore, the trainer performs four separate functions as the physician-on-the-spot:

1. He applies first aid when an injury occurs.
2. He is the liaison to the doctor, in determining whether an injury calls for the doctor's care, in reporting various details to the doctor, and in carrying out the doctor's instructions in the treatment of a player afterward.
3. He looks after the special physical needs of uninjured players (like giving rubdowns, taping ankles, and loosening up a pitcher's arm).
4. He looks after the general health of the club, checking weight, diet where necessary, dispensing pills for everything from sleep to colds to vitamins, administering various injections, and so forth.

In the above respects, a trainer's tasks at home and on the road are similar, except that he has a better-equipped room, usually, at home. In addition, however, he acts as an equipment manager while the team travels. He has the responsibility of seeing that uniforms, bats, helmets, and other items of team baggage are loaded and unloaded and delivered properly. Since a team rarely stays in one city more than three days, this gets to be quite a chore.

And on top of everything else, today's trainer is the twentieth-century counterpart of Figaro, the famous barber of Seville —the factotum of the town, the one on whom everyone calls for the solution of any unexpected little problem, from a broken shoe-lace on up.

Most teams, today, carry two trainers, a chief trainer and an assistant. During a game, one will be in the dugout and the other back in the clubhouse. A few carry an equipment man on the road (the best known was Eddie Logan, who moved from New York to San Francisco with the Giants in 1958; hearing a few words spoken by Eddie in his pure New Yorkese is testimony enough to his exceptional loyalty to the Giants).

All this is a far cry from the legendary idea of a trainer, based on practices of two generations ago. In the early days, a trainer was some old friend of the manager, with a gift of gab and a collection of patent medicines, with some secret-formula liniment in his secondhand doctor's bag, and as much alcohol on his breath as in the bag. His education was strictly haphazard and based only on experience, often someone else's experience imperfectly understood.

The gift of gab was important: the old trainer had to have the ability to kid an injured athlete along; if the injury was painful but not too serious, this kind of applied psychology might keep the man playing; if it was serious, at least the victim's spirits might be kept up, or at least attention might be drawn away from his suffering.

Such a talent in a trainer today is also desirable, but it is no longer the main therapy at his command. Modern trainers usually have formal preparation, in a trainers' school or elsewhere, which gives them a working knowledge of physiology, drugs and medications, diagnosis, and various therapeutic mechanisms.

In the dressing room of a modern stadium, one will find a special room for the trainer, usually between the locker room and the showers. It will have at least two rubbing tables, on which a man can stretch out full length to be massaged or otherwise worked upon. There will be a rather large medicine cabinet, and several machines: a whirlpool bath (a four-foot-high metal tub in which hot water circulates violently while arms or legs are immersed), some sort of diathermy machine (which uses electric heat or ultrasonics for deep heat treatment), and something that makes plenty of ice (a refrigerator is part of the standard furniture). One does not find, however, X-ray machines: for such examinations or treatments, players are sent to hospitals, where qualified personnel can handle them.

A trainer's bag usually has trays that set up when it opens, like some types of tool chests, and it is crammed with an incredible number and variety of objects: scissors, gauze, bottles of liquids and pills, cotton, spatulas, and ointments in bewildering combination.

Taping ankles, or wrists, is as much an art as a medical science, because the comfort of the athlete is as important as the structural support being given—and athletes can be pretty finicky about the comfort of a joint they have to use heavily. Good taping can keep minor strains operational and prevent injury.

Before a game, the starting pitcher, and perhaps a couple of other players, want their arms "loosened." This is a rubbing, kneading, stretching process that stretches the muscles about to be subjected to such unusual strain.

Every sport has it own pattern of common injuries. In baseball, in order of frequency, these are muscle-tearing injuries, twists at the joints (ankle, knee, wrist), bruises and cuts.

Broken bones are relatively infrequent, and when they occur are often "hairline" fractures.

The most common injury of all is a charley horse. Essentially, this is a hemorrhage under the muscles of the thigh: it can be the result of a blow, or of a stretching-tearing damage from excessive effort or insufficient warm-up. In general, because baseball is a game of quick starts (in fielding and in getting away from home plate or a base), legs are subjected to muscle "pulls" and tears. In a "tear," muscle tissue is literally torn, that is, separated at some point; a "pull" is a less severe version of a tear, and a "strain" is a stretch short of the breaking point. Because the ball must be thrown hard, often from awkward body positions, muscular arm injuries are common—and pitchers, of course, generate their own exceptional pressures.

The twisting injuries happen mostly in hitting the ground or taking a bad step—while sliding, while trying to make an acrobatic catch, or while slipping on a rain-soaked or otherwise tricky surface. Sprained ankles are more common than sprained wrists, but both are standard baseball hazards.

Bruises, in baseball, can be inflicted in four ways: by being hit by the ball, whether it's thrown or batted; by collision with another player, either a teammate trying to make the same fielding play, or an opponent guarding a base (especially the catcher); by running into a barrier, the outfield fence, or the box fronts in foul ground, while fielding; or by contact with the ground in sliding or falling. Most of the ball-inflicted bruises, of course, involve the hands and fingers, but some pitchers and infielders take their share of painful whacks on the leg or body from line drives traveling 100 miles an hour or more. It's remarkable that they survive these as well as they do.

Cuts are, by and large, of two types (although any collision can also produce them): spike-inflicted and ball-inflicted. The spike wounds, which often require half a dozen stitches or more, are the result of slides the vast majority of the time. Ball-inflicted cuts are the special torture of catchers, who suffer innumerable "split" fingers from foul tips. A split finger is one in which the blow by the ball has caused the skin to split, usually lengthwise.

Catchers seem to be well protected by their chest protectors, shin guards, and mask, but there are many vulnerable points, and foul tips seem to find them all. When a bat deflects the pitch just a trifle, too much for the catcher's gloved hand to re-act in time but not enough to make it miss the catcher, the ball still has practically all of its original force behind it. The points of the shoulders, the insides of the thighs and of the knees, the neck and Adam's apple, the top of the head, and, of course, the arms—all these are places exposed to the foul tip.

And, it should be realized, the umpire behind the catcher is almost equally unprotected from the foul tip that misses the catcher.

The elbow is a potential trouble spot for those who must throw a lot—pitchers and catchers, especially pitchers, and some outfielders, third basemen, and shortstops. Pitchers are far and away in most danger, it goes without saying; not only do they throw harder and longer when they pitch, but, by try-ing to put special spins on the ball, set up particularly severe unnatural stresses. A most common pitching injury, therefore, is a loose bone chip in the elbow. This can be removed sur-gically, but many men pitch successfully for several years with this condition before it gets so unbearable that it has to be corrected.

And a batter is subject to a special kind of injury that often goes unnoticed from the stands: a bruised instep, ankle, toe, or shin from his own foul tip.

The degree to which a man is incapacitated by an injury is often out of proportion to ordinary standards of damage. A very small thing can put a man out of action—and he may be able to play with an intrinsically more serious ailment that would have an ordinary man home in bed. It all depends on how the par-ticular problem affects the player's key actions.

For instance, just plain blisters on the palm of the hand—if raw and painful—can prevent a man from batting effectively. But a man with two broken fingers can play, and even bat a little bit—if the fingers happen to be the pinkie and fourth finger. One of baseball's most famous injuries was Dizzy Dean's broken toe, which ended his career as a top-flight pitcher. When he tried to pitch before the toe was fully healed, he used an unorthodox stride in favoring the toe, and thus permanently injured his arm by the unnatural motion that resulted. A charley horse may slow a man down, but not prevent him from playing; but a pulled muscle in the back, not even painful while running or throwing, may make swinging the bat impossible.

The trainer must judge all these things, or at least help the individual player judge for himself. He must help decide when pain is just pain, to be borne without danger of further damage, and when it is unsafe to ignore damage that doesn't seem to hurt much.

A good trainer, then, can forestall a certain amount of injury by precaution, and can get men back into the lineup a game or two sooner by effective treatment and proper understanding of the individual case. Every man has his own rate of healing, and his own psychological as well as physiological responses. The trainer who can read these accurately, and take appropriate action, is of immense value to individual careers and team success.

When a rookie arrives, the trainer is often the first friendly human being he finds. When a veteran is on the way down, the trainer may be the last sympathetic listener he'll have. And to the trainer, more than to anyone else connected with a baseball team, the star and the fringe player have equal status, and are of equal concern. The trainer sees men when they are in pain, with their defenses down, dependent and frightened. He may not become the best character-reader in the world, but he has the best opportunity to become one, and most trainers are pretty hard to fool in that respect.

They are the most unsung of the unsung heroes in the baseball hierarchy, and the standards of their profession—recognized only recently—are rising rapidly. It seems that owners, after a century of professional baseball, have finally come to realize that since the main assets of their business are the physical capabilities of their ball players, it might be a good idea to put those bodies in the care of qualified people. Actually, for owners, that's about the normal rate of speed for seeing the light.

One final point should be made. Why, the modern fan might ask, if trainers are better and more appreciated and given better equipment, do there seem to be more injuries than ever?

The answer is, there aren't more injuries. It just seems that way because today, through radio, television, and a different reporting attitude, the fan hears all about every injury, sometimes *ad nauseam*. In the old days, not only were injuries to familiar players less documented, but no one was aware of how many careers ended prematurely, before the player in question became familiar. Today, many players, who simply would have had to quit under the conditions of two generations ago, are kept going, and some thoroughly repaired.

15

Beating the Bushes

It all begins back in the bushes.

Among baseball people, the word "bush" has special connotations. It is usually an insult, or at least an expression of disrespect. It's short of "bush league," the opposite of "big league," and it usually refers to behavior—being cheap, or mean (in the sense of cheap); showing up a teammate or a friend; showing off; acting, in whatever way, small, petty, unsophisticated, crude. A man who has "no class" is termed "bush"; so is a situation not worthy of major-league conditions.

But almost everyone in baseball starts in the bushes, or comes through them. The number of players who come from farms, tiny towns, or isolated areas is much smaller than it used to be, but with very few exceptions all players spend at least some time playing in the little towns that make up the lower echelons of the minor leagues. And the big-city boys, by and large, come from the poorer, and tougher, neighborhoods. More well-educated, upper-middle-class-bred young men are playing major-league baseball today than ever before—but they are still a rather small minority. So "class," in the sense of polish, is something most players have to acquire, while "class," in the sense of character, is put to some severe tests on the way up.

It is in the bushes, then, where basic baseball attitudes are formed and hardened—and it is in the bushes, literally or figuratively, where most baseball talent is sought.

And the men on whom the whole elaborate structure of the multimillion-dollar business rests are the scouts.

It became an axiom, in the 40 years between the development and the universal application of farm systems, that no major-league organization is any better than its scouts. Before that, this wasn't true. When most minor-league teams were independently owned, and when the majors were relatively young, scouting was a haphazard business, although great energy went into it. The key man, usually, was the manager, who hired and fired players (no general managers then); in the minors, and on some major-league teams, owners were very active. They used their own observation, word-of-mouth reports, and letters of recommendation from friends and former associates. It was common for one player to recommend others to his manager. The inducement of a proferred contract, and occasionally transportation, was enough in most cases up to World War I and beyond. Major-league teams then bought minor leaguers who had done well.

When farm systems began in the 1920s, the traditional methods of personal recommendation and brief tryout of self-professed prospects proved inadequate. To stock a farm system, one parent organization had to sign hundreds of players—and to do this, the organization hired full-time, professional scouts.

In 1965, the painfully constructed scouting-and-farm-system operation was knocked into a cocked hat by the adoption of a free-agent draft, patterned on the football and basketball drafts of college stars. This revolutionary step altered many of the accumulated skills and known conditions of scouting, and its eventual effects could not be predicted.

But the basic structure remains.

A major-league team's scouting department has three major areas of operation. The most important scouts are the ones who deal with the primary source of raw material—players who have not yet signed a professional contract. These scouts are assigned geographic sectors, and watch high-school and college teams, sandlotters, American Legion, and other organized amateur leagues, semipros, industrial teams, and so forth. Each scout has several "bird dogs" working for him—friends or associates who are his pieceworkers, not really part of the ball club's organization but a vital network to the scout himself.

The second level of scouting is the minors. A parent team must have some evaluation, preferably a detailed one, on every player on every minor-league team. This has become all the more important under recent regulations which promote the drafting of players from rival organizations. Minor-league scouting has two basic purposes: knowledge of abilities of players who may be acquired in trades, and a standard of comparison for judging the performance and development of one's own players.

The third level is fairly recent: systematic scouting of other major-league teams. The practice of sending scouts to "get a book" on a prospective World Series opponent used to get a lot of attention; it was inevitable (under Parkinson's Law, that work expands to fill the time of an increasing staff) that this would spread to regular-season activities. If it was worth scouting the leaders in the other league before a World Series, why wouldn't it be just as useful to scout the teams you had to play to get into the World Series? It would.

The two purposes of major-league scouting, then, are to evaluate men for possible trades, and to keep up with current information on an opponent's form immediately prior to playing him.

The real work, however, is done at the lowest level: digging out raw talent in the first place.

No one in an important baseball position is more anonymous than a scout, yet for the success of an organization he is more important than well-publicized managers and front-office executives. The basic job of the front office, in fact, is to hire good scouts. In a way, that means scouting scouts, and, obviously enough, being willing to pay them better than some other organization.

Who are scouts? Former players, by and large, some with

recognizable names because they played in the majors, most unknown because they didn't. Most of them have some local business interest at home, because most scouts aren't paid much. Their expense accounts, in fact, mean more than their salaries. They travel a great deal, within their areas, seeing as many games as they can, running down reports from bird dogs.

What makes a good scout? Judgment and luck.

What does he judge? Basic talents. Obviously, the records compiled by a high-school player don't mean much, because of the level of competition. And his skills, at that point, aren't really important; what count are the skills he can acquire. So a scout looks for certain fundamentals, and tries to project in his mind how far these can be developed. How fast can he run? How hard (in absolute terms) can he throw? How quick are his wrists when he swings a bat? How relaxed and sure are his hands when he catches a ball? How quick are his reflexes, responding to a batted ball or an unexpected situation?

Has he reached full growth? Is he skinny and not too strong, but likely to fill out? Is he strong now but likely to be heavy-legged or overweight by the time he's 25? Is he effective now only because he had matured faster than the kids around him, or is early maturity a permanent advantage for him?

What's his mental and emotional makeup? How competitive is he? How much does he really want to play baseball? Is he clean-living, reliable, teachable?

These are the questions scouts ask themselves.

Branch Rickey, who was a farm-system pioneer and a great judge of talent, always spoke of five basic abilities: to run, to throw, to field, to hit, and to hit with power. George Weiss, another fabulously successful farm-system operator, was less a judge of player talent than a skilled administrator of good scouts.

As one can imagine, it's a tremendous roulette game. No one can really tell what a 17-year-old boy will develop into as a 30-year-old man. Yes, a Willie Mays or a Mickey Mantle is obviously a great talent, and you don't have to be a wizard to spot him; almost any fan, watching such superstars in the raw, could recognize their potential. But many others, perhaps equally gifted at 17, never went on for one reason or another—an injury, an illness, a lack of desire.

Discovering a Mantle or a Mays is luck—not luck in seeing them, since that's the product of hard work, but luck that they went on to fulfill their promise. The scout's bread and butter, though, is not superstars, but usable players—the ones who, alongside a Mays or a Mantle, can round out a winning team.

That's what's so tough, judging the eventual usefulness of a player with some clear-cut abilities, some evident weaknesses, and large gray areas of possibilities. Is this one worth signing, and (in the days of competitive bonuses) for how much?

Before the free-agent draft, a scout's most important skill lay in signing the player he had decided was worthwhile. Twenty clubs, presumably, were in competition. After World War II, it was no longer likely that any "sleeper" could be turned up, that any player of promise existed anywhere without the full knowledge of at least a half-dozen organizations. The trick was not to know of his existence, but to persuade him to choose your organization over another.

This involved cultivating the family, befriending the boy, keeping others at arm's length. In a bidding contest, finally, the amount offered would be crucial, and the scout had to decide how big a bundle the particular prospect was worth, in the context of a club's yearly budget. And when he did decide, it was up to him to see that his bid was favored over any reasonably similar bid from another direction.

Sandy Koufax, who did little pitching in high school, was comparatively unknown when scouts discovered him in Brooklyn. Yet, the first place he tried out was the Polo Grounds, for the Giants. (He was terribly wild, and Bobby Hofman, who caught him that day, told him, "Make sure you get a good college education, kid, 'cause you won't make it in the majors.")

The team that pursued him most assiduously was Pittsburgh, then run by Branch Rickey, and Sandy and his parents actually made a trip there to meet Mr. Rickey—who didn't make a good impression by neglecting to mention the bonus figure they were waiting to hear, a modest $10,000. The Braves were also interested, but finally Sandy's father, who was a lawyer, made a face-to-face agreement with Walter O'Malley, and the Dodgers got him.

Luck, coincidence, fate—these play a role in many signings. In 1966, a young Georgian named Jim Nash came up to Kansas City and posted a 12-1 won-lost record. "Best young pitcher I've seen in years," declared half a dozen rival managers.

Well, Nash had signed with the Kansas City organization four years before. He had been a high-school hotshot, and a dozen scouts came to see him pitch his last game. He was terrible, because, it turned out, he had pitched several innings only the day before. Only two scouts remained interested enough to find that out—one from Kansas City, one from the New York Mets. Nash told them both he wasn't interested in signing then, but in going on to college.

The next day, Nash says, his aging car expired. He had no summer job. The modest bonus being offered—around $1,000 —suddenly looked desirable. He decided he'd turn pro after all. (It is permissible, at this point, to have reservations about his whole-hearted devotion to higher learning.)

Naturally, the first scout he tried to contact was the one he knew best—Julian Morgan, of the Mets, who lived exactly two blocks away from Nash's home in the metropolis of Marietta, Georgia.

But Morgan wasn't home. He was off scouting players in the next town (since this was graduation week, the busiest portion of a scout's season in the nondraft, competitive days).

All evening, Nash tried to get Morgan. He couldn't. But he really wanted that money.

So he called the Kansas City scout, got him in (at whatever hotel it was), and signed with the A's.

The free-agent draft all but eliminated persuasiveness as a basic consideration, since the player could negotiate *only* with the team that drafted him, and made coincidence irrelevant. A scout's analytic powers (and prophetic powers) became much more important in the scheme of things.

A major-league club today has approximately 25 full-time scouts. They file reports on all players in their areas, and on all the minor-league players they see, every year.

A typical reporting system (as used by the New York Yankees, for example) rates every prospect by the highest baseball level he may ever reach in the opinion of the scout. A player is rated single-A, double-A, triple-A or major league *in potential*; then there is a final select category called "Yankee," presumably one step above major league. Until 1965, that was true enough.

Each player is reevaluated every year as he moves up through the system, and his ratings may change—but it is astonishing how often original opinions prove correct years later. In the course of, say, three years in the minors, a player is evaluated by half a dozen scouts (including his manager and various roving coaches). Each comment on each player runs to about half a page.

It is easy to be wrong, because living human beings, and very volatile ones at that, are the subject of these neat office procedures. Mistakes are made again and again. But very little is left to chance, and the amount of work done is prodigious.

It is safe to say that there is no baseball player in America, 18 years of age or older, who has played a dozen games with any organized team at any level, who has not been written up (or viewed and rejected) by some major-league organization.

Gradually, the bushes themselves are disappearing in an ever more urbanized society permeated with ever-improving transportation and communication. But whatever the bushes turn into, scouts will continue to beat them for talent—as long as professional baseball exists; if they stop, it won't exist.

Today the competition for talent is against other facets of life—college, well-paying jobs (minor-league pay is laughably inadequate and out of date), and other professional sports. The most gifted athletes of 1900, by and large, played mainly baseball as kids and stuck to it as they grew older, because it was the only game in which one could make a living. Today, the talented athlete of 15 or 16, not yet committed to any one game and exposed to all, may well choose football or basketball as a means of getting a college education, with the possibility of a well-paying pro career afterward.

At the same time, the players themselves are incomparably better educated about the game, exposed to fine points as children through television and Little League; much better coached at earlier stages; much more sophisticated, more sensitive, more arrogant, more independent, bigger and more powerful physically, less able and less willing to put up with hardship. All this makes scouting more important, and more difficult, than ever. The veneer of too-early experience can be misleading; character, under pampered conditions, may be harder to read.

But for every player on a pennant-winning team, there is some scout, somewhere, who saw something in him and decided, "sign him." It's an obscure, thankless job most of the time, but it is indispensable and no picture of Organized Baseball would be complete without the ubiquitous scout.

16

- Baseball is in its infancy.
  Charles H. Ebbets, 1913
- The very rich are different from you and me.
  F. Scott Fitzgerald, 1926

Who Owns Baseball?

Nowhere is myth more deeply entrenched than in the area of baseball ownership. The word associations of "sportsman" and "moneygrubber" represent the opposite ends of the scale by which our society measures the men whose money is invested in major-league teams. Neither term comes anywhere near the truth.

Baseball owners are capitalists, pure and simple, in an age when pure and simple capitalists are harder to find every day. Without exception, but in varying degrees, they are wealthy men, since only men who are already wealthy have the money to buy their way into this extremely exclusive company. But "wealth," of course, is a relative term: the millions commanded by a Phil Wrigley, who owns the Chicago Cubs, are incomparably greater than the hundreds of thousands a Walter O'Malley was able to control in acquiring the Brooklyn Dodgers. O'Malley was a successful lawyer with a shrewd eye for politics, finances, and promotional manipulation, and he qualifies as a "self-made man"—but the point is that he made himself first, outside of baseball, and then got into it.

They are also, in attitude, closer to the robber-baron image of the nineteenth-century industrial autocrat than any other surviving segment of the business community. They exercise absolute power within each 24th of their monopoly, and collectively maintain a policy of internal *laissez faire* and external imperialism. In their prime commodity—player talent—they held off any taint of trade unionism until 1969. In matters of government subsidy and supervision, they have remained unsullied, while taking full advantage—like all good nineteenth-century capitalists—of governmental protective and favor-granting powers.

Thus baseball owners, as a group, tend to be extremely conservative politically, and—perhaps with all sincerity, perhaps not—to equate their peculiar ways of doing business with the Foundations of the Republic. Mom, apple pie, and the unhindered operation of the baseball monopoly are obviously equally sacred to the American Way of Life. That tax laws should make possible baseball profits; that antitrust provisions of the law must have exemptions for baseball; that municipalities and counties should indirectly subsidize a ball club by paying for a new stadium and roads; and that any attempt to set up a rival organization in the same business must be ruthlessly stamped out—these are the ideas taken for granted by the baseball community, and they are quite in tune with a philosophy that sees the function of government as helping business and keeping its hands out of most other things. The principles of high tariff (restrictions of players' activity outside of Organized Baseball); colonialism (the farm systems); labor as a commodity (the reserve clause, trades, blacklists); *laissez faire* (free movement of franchises regardless of local conditions); a "public be damned" attitude whenever an owner's desires conflict with the public's; a certain amount of *noblesse oblige* charity (the pension plans); these principles are still the reality of baseball half a century after they had been modified or abandoned, or at least modernized, in most other activities.

Does this mean that baseball owners are ogres, to be shunned by liberal-minded contemporaries? Or to be looked upon as heroes by the new wave of conservatives? Not at all. It simply means that they should be seen for what they are: prosperous businessmen, each with his own character and mind, but sharing with all the others the common desire to make money and get personal attention.

All owners are in baseball to make money. It doesn't necessarily follow that the money they hope to make will come directly from the operation of the baseball club; the indirect benefits of baseball fame to other business were mentioned in Chapter 10. The means of financial advantage—taxes, other business, publicity—may vary, but the goal is always the same: profit.

All owners want public notice, or at least the notice of some prominent local group important to them. If the owner wanted *merely* profit, he could make more in surer ways by other investments. It is the combination of profit *and* a certain kind of fame that brings an already successful man into baseball.

Most owners—but definitely not all—are sincere baseball fans, with a deep rooting interest in their club, and perhaps in baseball generally. What must always be remembered is that this emotional attachment, while real, always comes *second* to economic necessity. Owners will put up with financial loss in order to remain in action; they will rarely *choose* financial loss for sentimental or "sporting" reasons. The sad fact is that, with rare exceptions, when a clear-cut choice arises between more victories and more profit, the path toward more profit is chosen. (Fortunately, this wrenching emotional experience isn't confronted too often, since as a rule victory on the field promotes profit; but there are situations when that isn't true—such as in a stubborn holdout by a star—and in such situations, the resolution is almost always in the direction of profit.)

No one but an owner has any real power in baseball on any guts issue—not the Commissioner, not the league presidents, not the general managers, not the public interest, and not the press (which can manipulate public response). Much flimflam surrounds the exercise of authority by all these other people, but it is illusory: it is true that 99 percent of the time the owners don't bother to interfere with routine matters. But when anything really fundamental is involved—expansion, or television money, or rules of operation, or pensions, or player relations—the owners and *only* the owners decide. The Commissioner, theoretically, is at the top of the baseball structure, but in reality he is the *employee* of the owners, and anytime one loses sight of that fact, one loses his ability to comprehend clearly what is happening in baseball.

Some owners, sometimes, feel civic and public responsibility and act accordingly. Only some.

All owners are surrounded by employees, assistants, and advisers whose prime interest it is to keep the owner convinced that he has an excellent staff. It is the staff that handles the day-to-day details.

Most owners have little understanding of the nature of baseball, the feelings of its participants and spectators, or the true dimensions of baseball problems—because they did not spend their early or even youthful years around baseball, and because they can give it only a small portion of their time and attention now. Their assistants, at the general manager level, do have the necessary knowledge, contact, and understanding of the ground roots, but often fail to make the right points to their employers because of the difficulty in making an unprepared boss—even a bright boss—grasp the subtler issues.

One consequence is that the owner who is a full-time baseball man, and who is exceptionally smart—like Walter O'Malley—can wield an influence far out of proportion. It isn't that Walter is necessarily smarter than *any* other owner, but that those owners who are as smart spend most of their time and thought on other enterprises. Walter's fertile brain concentrates on baseball, and on his own position in it—and he can often swing baseball as a whole to a position he feels is right. This may or may not be good for baseball, but it's usually good for O'Malley.

Another set of factors magnifies the gap between most owners' conception of the baseball world and the real thing. Since they are already capable, successful men in their own fields, with plenty of money, they tend to refuse to accept the idea that they *don't* understand. Like most successful people, they come to believe that methods they *know* have proved successful in the past can be used in a new situation. (We saw a similar problem in changing a hitter's style.)

The successful industrialist, or the heir to a fortune, is usually confident of his own judgment: he has the money to prove it, and he is accustomed to having his orders followed unquestioningly. Whatever else Fitzgerald might have had in mind in the opening words of his story "The Rich Boy," he was dealing with one pertinent facet of this chapter: the habitually rich live in a different environment than the ordinary man, and therefore develop different responses—but while this difference can be more or less sidestepped in other pursuits, in baseball the very rich man (the owner) is dealing directly with the emotional reactions of the definitely not-rich (the fans), and it's not surprising that an empathy gap results.

And this is further complicated by the probable character of a man who chooses to buy a baseball club. He is money-oriented, if he is self-made, because that's what it takes to be self-made; he then tends to measure success and failure in money terms. He is not of deeply intellectual bent, since he has chosen being a baseball owner over collecting art or endowing symphony orchestras. He is outgoing to some degree, at least within his peer group, or he wouldn't have chosen so public a position.

Such men, with such interests, are likely to make mistakes precisely when it counts: in those few, but important, situations in which the subtle peculiarities of baseball life require a different solution than apparently similar circumstances in other fields call for. Such men find it hard to accept that they *don't* know, and hard to listen to those who do.

At the end of the 1966 season, the men who acted as principal owners of the 20 major-league teams could be classified in this way:

Three relied on baseball for their primary source of income: Walter O'Malley (Dodgers), Horace Stoneham (Giants), and Cal Griffith (Twins).

Two were essentially career baseball executives who had reached the status of part-owners: Gabe Paul (Indians) and Bill DeWitt (Reds).

One had become a full-time baseball operator, but was really as much involved in promoting the building (the Astrodome) as the ball club, and was not necessarily finished with politics: Judge Hofheinz of Houston.

Three were immensely wealthy individuals who considered baseball simply a sideline: Tom Yawkey (Red Sox), Phil Wrigley (Cubs), and Mrs. Joan Payson (Mets).

The other 11 clubs were owned by syndicates, or were divisions of larger corporations, or were operated by men who had many larger business interests that took up more of their time.

Of the 20, less than half could be found inside a ball park with any degree of regularity.

Six years later, the lineup was only a little different, and both the changes and the stabilities were instructive.

O'Malley (with most functions turned over to his son Peter), Stoneham, and Griffith were still at it.

So were Yawkey, Wrigley, and Mrs. Payson.

Hofheinz, his activities curtailed by illness, was less visible but still boss of the Astros, who were now part of a complex that included a circus, a hotel, and an amusement park.

Paul had moved from the Indians to the Yankees, who were purchased from C.B.S. by a 15-man syndicate headed by George

Steinbrenner, a Clevelander of many interests whose prime business was shipbuilding.

The Cleveland club, in turn, had been purchased by a syndicate put together by Nick Mileti, a Cleveland lawyer who had also acquired basketball and hockey franchises there and had started to build an indoor arena in the suburbs.

Charley Finley, who had moved his Athletics from Kansas City to Oakland, had branched out into hockey and basketball as well, but still had his insurance business as a basic resource.

Bob Short, a man of only marginal affluence who had once moved the Minneapolis Lakers basketball team to Los Angeles and had sold it there for $5,000,000, purchased the Washington Senators in 1968 for nine million borrowed dollars. By 1972, he had moved them to Texas, and high interest rates were hurting his hotel and trucking operations as well as his baseball.

DeWitt was out of baseball, having sold the Reds to a syndicate of prominent Cincinnati people who also invested in the Cincinnati football team. Heading the group was Francis Dale, a lawyer and newspaper publisher.

The other eight were in the hands of the same syndicates or parent corporations as they had been: St. Louis (Anheuser-Busch), Chicago White Sox (Artnell), Detroit and the California Angels (radio-television networks), Philadelphia (Bob Carpenter of the DuPont family), Atlanta (the combine of Chicago financiers that had moved the team out of Milwaukee), Pittsburgh (John Galbreath and his son Dan, of worldwide construction activities, and other partners), and Baltimore (National Brewing Co.).

There were, of course, four new teams, too, as of 1969. Montreal was in the hands of the Bronfman family whose best known holdings were the Seagram distilleries. A new Kansas City franchise was set up by Ewing Kauffman, a self-made pharmeceuticals magnate. The San Diego franchise was owned by C. Arnholt Smith, a high-powered investment banker and close advisor to President Nixon. And the American League Milwaukee team, brought there after it failed in its first expansion year in Seattle, was owned by a local syndicate in which the Uehlein family (brewers) was most prominent.

Moneygrubbers? Not really. Sportsmen? Hardly. Perhaps the only suitable description is the most direct one: owners. They own.

And they don't like you to forget it.

17

· That man is killing the sport.

Gene Autrey, 1971

· We're not going to give them another God damn cent.

Gussie Busch, 1972

The Other Kind of Strike

Owners own. But players play. And today, at long last, there is some muscle on the player's side of the bargaining table. The players have a union, and the owners, who were able to operate in 1960 the way Andrew Carnegie and his friends could operate in 1890, have been dragged—kicking, screaming, and inflicting wounds on themselves—into the twentieth century.

The union is called the Major League Baseball Players Association. It was a long time coming.

Baseball—like all other professional team sports, which imitated baseball—has based its business on something called the reserve clause. It's a complicated system of interlocking rules, agreements, and contract provisions with a very simple effect: every player "belongs" to some club at any given time, and he can not agree to play for any club except the one that "owns" him (that is, owns his contract) at the moment. And no club may offer him employment while he belongs to another.

Now, anyone who signs a personal service contract to do anything is usually obliged to work exclusively for that employer—for the length of the contract. Where baseball differs is that the man continues to be "owned" between contracts. Once he signs the first one, a series of automatic self-renewals keep him under obligation forever, or until the club decides, unilaterally, to "release" him. It's the agreement among all clubs not to hire him that makes this work.

No one denies that this system is different from all other employee-employer relationships in our society, and that it flies in the face of the "free market" concept, which holds that any man is entitled to sell his services to the highest bidder. But those who run baseball (and those who agree with them, which seems to be most fans and writers), contend that this system is justified, necessary, essentially fair, and historically established as "the only way" to conduct orderly competition with well-balanced teams. And those who are against it (mostly players, lawyers, and a few writers) don't argue that it would be possible to have no rules at all. They do say that the system is far too one-sided in favor of management, and that all the restrictions evolved in the name of "even competition" have actually been designed to maximize profit and minimize salaries, even when the actual dollars in salaries appear high. They advocate a loosening, rather than a flat abolition, of the reserve system.

In broad outline, those two positions have been unchanged for nearly a century.

The controversy began as far back as 1879, when the National League was only three years old. All of major-league baseball consisted of six teams, while dozens of other teams had some players every bit as good as the major leaguers. The better players were being hired away right and left by more eager club managements, and the league members, who were the only ones sufficiently organized to take a common action, agreed to the following plan: each club would place five players —presumably the best five—on a "reserve list"; each club then promised not to try to hire anyone who was on another club's reserve list.

At first, it was something of a distinction to be "placed on reserve," since it meant you were one of the more desired players and guaranteed work for next year. But it took only a few years for the obvious trend to assert itself: from a list of five, it went to seven and nine and 11 and, finally, the entire roster; and as the National League grew, and another major league (the American Association) sprang up, independent teams were pushed into the background.

By 1887, the reserve system was so completely in control of player hiring that maximum (maximum, not minimum) salaries could be imposed. The players rebelled to the point of forming a union (remember, this was the 1880s—when unionism implied wild-eyed radicalism). The union and the club owners did not get along, and after the 1889 season, most of the major league players rebelled and formed their own league, the Players' League, which operated in 1890 in direct competition with the two existing leagues. Not surprisingly, such a frontal assault broke everybody, and the Brotherhood of Professional Baseball Players passed into history. The National League emerged as a 12-team monopoly in 1892.

Less than 10 years later, however, a new major league appeared, the present American, and once again competition for the services of the best players undermined the reserve system. So the two leagues quickly reached agreement about observing each other's reserve lists, and the modern structure of baseball was born in 1902.

There was another flurry in the next decade, when a third major league (called the Federal League) went through the same process. This time it was bought out and absorbed, rather than added to the existing structure. And finally, in 1946, right after World War II, a scheme to promote a Mexican League involved many American players, who were blacklisted when they tried to return.

That last bit of retaliation against the Mexican "jumpers," combined with the fact that almost all young Americans had just had experience with the armed forces and their emphasis on a pension as a reward for years of service, laid the foundation for the present Players Association.

The Mexican League incident made clear to many players, especially the less affluent ones, that they needed some sort of joint protection from arbitrary behavior by their contract-holders; and the pension issue was something everyone could identify with and rally around.

The Association's first goal, therefore, and its main activity for many years, was the establishment and development of a pension plan. It also procured a minimum major league salary ($5,000), systematic rules about meal money on the road and during spring training, and a few other housekeeping items. It got valuable outside professional help, first from lawyers named Robert Murphy and Norman Lewis and later from a Milwaukee Judge, Robert Cannon; but its stance, essentially, was one of collectively asking the owners for items that were granted or refused, rather than demanding any real negotiations.

No real change occurred until the middle 1960s. By that time, prosperity was rampant in all sports, most noticeably in football, and television's existence had accustomed everyone to the tremendous sums that could be generated by big sports events. The baseball scene, in particular, had changed through expansion and the construction of many new ball parks—both steps proving, even to the least aware player, that there was an awful lot of money in the pot. The players started to feel they weren't getting their appropriate share of the pie, and decided to hire a full-time negotiator.

His name was Marvin Miller, and he was an exceptional man. An economist by profession, he had worked for many years for the United Steelworkers Union. He had a sharp and painstaking mind, and experience, as well as factual knowledge, to bring to labor relations. Never—but never—had the club owners been up against anyone like this for collective bargaining. They knew such people in their other businesses, but in baseball? Ridiculous. Revolutionary. Radical. Red bolshevism. Rats.

They fought every step of the procedure, but in the 1960s it was a little late to stem the tide of labor organization that had reached all other parts of the society a generation before. The opposition of the owners—to the choice of Miller, to plans for financing his office, to the various items Miller brought up— had the predictable effect of solidifying the players. Miller's main task, from the beginning, was to educate his own Association members; the owners, by often ludicrous intransigence on trivial matters (before finally giving in on bigger issues), provided him with endless object lessons.

So the labor crisis became a standard feature of major-league life. No one enjoys it (not even Miller and Dick Moss, his legal counsel, since they would prefer less wearing negotiations), but it is here to stay.

Through this system, the players now have a comprehensive collective agreement that spells out their minimum salaries (now $16,500), severance pay (which didn't exist at all in the past), expenses, moving expenses when traded, permissible scheduling (like a ban on night games before day games involving a move between cities), and a host of other items. Most important of all, it provides for grievance procedures that lead to outside arbitration, even in a salary dispute, rather than to unappealable determination by the Commissioner of Baseball, who is chosen by, fired by, and paid by the owners exclusively.

This "general agreement" does not encompass the pension and benefit plan (medical insurance, death benefits, as well as pensions). That's a separate contract, separately negotiated, in which the owners and the Association are joint trustees of the Pension Fund.

Headlines—much to the annoyance of most baseball fans— have centered on the negotiating strife and the figures arrived at in settlements. But the most important day-in, day-out function of the Association is handling disputes, situations in which a player used to be entirely at the mercy of the views of the club owner or commissioner. These men might be, in any particular case, perfectly fair and even generous, but they might not. In any case, to the young men of the 1970s, it seemed entirely unnecessary and unacceptable to be in a position of being patronized, benevolently or not.

One landmark grievance involved Alex Johnson of the California Angels in 1971. Johnson, American League batting champion in 1970, had a history of conflict with various managements, having played for St. Louis, Philadelphia, and Cincinnati before coming to the Angels. The usual charges were failure to hustle, and he was fined from time to time by various managers. Midway through the 1971 season, after a series of similar incidents, he was suspended without pay for the remainder of the year.

The grievance concerned the propriety of the suspension, which amounted to a fine equal to half his year's salary (which was about $50,000). Johnson claimed that, for various reasons, he was emotionally upset and not capable of playing—and the argument advanced on his behalf was that he should have been placed on the disabled list, and therefore paid. This principle—that an emotional illness (Johnson was getting psychiatric treatment, and his doctor testified) could be viewed as an "incapacity" just as much as a broken leg—was upheld by an outside arbitrator.

Gene Autrey, the Angel owner, blamed Miller for Moss's success in presenting a persuasive case. "That man," he said, meaning Miller, "is killing the sport, and you can quote me on that."

There is no doubt that Miller has killed, once and for all, the "sport" of owners handling any problem any way they felt like it.

With Miller and Moss devoting their minds full time to advocating the players' side of all sorts of problems, the owners hired a full-time counterpart to do their negotiating. He was John Gaherin, who had held similar positions on behalf of railroad and newspaper managements.

So negotiations, in theory, work this way: Miller and Gaherin, as professionals, can present proposals and thrash out details. Miller's decisions must be ratified by his board of player representatives—active players chosen by their teammates, one representative and one alternate from each of the 24 teams— and, on the most serious issues, by a vote of the entire membership (about 900 players). Gaherin reports to a special negotiating committee set up by the owners, consisting of a couple of owners from each league and the two league presidents. Ultimately, the decisions of this committee must be acted on by all 24 club owners, voting within their leagues.

That's theory. Practice is different, because of practical and psychological realities. The player representatives can meet rarely, they change frequently (as players get traded and retire), they include virtually no one experienced in business or bargaining, and they follow Miller's advice. Gaherin, on the other hand, has 24 independent thinkers as bosses, each thoroughly experienced in business, each with his own large staff and his own established pattern of doing things. Gaherin's advice, inevitably, carries far less weight in the decision-making process on his side, however wise or perceptive it may be. Miller is, beyond question, the leader of his side; Gaherin, to his personal discomfort, is seldom more than a messenger.

So the owners, who hold almost all the economic and public-relations power, tend to dissipate their strength because of lack of unity and cohesive leadership; the players, who still have very little actual bargaining strength, make it go a long way because Miller provides highly co-ordinated thinking.

It was exactly this contrast that appeared in the first real strike baseball had, one which delayed the start of the 1972 season by almost two weeks.

The issue was a new pension plan contract, but hovering

over it was a general agreement that would have to be negotiated the following year. The Curt Flood lawsuit, attacking the reserve clause on antitrust grounds, was already in the hands of the Supreme Court that spring; and the owners were using as a defense the fact that they were "prepared" to bargain on reserve clause modifications, so that the whole thing should be a matter of labor negotiation and not law. The owners felt, therefore, that it was time to take a "strong" stand on the pension contract, to "draw the line somewhere." And the players realized that the 1972 test of strength, whatever the specific issues, would be reflected in the more far-reaching questions that would have to be fought over in 1973.

But the actual strike was a fiasco, on several levels. The players wanted a ludicrously modest improvement in pension rates—to cover, they said, rises in the general cost of living. They wanted $1,000,000 added to the fund each year, which amounted to about $40,000 per club—but even this should be "painless," they argued, since the essential source was World Series TV money, which was going up.

But the owners felt, with equal sincerity, that no increase in an already impressive pension plan was justified.

"Not another God damn cent. If they want to strike—let 'em," declared Gussie Busch, owner of the St. Louis Cardinals, after a meeting in which the owners voted unanimously to stick by their no-increase offer.

Just as spring training was ending, the players voted to strike. They had authorized the action by a vote of 663-10; the player reps voted 47-0.

But wait—by this time, Miller had discovered that the pension fund itself had been accumulating a surplus, and that the addition the players were seeking could come entirely from this surplus. So in announcing that they would strike, the players simultaneously offered to capitulate: they would accept the "not a cent" position of the owners, in the sense of demanding no new payments to the fund, and would accept any portion of the surplus an outside arbitrator would give them—without waiting for the arbitration to take place.

Here was something that would cost the owners zero in out-of-pocket dollars (the fund surplus could never be used for anything but pensions, anyhow), and a fine way to save face.

The owners didn't take the opportunity. The hard-liners won out. The strike began.

It was obviously a suicidal course for the players. They were scattered all over the country in spring training camps (in Florida, Arizona, and California); most of them had received no salary since the previous October (since players usually get paid only during the regular season), and many had already taken advances against their 1972 salaries. Most were insecure about their jobs anyhow, since these are determined by management's favorable opinion. And many had only a hazy idea of what was involved. Obviously, they would never stick together, and as soon as some players, or some whole clubs, got back to work, the strike would be broken. And the owners would show them, once and for all.

But, amazingly, it was the owners who couldn't stick together. For five days, before the first regularly scheduled games, they avoided having a full meeting. When they did, some of the owners learned the details of the surplus for the first time. Those whose clubs were in weaker financial situations wanted to settle immediately and open their gates; older, stronger clubs were adamant that the players "must be taught a lesson."

Five days after that, the internal stresses proved too strong for the owners. The players, remarkably, were sticking together; the owners, with no unified policy (like the one which Miller was presenting to his members), decided to offer what they could have offered in the first place: $500,000 out of the fund. Miller accepted within minutes.

But the "teach them a lesson" faction wouldn't give in. The players, individually, had to be made to "feel the pinch." So for five more days—days of mounting public alienation from the product they were selling—the owners kept baseball closed down while they argued about how the unplayed games would be made up. Here, again, Miller had a direct, coherent, simple position: either don't play the games at all, or pay us our regular pro-rated salaries for whatever games are made up. The owners kept insisting that the players should make up the games without being paid. Again, the players stuck to their guns. The season finally began with the unplayed games forgotten.

It was unnecessary bloodletting—but perhaps it did avert a longer, tougher conflict in 1973. The reserve clause question was not settled or even seriously modified in that negotiation, but an important breach was made in the agreement to send salary disputes to an outside arbitrator. The first time the arbitration procedure was tried, in February, 1974, more than 30 cases were presented to the arbitrators, an historic reduction of owner autonomy in salary matters.

Of all the aspects of baseball, this area of labor negotiation is without any question the most unattractive to the fan, and to many of the people who work in baseball. But its unattractiveness can't blot out its importance: nothing that happens in baseball today has as far-reaching effects on the entire game as the struggle, now more equal than it has ever been in the past, over who keeps what share of the income generated.

Perhaps the best position for the onlooker to take is this: players are no less selfish, nor more noble, than owners; owners, as individuals, are no less short-sighted, nor more self-centered, than players. But when it comes to arranging things to someone's advantage, the owners still have most of the power to do it their way—most, but less than they did.

And they will have still less as time goes on.

18

The Legal Status of Practically Everything

Slogans change. They used to say, "You can't tell the players without a scorecard." Now you can't tell the players without a lawyer. You can't tell them anything. You can't tell a club owner, general manager, league president, or many other people without a lawyer, either.

Lawyers are the newest members of the sports scene in America, and baseball has its share—at least.

The reasons for their omnipresence are clear enough: television, lawsuits, municipally financed stadiums, labor negotiations, higher earnings with complicated payouts, taxes—all requiring legal advice.

There were always lawyers involved in baseball, to a modest degree. Every club, like every business, has counsel on retainer. So does each league. So does the commissioner's office. And many players—like most people—have some more or less regular relationship with a personal attorney. But, until the last 10 years or so, they were pretty much in the background. Whatever they did, and whatever influence they exerted, didn't get much publicity.

Now it does.

And there has been a far more serious consequence of lawyer

prominence than mere annoyance on the part of the public, which turns to baseball for excitement and entertainment, not logic-chopping. The consequence is this: lawyer-presence has led to a dominance of lawyer-thinking in baseball's highest councils—and lawyer-thinking is far removed from promotional mentality.

Lawyers, by training and inclination, are careful, painstaking, and letter-of-the-law in their orientation. They examine every situation for its possible legal consequences and loopholes before making a decision, and are accustomed to moving slowly after extensive preparation. Above all, they value confidentiality.

Obviously, not every single lawyer everywhere is like this; and, just as obviously, this is a sensible and responsible way for any lawyer to proceed—in the practice of law. But for running commercial sports entertainment, making publicity, and selling tickets, it's the wrong approach. Lifelong training in seeking precedents and anticipating all possible opposing arguments does not stimulate originality or inspiration. Being legally correct is not the same as being a terrific salesman. Understanding the fine print is not the same as sensing the pulse of a volatile public.

What has happened, then, is a shift in power. Because legal aspects of nearly everything became so important in the baseball world after World War II, lawyers inevitably took a larger and larger share in the decision-making process. From a situation in which the lawyer was asked what an action's legal ramifications might be, we have moved to a point where the action (or decision) itself is determined by legal minds.

Certainly this process has not been limited to baseball, as any sports fan (or anyone who followed the Watergate hearings) knows. This is an age in which lawyers are more and more prominent in every field. But the effect on baseball has been striking.

The first Commissioner of Baseball, selected in 1920, was a

federal judge named Kenesaw Mountain Landis. The overwhelming problem at the time was restoring public confidence in the honesty of baseball games, in the wake of the Black Sox scandal. But no one who has studied the career of Judge Landis would mark him as an exceptional "legal mind": quite the opposite, he was a forceful, free-wheeling personality who placed his own concepts of "justice" above any written laws. And, as a matter of policy, his basic approach to ruling baseball was to keep it out of the courts at all costs, because he was a good enough legal mind to appreciate its antitrust vulnerability.

The second commissioner, after the death of Landis, was a professional politician: Senator Albert B. (Happy) Chandler of Kentucky. Chandler did not succeed in keeping baseball out of the courts, and that was a principal reason for his dismissal after a costly (by the standards of that day) settlement of an antitrust suit brought by Danny Gardella.

Chandler was succeeded by Ford Frick, whose regime lasted 14 years. Frick had been, orginally, a highly successful sportswriter and radio commentator. He became publicity man for the National League, then the league's president, and finally commissioner. He was often criticized and ridiculed by the outside world, but he was a "baseball man" through and through.

During Frick's term, an endless series of Congressional hearings on baseball's antitrust exemption began, and a major role of the commissioner became lobbying in Washington. Another new role for the commissioner was the extensive negotiation of combined television packages, not just for the World Series but for game-of-the-week programs.

When Frick retired, after a long and ludicrous search, the owners found General William D. Eckert, as non-baseball a man as one could imagine. Gen. Eckert was a retired air force general whose specialty had been negotiating defense contracts. He wasn't a lawyer; he was a military man. But his examination of fine print was lawyer-like in its effects, and his awareness of baseball reality was nil.

So the owners fired Eckert, and had a beautiful public row, as they were unable to agree on a successor from within baseball's ranks. They finally decided, in February, 1969, out of sheer desperation, to make one of their lawyers an "interim" commissioner, in the hope that he would help them find a permanent one. His name was Bowie K. Kuhn, and he had been taking a gradually larger role in baseball affairs as a member of the Wall Street firm representing the National League. He had also become, in the previous couple of years (before the advent of John Gaherin), the chief negotiator opposite Marvin Miller.

It took only a few months for the "interim" commissioner to emerge with a seven-year contract at $150,000 a year, or more than double what Eckert was getting.

Under Kuhn, the commissioner's staff has tripled in size, while his internal baseball power has shrunk under determined attack by Miller.

When Frick was commissioner, his No. 2 man was Charles Segar, also a former sportswriter. Eckert's No. 2 man was first Lee MacPhail and later John McHale, both lifelong baseball men who came up through the ranks to general managerships of ball clubs. Sandy Hadden, who had been the American League attorney while Kuhn was representing the National, became Kuhn's No. 2 man.

At league meetings, nowadays, lawyers for each club are usually present. The negotiations between players and owners on collective contracts (the general agreement and the pension plan) are conducted primarily by lawyers on the owners' side. As of 1973, no individual club owner had ever attended a negotiating session.

As for the players, the more successful ones have turned more and more to being represented by a lawyer, rather than an old-fashioned "agent" or "personal manager." An agent "sells" his client after bargaining; but since the most important factors these days are tax breaks, deferred compensation, and loopholes in the reserve rules, an agent would have to go to a lawyer anyhow. So most players get a lawyer in the first place. And that makes the legal thicket thicker.

Hanging over all these generalities is the special position of baseball with respect to the antitrust laws, from which it is exempt. The true position is not easy to understand, and many baseball people have failed to understand it. That's one reason lawyers have moved into a sort of vacuum. But it's worth trying to grasp it, because it's the determining feature of the whole baseball business.

When the reserve system was invented, in the 1870s, there were no federal antitrust laws. These date from the 1890s.

Under the antitrust laws, certain business activities are clearly illegal. "Combinations in restraint of trade" certainly include agreements among employers not to hire one another's employees if an employee wants to move; they certainly forbid joint action for selling all television rights; they make very questionable the cutting up and parcelling out of exclusive market areas through franchises. And in addition to the federal antitrust laws, there are many separate state antitrust laws.

In 1915, when the Federal League ended its challenge to the older National and American Leagues, some of the club owners in the Federal League were promised that they could buy into established clubs. A dispute arose about the honoring of this promise, and the owners of the Baltimore Federal League club, who had been denied the purchase of the St. Louis Cardinals, sued the National League on antitrust grounds.

It was 1922 before the case was decided by the Supreme Court. In an 8-0 decision written by Justice Oliver Wendell Holmes, the court in effect refused to decide the issue. It simply said that the antitrust laws weren't intended to apply to a business like baseball.

It's important to keep clear what the court did not say, as well as what it did. It did not say, "Baseball is a sport, not a business." And it did not consciously make a distinction between baseball and other big-business sports, because at the time there were no other big-business team sports: professional football, hockey, and basketball simply didn't exist on any large scale.

What it did say was that "the giving of baseball exhibitions" was not really interstate commerce (which is all that the federal government can regulate), because even though players were transported across state lines, it was incidental to the local event when staged; and that playing baseball games was not the kind of manufacturing or trade or "commerce" intended to be covered by the antitrust laws.

It didn't matter, therefore, whether the specific action violated the antitrust laws or not, and the Court didn't even consider the merits of the case. The laws simply didn't apply.

The legal philosophy behind this view of the baseball business was considered strange even then; but by the 1930s, in countless other decisions, it was abandoned. No one doubted that things "like" baseball—other sports, movies, all kinds of entertainment—were "commerce" in the sense that the laws did cover. And once radio and television entered the picture, there was also no question that interstate commerce was clearly involved.

That's why Landis was so careful to keep baseball out of the courts. It was widely assumed that if the Supreme Court ever got another crack at the subject, it would reverse the 1922 ruling and leave the whole baseball structure—especially the reserve system—open to attack.

But this assumption proved false in an unexpected way.

In 1952, the Supreme Court did rule again (in a case directly concerned with the reserve clause, involving a Yankee farm chain pitcher named Toolson). And it said, in effect: "For 30 years, baseball has been allowed to develop its policies with the specific assurance that it was exempt from the antitrust laws. Many people have invested money in it on that basis. To overturn that ruling now would lead to damage suits and chaos for people who have been acting in good faith. Without considering the merits of the reserve system, we feel that the court should not be the one to upset the existing system. We think it's up to the Congress—which has the capability of examining through hearings what the right relationships should be—to pass a law saying that baseball should or should not be subject to the antitrust laws. But for now, the exemption stands."

That decision, by 7-2, started all the Congressional hearings, the first and most famous of which was conducted by Representative Emmanuel Celler of New York, chairman of the House Judiciary Committee.

Meanwhile, throughout the 1950s, in a series of other decisions, the Supreme Court ruled against antitrust exemption for football, boxing, movie theaters, and so on. Each time it noted that baseball was an exception only for historical reasons; each time it noted the contradiction and said it was up to Congress to resolve it. And each time no new law was passed.

By the middle 1960s, the special exemption granted baseball, and only baseball, was considered a joke by most outsiders. Baseball lawyers, of course, argued that the exception was justified because baseball was "different": it had to support farm systems while other sports got stars ready made out of college. And it certainly believed other sports were entitled to the same exemption; but it didn't want its own exemption revoked.

In 1969, Curt Flood was traded by St. Louis to Philadelphia, and he decided to sue, to try to get the reserve clause issue to the Supreme Court once more. As a $90,000-a-year, 31-year-old veteran of 12 major-league seasons, he was not the sort of player Miller and the Players Association would have chosen for a test case, which they did want sooner or later. But since Flood was determined to go ahead, they supported him and took over his case, on the theory that they couldn't afford to have him lose an under-supported test.

The early stages, while colorful, were predetermined: no lower court had jurisdiction. No one could reverse the Supreme Court decision but the Supreme Court itself.

And in June, 1972—after the player strike had run its course, incidentally—the Supreme Court let the exemption stand by a

5-3 vote. Again, it refused to consider the merits of the case. Again, it gave as its sole reason the existence of previous decisions that it was unwilling to "correct." Again, it recognized that it was "illogical" to make only baseball exempt. And again, it called upon Congress to resolve the situation with new legislation.

One thing that was hard for the layman to grasp was why it was up to Congress, which never offered any exemptions in the first place, to untangle a mess made entirely by the Supreme Court. But that's why lawyers have moved into ascendancy: because laymen find so much that is hard to understand.

Aside from the antitrust question and all its fallout, there is another area in which the lawyers are needed: taxes.

Baseball financing is based—entirely legitimately—on tax advantages to wealthy individuals or corporations. The possibility of writing off player contracts as depreciation, the possibility of capital gains, the possibility of charging the losses in one sphere against the profits in another and thus avoiding tax liability—these are things that Charley Ebbets would have had a hard time handling on his own. It takes lawyers to get the details correctly. But getting the details right often means deciding what to do in a certain fashion long before the first step is taken, so the lawyers enter the decision process much sooner than they used to.

It was the mythical twentieth-century philosopher Jake Popper (also known as the Sage of 114th Street) who summed up the quintessential cry of twentieth-century man: "Get me a law-yeh!!!" he is supposed to have howled, from the heart, on general principles. He was ahead of his time, early in World War II, but in this way too the totality of life has reached out to encompass even baseball.

Only one group remains on the daily baseball scene without effective, constant—and expensive—legal representation: we writers.

SECTION

3

*Personalities
and Propositions*

19

The Great Debate: Mays or Mantle?

New York City has always enjoyed a lion's share of baseball history and glamor. The first real baseball club, of course, was the Knickerbocker Club of New York, which played the first recognized game in 1846. The dominant personalities of the two major leagues—John McGraw in the National and Babe Ruth in the American—operated in New York in their years of greatest achievement. There were 61 World Series between 1903 and 1964, and at least one New York team (including Brooklyn) took part in 37 of them; 13 times the championship of baseball was decided in a "subway series," involving two New York teams.

The Golden Years ended, actually, in 1958, when the Dodgers and Giants set up shop in California, leaving the Yankees in lonely splendor. When the Mets came along four years later, they filled a great vacuum, but they didn't really replace the established rivalries the Giants and Dodgers had represented. The Yankees never did cash in on their position of monopoly while they were alone, and Met success at the gate was based on the return visits paid by the Dodgers and Giants. This may have surprised a lot of casual observers and doctrinaire economists, but the explanation was simple: baseball fans live off argument, comparison, discussion, and opinion; with three teams in one city (two of them in the same league), there was an endless supply of material for barroom conversation, and a wide choice of loyalties; with only the champion Yankees around, what was there to argue about?

In many respects, therefore, the most Golden Year of all was 1951. That year, for the only time in baseball history, all three teams finished first. The Yankees won the American League pennant, fighting off Cleveland in a tight battle through September; and the Giants, trailing the Dodgers by 13½ games in mid-August, caught them on the next-to-last day and finished in a tie for first. Then the Giants won the three-game play-off, on Bobby Thomson's three-run homer in the last of the ninth of the third game. And finally, the Yankees defeated the Giants in an eventful World Series, four games to two.

Among other things, Allie Reynolds pitched two no-hitters for the Yankees, and Joe DiMaggio played his final season; Gil McDougald hit a grand slam in the World Series; and the city had six 20-game winners—Vic Raschi and Eddie Lopat of the Yankees, Preacher Roe and Don Newcombe of the Dodgers, Sal Maglie and Larry Jansen of the Giants. The three managers —Casey Stengel of the Yankees, Leo Durocher of the Giants, and Charlie Dressen of the Dodgers—were three of the most talkative, colorful, controversial, and knowledgeable figures in the history of the game. It is small wonder, in a year like that, that 4,634,251 tickets were sold for games at Yankee Stadium, Ebbets Field, and the Polo Grounds.

An yet, the most lasting effect of 1951 was none of those things. It was the arrival of two rookies, instantly recognized by the fans as superstars: Mickey Mantle and Willie Mays.

It is amazing how accurate the instincts of the dedicated fan can be. The bleacherites were far ahead of the experts in accepting Mantle and Mays as larger than life-size. The registered experts, well informed by baseball men who had seen Mickey and Willie in action, nevertheless clung to small hesitancies, reservations, doubts, and supercilious calm; they had to, after all, maintain their self-image as objective critics, even if they were willing to forgo their public pose as hard-to-impress New Yorkers.

But the fans made no such mistake, and indulged in no such delayed response. Their imaginations were inflamed as soon as they saw them—Willie, his cap flying off, catching the ball in that ridiculous fashion with his hands at his belt; blond Mickey, with blinding speed in his legs, swinging the bat from either side of the plate. The fan had no more trouble identifying baseball godhead when he saw it than an ancient Athenian would have had identifying a huge, bearded man with a bolt of lightning in his hand as Zeus; only an expert could miss it. (However, in fairness to the experts, it must be noted that most of them quickly switched status and began to react as fans.)

And so, the Great Debate began.

Who do you like better, Mantle or Mays? Which one is greater? Which one will be greater?

In bars, on street corners, in school hallways, in living rooms, in country clubs, in restaurants, at work, during lunch, over cocktails, in the subways and buses, and most of all around the ball parks, the discussion flourished.

Mantle could hit the ball farther than anyone, and do it lefty or righty—and still run faster than anyone. How could anyone top that? But Mays moved even better on the ball field, and made a new incredible catch every day—and also hit homers while maintaining a high average.

Fifteen years later, the argument had been settled in one sense, but was more fascinating than ever in another. By 1966, Mantle had been crippled so often by a succession of injuries that his ability to play at all was in question, while Mays was accomplishing things in his mid-30's that he had not done in his late 20's. From the standpoint of continuous, cumulative, and still fully effective achievement, Mays had come out ahead; but admiration for Mantle is stimulated by contemplation of what he might have done if granted the normal amount of freedom from injury.

Their careers followed quite different rhythms.

Mantle's buildup came first. Before the 1951 season, the Yankees conducted a "rookie school," an innovation at the

time. That year, incidentally, the Yankees and Giants had arranged to "trade" training camps, and the Yankees were based
in Phoenix, Arizona, while the Giants trained at the traditional
Yankee site in St. Petersburg, Florida. By March, many tales
had started to trickle back to New York about the "pheenom"
the Yankees had found.

He was 19 years old, and his father had named him after
Mickey Cochrane and had started training him as an infant. He
had played half a season of professional baseball at Independence, Missouri, and then all of the 1950 season at Joplin,
Missouri, as a shortstop. He had hit .383 with 26 homers and
136 runs batted in. He was shy and socially awkward, the son of
a lead miner from a small Oklahoma town. He was a switch-
hitter, and incredibly fast.

In those days, few players made the jump from the low
minors to the majors in one year. Even McDougald, who was to
join the Yankees that season and become American League
rookie of the year, was considered remarkable because he had
come up from the Texas League, a double-A classification. But
Mantle, who had played no higher than Class C at Joplin—
that is, five steps below the majors—was already tabbed "can't
miss."

He had, the most critical veteran observers admitted, two
weaknesses. The physical one they shrugged off; from a football
injury, he had osteomyelitis of the right leg—a persistent bone
infection that could be controlled but might act up at any time.
The other was his mental-emotional makeup: the young Mantle was simultaneously uncontrollably eager and stubborn. He
was slow to learn, intent on hitting everything as far as he could,
enraged with himself at every failure, capable of deep depres-
sion, and not at all analytic in his approach to the game.

The man most impressed by Mantle's potential was the
Yankee manager, Casey Stengel. Looking at Mantle's physical
equipment, and especially his ability to hit from both sides of
the plate, Stengel saw the perfect player in the making. All the
knowledge, slickness, and information Casey had accumulated

in 40 years of baseball would be imparted to this unformed but unlimited talent, and the mature Mantle would emerge as the monument of Stengel's career, his masterpiece.

So Mickey Mantle opened the season in right field at Yankee Stadium, wearing a very pointedly significant No. 6. Babe Ruth had worn No. 3, and Lou Gehrig No. 4, and both numbers had been "retired," never to be worn again by Yankee players. Joe DiMaggio was No. 5, and he was still the center fielder. The Yankees were making no bones about the progression they expected Mantle to maintain.

In his first Yankee game, a 5-0 victory over the Red Sox, Mickey's modest contribution was a single. The hitting star was another rookie, Jackie Jensen, who played left field.

But the burden was too great, the leap too wide. By mid-season, Mickey had bogged down in a strikeout streak. On July 15, with his average at .260, he was sent back down to Kansas City (then the triple-A farm club) to get straightened out. Despondent, he thought of quitting, but his father snapped him out of that by telling him, "If that's all the courage you have, go ahead and quit." In 40 games at Kansas City, Mickey batted in 50 runs, hit 11 homers, and batted .361. On August 24, he was back with the Yankees.

But when he came back, he didn't put on No. 6. He took No. 7, and wore it from then on.

Meanwhile, New York had remained unaware of Willie until May.

Jackie Robinson had become the first black major-league player only in 1947. The chief source for new talent, still being tapped, was the established Negro-league structure. In 1950, the Giants' organization signed Mays, who was 19 years old and playing with the Birmingham Barons. He finished out that season at Trenton, New Jersey, in a Class B league, hitting .353. For 1951, he was assigned to Minneapolis, the top Giant farm club, in the American Association—the same league in which the Yankees had Kansas City.

By May 24, Willie was hitting .477.

Not .377.

.477.

And remember, this wasn't the low minors. This was the last step below the majors and, at that time, a considerably tougher league than the triple-A leagues now in existence. And yet, when the Giants called Willie up, it was for his fielding—and they were right.

The Giants' home field was the Polo Grounds, which had the largest center-field area in the majors, and Willie played center field in a way that had to be seen to be believed. (Eventually, tens of millions saw and believed.) His range was limitless, and his arm so strong that he could make effective throws from the most unlikely locations and from the most unlikely body positions. Because he could go back so well and so far, he could play closer to the infield, and catch innumerable possible singles —and still always get back to the boundary of the particular field to prevent a ball from going over his head for a double or triple.

The Giant management (Leo Durocher was the field manager) appreciated these qualities from prior knowledge (through reports)—and was confident that he would hit, too. The Giant players—especially the pitchers—saw for themselves in the first few days after his arrival. But even the fans recognized the full value of these magnificent skills, because it is a fact that they accepted Willie's greatness even before he did any real hitting in the majors. (He finished the year at .274, seven points higher than Mantle, and had 20 home runs.)

When Willie joined the Giants, they were just getting back to .500 after a disastrous start. Since the team's main assets were great pitching and Durocher-style opportunistic offense, the improved defense provided by Mays was exceptionally important. The Giants straightened themselves out—but the Dodgers were running away.

In mid-August, the Giants began a 16-game winning streak. The day that Mantle rejoined the Yankees, the Giants won No. 12 of their streak. The Yankees, at that point, were a couple of games behind the Cleveland Indians and driving. Mays and Mantle, as individuals, were overshadowed by the steady stream of dramatic events as that season came to its end, but they played important roles in them. The day that the Yankees clinched the pennant, Reynolds pitched his second no-hitter; the Giants didn't win theirs until Thomson hit his home run—with Willie, admittedly scared, kneeling in the on-deck circle.

And so, on October 4, the World Series began with Willie Mays in center field for the Giants and Mickey Mantle in right for the Yankees. In the first game, both went hitless (Mickey walked once) as the Giants won. Mantle led off for the Yankees in the second game with a bunt single, and struck out in the third.

In the fifth, a routine play set the stage for the theme of the whole Mantle-Mays comparison. Mays, still hitless, hit a fly to right-center. Joe DiMaggio drifted to his left to catch it. Mantle eagerly raced over from right field to be alongside, back up, help, or catch it himself if necessary.

He was within 10 feet of DiMaggio when his right foot stepped on the wooden lid of a drainpipe imbedded in the outfield grass. His right knee buckled. He went down, as so many people have described it, "as if shot."

Mickey had a torn knee cartilage. He played no more in that Series, and his legs were never 100 percent sound again. And few people remember that Mays hit the ball that started Mantle's troubles.

Mays played out the series with a .182 batting average, and the Yankees won it in six games.

In 1952, Willie played 34 games and then went into the Army, where he stayed through 1953.

In 1952, Mantle had to start slowly because of the knee operation he had undergone—and he was medically deferred from the draft. A certain segment of the public persecuted Mantle for many years on this score. Also, he had endured a spiritual crisis—his father's death at the age of 41.

DiMaggio had retired, and Mantle was heir apparent to the

center-field job—but he wasn't ready physically, and opened the season in right field. In May, as his leg got stronger, he shifted to center. He had a fine year, hitting .311 and 23 homers, and the Yankees won another close pennant race. In a seven-game World Series against the Dodgers (the Giants had finished second), Mickey was spectacular, hitting .345. It was this World Series that established the idea nationally that Mickey was the next leader of the Yankees.

In 1953, a deteriorating, Mays-less Giant team finished fifth. The Yankees, however, won their fifth pennant in a row. Mantle, becoming famous for "tape-measure homers," hit .295 and a grand slam in the Series, as the Dodgers were beaten again, this time in six games.

When the 1954 season began, Mantle was fully established as a national sports hero. Willie, except to dedicated Giant fans and less secure Dodger fans with long memories, was just another promising player coming back from military service. And there was more to the publicity gap than the fact that the Yankees had just won five straight World Series while the Giants had faded with Willie away.

It must be realized that this was less than a decade after World War II. The recognition of teen-agers as a distinct class was relatively new—and Mantle had played in the majors as a teen-ager. Physically, he combined the most glamorous attributes of a classic hero—Herculean strength (those 500-foot homers), incredible speed (he could get down to first base in 3.1 seconds), good looks, youth, unprecedented versatility (there had never before been a switch-hitter with such power), and unlimited potential. If ever a "perfect" player was in the making, Mantle was the one—and it's hard to exaggerate how stimulating he was to the fan's imagination.

The degree of identification—always the basic ingredient in the creation of any superstar—was, in Mantle's case, of exceptional depth. His physical flaw, the bad leg, almost literally an Achilles' heel, only added to the drama.

And, of course, Mantle was white. This was only 1954, the

year of the Supreme Court's school desegregation decision. Whatever more complicated guilts or resentments might arise in the collective mind later, at that time there was simply no comparison in emotional appeal. Willie was black and, no matter how sincerely admired and enjoyed, could not arouse the same level of personal identification in whites that Mantle could.

Ten years later, this factor meant much less, because the whole context of life was changing, and because each man's achievements had created an individuality beyond his outer aspects. But, at the beginning of 1954, they didn't yet have any overwhelming achievements—just promise.

Then they started to make the promise good.

In 1954, the Giants won a pennant unexpectedly. They fought off the Dodgers and Braves, who were fundamentally more talented teams. The Giants had great pitching and an experienced first-string lineup, but the real difference was Mays. In one sense, he gave the most remarkable performance of his entire career.

It was remarkable in this way: in June, Willie went on a home-run spree, and by the end of July, he was running well ahead of Babe Ruth's record pace of 1927. But his batting average was not too high, as he swung for the fences, and the way the Giants played, they needed more singles than homers. So Leo told Willie to stop swinging for homers, and to hit the ball to right field. In the team's first 99 games, Willie had hit 36 homers; in the last two months of the season, he hit only five more—but raised his average to .345 and won the league batting championship on the last day of the season.

The Giants went on to sweep the World Series in four straight games from the Cleveland Indians, who had finally beaten the Yankees by setting an American League record of 111 victories. Mays was the Most Valuable Player in the National League. Mantle had hit .300 and 27 homers for the Yankees, but he had been overshadowed.

From that point on, the Great Debate was firmly established.

In 1955, the Dodgers reclaimed the National League championship as the Giants finished a distant third—and Willie, with no reason not to swing for the fences, blasted 51 home runs, giving Ruth's record a good challenge most of the season.

In 1955, the Yankees started another string of pennants, which was to reach four. Mantle emerged as the American League home-run champion (with 37) and hit .306. (Mays hit .318.) But during the World Series, Mickey's legs kept him out of action more than half the time as the Dodgers (for the first time) won the World Championship in seven games.

In 1956, Durocher was gone from the Giants, and they became a second-division club. Mays had one of his least distinguished batting records—.296 with 36 homers—but those who followed the Giants knew that he was performing new prodigies in the outfield every day. He also led the league in stolen bases, with 40, a department in which he was to lead for the next four years.

But Mantle, in 1956, hit the jackpot. He won the "triple crown"—batting title (.353), home runs (52), and runs batted in (130). Many of the home runs were of fantastic length. In the World Series, in which the Yankees got even with the Dodgers by winning the seventh game, Mickey hit three more homers. Now it was Mantle's turn to have a MVP Award.

By now, several facets of the Great Debate had become well-established.

As base runners, both men were fabulous. Mantle never approached the statistical record of Mays in stolen bases, but there were two good reasons for it: the Yankees didn't play that kind of baseball, and there was no sense risking Mickey's vulnerable legs too much. (In 1956, when Willie stole 40 bases, the whole Yankee team stole 51.) But Mantle, when it was desirable, could steal as effectively as Willie, and over the years succeeded in about 80 percent of his attempts.

In fielding, Mays was obviously superior in skill—but Mantle could run so fast that he made up for much of the difference.

At bat, Mantle was obviously more dangerous, since he could turn around.

And in personality, there was a striking contrast. Mantle was always a figure tinged by tragedy, moody, at times frustrated, stubborn (he was still swinging for the fence every time, striking out too much), shy and suspicious, often troubled. His mainsprings were pride and determination. But he also had playboy tendencies, and was often mentioned in gossip columns.

Willie's mainspring was uninhibited joy. He played baseball with a cheerful abandon that made everyone who saw him smile involuntarily. With his squeaky voice and high-spirited laugh, he was the butt of playful gestures by teammates and rivals alike. He had an open manner, friendly, vivacious, irrepressible. Whatever his private insecurities, he projected a feeling that playing ball, for its own sake, was the most wonderful thing in the world; and when the major-league game was over, there was stickball to be played in the streets of Harlem.

Later, this changed. Willie, as he grew older, became more withdrawn and suspicious, more cautious, more vulnerable—and with plenty of reason. Life, both personally and professionally, became more complicated for him and he had his share of sorrow. He married, adopted a child, then went through a painful divorce. Mantle, on the other hand, became somewhat more expansive—at least, at times—as he matured. But the basic images always remained true: joyful Willie, unfortunate Mickey.

In 1957, the Giants finished their New York career (as a sixth-place club) and moved on to San Francisco. Willie hit .333 with 35 homers, and the New York public considered his departure a much greater loss than the franchise itself.

That left Mantle with the metropolis to himself—but even as Mays was leaving, Mantle was suffering another injury which was to have a lasting effect.

In 1957, Mantle was MVP again. (He hit .365 and 34

homers.) In the third game of the World Series against Milwaukee, Mickey was on second when the pitcher (Bob Buhl) tried to pick him off. It was a high throw, and Red Schoendienst, the second baseman, had to leap. He came down on Mantle's right shoulder.

Mickey finished that game (and hit a home run), but the shoulder was damaged. Gradually, from that point on, he developed more and more difficulty in throwing, and in batting left-handed. (From that side, the right shoulder is the front one, and the arm must be lifted higher to lead the bat; Mantle always was a better hitter right-handed, but this injury increased the difference.) Eventually—in 1965—the shoulder became so painful that he couldn't throw at all, or hit effectively, and he was ready to quit baseball. Only then, in January, 1966, was surgery performed to remove bone chips and inflamed tendons, making it possible for him to continue.

How much this injury hampered Mantle can never be measured; it never got as much publicity as his legs, but it was a constant problem.

From 1958 on, the Great Debate lost its local intensity but gained a sort of diffuse momentum nationally. San Franciscans, believe it or not, resented Mays at first. Mantle, although he led the American League in homers in 1958 and 1960 (with 42 and 40), was dropping in all-around efficiency.

The Yankees didn't even win a pennant in 1959, and Stengel's regime ended when they pulled one out in 1960 but lost the World Series to Pittsburgh. Willie, meanwhile, played 1958 and 1959 in little Seals Stadium in San Francisco, while Candlestick Park was being built. His fielding brilliance, while no less effective for the club, was cramped and less noticeable to the public. And when the Giants moved into Candlestick in 1960, it turned out to be too large to hit many home runs in.

In those years, then, the debate cooled off, but it regained pertinence in 1961.

That was the year Mantle and Roger Maris went after Babe

Ruth's record, and Maris got it. Roger hit No. 61 on the last day of the season, but Mantle wound up with 54 and kept pace until the last four weeks. When Maris had 53, Mickey had 51, on September 5. Soon after that, a virus weakened Mickey, and kept him out of most of the World Series, but he won more finishing second than Maris did finishing first.

Maris carried two huge handicaps: the burden of attacking Ruth's hallowed record, and his own inability to deal with the pressures of instant fame. Commissioner Ford Frick added to his problem with a ridiculous ruling about "154 games" (since this was the first year of expansion and the 10-team league meant a 162-game schedule). To many fans, therefore, Maris became a target for resentment—and by reaction, Mantle became a hero in the eyes even of those who had criticized him up to then.

In Candlestick Park, that year, they moved the fences in, and Willie returned to the 40-homer class.

In 1962, Mantle was MVP again as the Yankees won the pennant for the 10th time in his 12 years with the club. A succession of leg injuries kept him from playing almost one-fourth of the time, but he hit .321 and 30 homers.

And they met again in the World Series, for the first time since their rookie year.

Willie had hit 49 home runs and a key single in the ninth inning of the third play-off game at Los Angeles. This was another seven-game Series, and it ended with Willie on second base with the potential winning run as Bobby Richardson caught Willie McCovey's line drive for the final out of a 1-0 victory. As a confrontation, though, it was a bust: Mays hit .250 and Mantle .120.

In 1963, in June, Mantle suffered the injury that made him a semicripple for the rest of his career. Running into the wall in Baltimore, he broke a bone in his left foot, and also tore the knee cartilage. He missed two-thirds of that season, limped through 1964, and, in 1965, came to the point of retiring.

But Willie was getting his second wind as a slugger. Still superb, he was no longer quite the incredible outfielder he had been in the 1950s. As the team acquired more power, he did less base-stealing. His batting average stayed pretty stable—.314 in 1963 (the same as his lifetime average through 1965), .296 in 1964, and .317 in 1965. His home-run production, however, soared—38 in 1963, 47 in 1964, 52 in 1965. Early in 1966, Willie hit No. 512 of his career, breaking Mel Ott's National League record. Soon only Ruth's 714 was ahead of him.

At the end of the 1965 season, an interesting statistical coincidence showed up: Mantle and Mays had each played 2,005 games. Comparison was inevitable.

Mays had come to bat 220 more times.

Mantle had reached base 216 more times—because he had 1,464 walks to Willie's 949.

But Willie had a higher batting average, .314 to .306.

Willie had 32 more home runs and 58 more runs batted in. He had almost twice as many stolen bases (276 to 145), but Mantle had a better percentage of success in stealing—81 percent to 76 percent. And Willie had hit into more than twice as many double plays (174 to 86).

But Mantle struck out much more—1,424 times (a major-league record, surpassing Ruth) to 893.

However, Mantle also broke Ruth's record for home runs in World Series play, with 18. (The Babe had 15.) Mays never did hit a World Series homer, in 17 games played.

Finally, in the very rudimentary category of fielding statistics, Willie's big advantage showed. He played 1,987 games in the outfield, 65 more than Mickey—and made 980 more putouts.

Neither career ended, of course, in 1965, but that was the last time their figures were comparable. Mantle, as might have been expected from his physical difficulties, deteriorated quickly. In 1966, as the once mighty Yankees sank to last place, he could play only 108 games, although he did manage to hit .288 with 23 homers. Over the winter, the decision was made to switch him to first base, where he wouldn't have to run; and despite his fears that he might "embarrass" himself, he played out two more seasons at that position, being deified by the management. But he couldn't even hit .250, and that did embarrass him. After the 1968 season, having hit his 536th home run, he retired at the age of 38.

But Mays, at 38, was going strong. It didn't seem likely that he could reach Ruth's hallowed total of 714 homers, but people were taking the attempt seriously (and no one, yet, was paying attention to Hank Aaron, some 75 homers behind Mays but three years younger). Willie had aching legs now, too, and needed his rest, and could no longer hit .300 (in a baseball world in which .300 hitters were ever fewer). Now and then, though, he could be as exciting as ever, and day after day he could still help a contending club. He hit 37 homers in 1966 and 28 homers as late as 1970. In 1971, helping the Giants win a divisional title, he stole 23 bases at the age of 40—more than he had in any of the previous ten seasons.

Early the next season, though, a deal was arranged for Willie to return to New York, to the Mets, to play out the string and be assured of income and adulation to a degree Stoneham and San Francisco could not afford.

When it was all over, Willie's statistics could be found among the top five in all major offensive categories—in some order or other, you'd find him along with Cobb, Aaron, and Musial in longevity, and among Ruth, Aaron, and Musial in slugging categories. Mantle, for all intents and purposes, had an effective career five years shorter.

No one knows what a healthy Mantle might have done; still, in the early years, Mays surpassed him in rate of development. As a batter, Mantle was more dangerous and more consistent than Willie, who was notorious for all-on or all-off hot streaks and slumps. In effective speed, they were equal. Defensively, Mays was much, much better.

To players, Mantle has always been an object of special awe.

They have been impressed not only by his exceptional strength and other abilities, but by his determination and courage in forcing himself to play—and to play so well with so many physical handicaps.

But the phrase usually applied to Willie is a sort of inarticulate appreciation: "Willie? He's just too much."

For myself, comparison isn't exactly equal, because I saw most of Mantle's career, but only pieces of Willie's since the Giants moved to California. Only a handful of players, in all baseball history, have been as important to winning teams, and have been able to contribute as much to eventual victory, rather than to statistics, as has Mickey Mantle. Willie, on the other hand, I can sum up very simply: he's the best baseball player I ever saw.

20

Socrates in the Dugout

More words, probably, have been written about Casey Stengel than about any other sports personage, anytime, anyplace, from Achilles through Y. A. Tittle. No other face, reproduced countless times by all of modern man's technical marvels, became as recognizable to so many people.

And yet, despite all the attention lavished on this octogenarian gnome, his true nature remained a mystery to the public at large. Casey Stengel, to the millions who took some sort of interest in his existence, remained a collection of one-dimensional stereotypes—a clown, a genius, a grand old man, a senile fool, a father figure, a tyrant, an ultimate symbol of fighting spirit, a cantankerous publicity hound, a peerless leader, a lucky stiff, a wit, a phony, a wizard, a myth.

The particular image applied in a given case always varied with the experience, bias, and perceptiveness of the particular beholder, but anyone who had more than casual contact with Stengel himself soon realized that at least some of the above images blended into a composite.

The totality (a more humble but no less ambitious concept than "truth") is harder to come by. For one thing, no one has ever been able to be close to Stengel without developing some sort of bias, for or against. His personality, however one interpreted it, never failed to make an impression. In a nationwide poll for "The Most Unforgettable Character I Ever Met," Stengel would surely win because he made a point of meeting so many people who, in the ordinary course of their lives, couldn't possibly have run into anyone more startling.

Besides, Stengel was in the public eye for more than half a century, and he wasn't the same person in all circumstances during that time. In fact, one of his chief characteristics (and biggest assets) was his ability to respond to change—quickly, almost mercurially, and certainly over long periods of time. Since so many people formed their basic idea of Stengel at such diverse stages of his life (and theirs), it is not surprising that the consensus description contains contradictions.

The Stengel we will look at is the Fifth-Stage Stengel, the period in which he managed—or rather created—the New York Mets, from 1962 until the night he broke his hip a few days before his 75th birthday in July, 1965. The fact that it is the fifth stage, quite distinct from the first four, is pertinent to the portrait.

Stengel was born in 1890 in Kansas City, Missouri, and was a star high-school athlete there in baseball, basketball, and football. He studied dentistry briefly, but became a professional baseball player in 1910 in Kankakee, Illinois. He reached the Brooklyn Dodgers at the end of the 1912 season and was with them when shiny, new Ebbets Field was opened in 1913. He was a regular outfielder with the Dodgers through 1917, and was traded to Pittsburgh (while serving in the Navy as a meat-packer in the Brooklyn Navy Yard). He went to the Phillies in 1920 and to the New York Giants in midseason of 1921. After making headlines by hitting two home runs in the 1923 World Series (the first played in Yankee Stadium), he was traded to the Boston Braves. After the first few games of the 1925 season, he went back to the minors.

That was Stage One of his life: professional athlete. He was 34 years old, he had been married to Edna Lawson for less than a year, he had played 1,277 major-league games—and he was washed up.

"When I started with the Kankakee club and the club folded in midseason, I kept the uniform in loo of my salary

*and what do you suppose they did years later? A bank in
Kankakee wrote and asked for the uniform back so they could
put it in a museum—and offered me $10 for it.*

*"One place I played they had an insane asylum—that's
right, a crazy house—right outside the center-field fence, and
they used to watch us play. Now I figured out, how many
times do you come in from the outfield and go back out in a
game, right? Every inning, that's right, that's 18 times both
ways. So I figured I could practice my sliding 18 times every
game by sliding into second base on my way out and on my
way in. It didn't interfere with the game, did it? Well, the
loonies loved it and the people in the stands kept sayin', Look
who's out and look who's in—but I learned slidin'.*

*"I met Edna in the Polo Grounds in 1923, and she still likes
to tell me what to do, like when she says, 'Oh, my, you can't
go and fire that nice young man with that pretty wife and
all those lovely children'—and she don't even know whether a
baseball curves."*

Stage Two began immediately. In this phase, he was a professional baseball manager with little success. When he went to
the minors, in 1925, it was as president and player-manager of
Worcester, an Eastern League team the Braves had just bought.
He played 100 games, batted .320, managed the team to a third-
place finish—and, at the end of the season, when an opportunity to move up presented itself, wrote himself (as president) a
release (as playing manager) and took over Toledo, in the
American Association.

He stayed there until 1932, when he became a Dodger coach,
and two years later became the Brooklyn manager for three
years. In 1937, he sat out the remaining year of his Dodger
contract, being paid "not to manage," a humiliation he never
forgot. From 1938 through 1943, he managed the Boston
Braves (then called "Bees") and invested about $40,000 of his
own money in the team.

By December, 1943, he had been managing, on and off, for

19 years. He had a newly acquired limp, as the result of being struck by a taxi. His interest in the Braves was bought up, he was fired as manager, and Stage Two was over. He had managed nine seasons in the National League and had never been out of the second division.

> *"Let me show you what a smart man I was. We're playin'*
> *the Cardinals and they got this kid, just up from the minors*
> *at the end of the year. I know all about his record and how*
> *he's supposed to be great and a left-handed hitter and all.*
> *But he's a kid. And I know how it is with kids, they can all*
> *hit fast balls, but they can't hit the soft stuff, because they've*
> *just come from the minors and who's down there that's a good*
> *experienced pitcher and knows how to mix it up, right? So*
> *he's been lookin' at fast balls and wild men and now I tell*
> *my pitcher, don't worry about it, just give him those little*
> *soft curves and he'll break his back swingin' at it—and he hit*
> *two singles and two doubles off my pitcher, and that's when*
> *I found out this Mr. Musial was a pretty good hitter whether*
> *he was young and had seen old pitching or not."*

Stage Three was the low point, professionally. He started 1944 without a baseball job. In May, when Charley Grimm left the Milwaukee Brewers (of the American Association) to manage the Chicago Cubs, Stengel took over the Brewers and won a pennant for absentee-owner Bill Veeck, then in the Marines in the Pacific. In 1945, Casey managed the Yankee farm club at Kansas City.

By now, Mrs. Stengel's real-estate business in California was requiring more time, and Casey's oil investments were doing well, so they decided that California was the place to be. Stengel became the manager at Oakland, in the Pacific Coast League, and had three rather successful seasons there.

Stage Four began with a wholly unexpected rocket ride to the top of the baseball world. The New York Yankees suddenly called upon him to take over baseball's most successful team, which hadn't been quite so overwhelmingly successful in the preceding five years. George Weiss, who had become friendly with Casey more than 20 years before, when Stengel was at Worcester and Weiss was running New Haven, had emerged as effective head of the Yankee operation. He brought Casey to New York.

Stage Four, then, turned out to be 12 years of glory unparalleled in baseball history. Stengel's Yankees won ten pennants, and seven World Series (including the first five in succession). Casey's universal fame was established. Until he became manager of the Yankees, at the age of 58, Casey was known only to the more dedicated baseball fan; within a year, he was a world figure, and still is.

In 1960, shortly after the Yankees had lost the seventh game of an eventful World Series to Pittsburgh, the Yankees carried through a prior plan to fire him. They called it, sincerely enough in their own minds, retirement; a little later, they disposed of Weiss (who was 67) the same way. But Stengel wouldn't hold still for the euphemism. "I was discharged," he said later, "because there was no question I had to leave."

Offers poured in from many sides, but Casey and Edna retired to Glendale, where Casey had become a bank director. Apparently, his long, eventful career was over.

Meanwhile, however, obscure forces were preparing Stage Five. The majors were expanding, and there was to be a new National League team in New York City, abandoned by the Giants and Dodgers in 1957. The new team, the Mets, could never compete with the Yankees in playing ability, since it was to be stocked with castoffs. But it could, certainly, compete for public attention in other ways.

So the owners of the new team hired Weiss as president, and Weiss urged Casey to become the manager. Casey accepted, in the fall of 1961, and started his new job in Florida in February of 1962.

"It is a great pleasure," he declared in accepting the job with the Mets, whose nickname had just been adopted with great fanfare, "to become a part of the Knickerbockers, and we will offer the Yout' of America to the fans." Did he mean the Basketball Knicks or the original baseball team of 1845? No one had the nerve to ask.

Ten months later, the Mets, their name clearly established and their roster dotted with fading veterans, kicked away another of the 120 games they lost that first season. "We," rasped Casey confidentially, sweeping his arm toward the large crowd filing out of the Polo Grounds, "are a fraud."

All this historical material is essential to an understanding of the Fifth-Stage Stengel, because its influences remained so very much alive.

Over the years, I had many occasions to seek colorful identities for Casey. Once I called him a 72-year-old Figaro, another time King Lear; he had been compared, facetiously, to Albert Einstein and Albert Schweitzer, and at times he spoke like Baron Munchhausen.

The most suggestive association, however, was Socrates. Like Socrates, Casey asked questions as a method of instruction, he challenged all established ideas, and very likely, in some sense, he corrupted the youth. His talk irritated many but fascinated others; it took time and effort to learn his dialectic, but many who did, became disciples. In his own context, he sought the "truth" uncompromisingly—the truth, in this instance, being not justice but whatever would win more ball games. Endless words, challenging ideas, imparting knowledge by making you think—that's the pattern of the Stengel who managed the Mets. The recurrent phrases were: "Why wouldn't ya . . ." and "You're fulla bull and I'll tell ya why. . . ." and "Now *wait* a minute, that's what I been tryin' to *tell* ya" and "What's wrong with . . ." followed by some unorthodox suggestion.

Considerable insight into Stengel's character may be gained from the bare decision to come to the Mets. He was, after all,

71 years old. He had all the money he could ever use, and in his profession had achieved every honor possible to a manager. If pure egotism, self-aggrandizement, and the promotion of his image as a genius were his true motivations—as his detractors often insisted—it made no sense to tarnish his Yankee record by taking on the Mets. When he was finally named to the Hall of Fame in 1966, it was essentially for Stage Four, the Yankee years.

His real motives were, in fact, quite the opposite, although they seemed to be related. Retirement in Glendale for the childless Stengels was simply unbearably dull. In the sense that Casey craved the spotlight and constant attention, a return to action was self-indulgence. That he needed listeners, admirers, arguers, and agreers was a fact. But if that were all he wanted, he could have accepted the managership of much better teams than the Mets during 1961.

What really attracted him to the Mets was his dominant desire: to teach. In that respect, the very fact that the Mets were starting from scratch was an advantage and an incentive. There was, to be sure, a subsidiary desire for some sort of indirect revenge against the Yankees. But the opportunity to build was the main thing—and remained the main thing right to the end, although so little was built.

To himself, Stengel was primarily a teacher.

His egotism, so immense, was really concentrated on the teaching function. He wanted to mold, to create. His pride was attached not to mere winning, but to winning through his instruction and leadership. He didn't want to be hailed for the sensational statistics the Yankees compiled, but for the fact that they were compiled by men he chose and guided.

There were two principal roots of this desire. The first was frustrated fatherhood: having no children of his own, Stengel made many a young ball player into a surrogate son. The results were remarkably true to life—not all sons are comfortable with their fathers, especially when the fathers drive them toward an achievement the father chose; and not all fathers understand the best way to handle their sons. And, as happens so often, it is only when the son is older and more mature that he comes to appreciate what the old man did, or tried to do, for him. It was common to hear players (Hank Bauer and Gene Woodling became prime examples), who chafed under Stengel's authority and hated him passionately, admit afterward that they had better records and longer careers because of Stengel's handling.

The other root was Stengel's personal experience throughout Stage One, as a player. He was not especially gifted in size, speed, strength, or miraculous coordination. Everything he could do on a ball field he learned by long practice and sharp observation. To players of his type, "slickness"—the word he always perferred—was the means of survival. Only by noticing every little potential advantage, and making full use of it, could Stengel compete with bigger and better players. He learned enough, and applied himself hard enough, to play 1,277 major-league games and to hit .284.

His baseball religion, therefore, listed hustle, alertness, practice, study, and correction of weakness as the five cardinal virtues—and these are precisely the things that can be taught. No one can give a player better reflexes, or more speed, or a stronger arm; and if the player depends only on his natural ability and early habits, his limitations are pretty clear. But he can be driven to try his best at all times, taught what to look for, shown tricks, trained to recognize lapses in others, prompted to analyze techniques and situations, and forced to practice. Whether or not a teacher succeeds in any particular case, he can try, at least, to do these things.

Thus, in Stengel, a lifetime of looking for the little edge that smartness brings was combined with a deep personal desire to impart that knowledge. It is, of course, ego gratification that Stengel sought, but the gratification was tied to the performance of his pupils.

Like all the greatest teachers, Stengel was a superb actor.

Every gesture, every facial expression, every tangled word was put to use—first to get attention, then to deliver the message.

The same skills, of course, served perfectly in Casey's other activity: promotion. He was an instinctive genius, as well as a shrewd practitioner, at public relations. As a Yankee, his bizarre behavior, his incomprehensible speech, his history of failure all helped to counteract the image of cold efficiency the pre-Stengel Yankees had created. As a Met, with the circumstances of his Yankee eviction added to his other assets, Stengel alone constructed the remarkable conglomeration that became the "Met image"—off-beat, youth-oriented, the ultimate underdog, deliciously illogical, steadfastly pugnacious in the face of endless frustration, rebellious, nonconformist, ever hopeful—in a word, crazy.

"We're going to have in our new ball park," Stengel told a Detroit broadcaster in Florida, "21 escalators and four restaurants and lovely rest rooms and soft chairs so you can rest and not get tired watching the Mets, that is, if your heart is weak."

"Look," said Stengel on a St. Valentine's Day, pointing to dozens of squealing ladies in the little wooden stand at the practice field in St. Petersburg—ladies averaging at least 65 years of age. "Look, I've got to get back to my charm school."

"From Little Rock, eh?" said Stengel to six teen-agers in the lobby of the Chase Hotel in St. Louis. "Now you must be 17 years old. Why wouldn't you want to come and sign with the Mets and get a big bonus and become famous and go back to Little Rock and open up a big restaurant like Mr. Musial has here, which I understand you couldn't get a table in last night?"

"Hey, Heffner," yelled Stengel to Coach Don Heffner, who had been holding an infield drill for rookies on one of the three diamonds on the practice field at St. Pete, "take 'em down to that other field and find out if they can play on the road."

"All right," said Stengel to Solly Hemus, an earlier Met

coach, who had asked if the team should take fielding practice before a game in San Francisco, after strong winds had forced cancellation of batting practice. "Go ahead, but just hit them some pop flies. Don't bother with grounders—there ain't gonna be no earthquake."

Casey's promotional fervor had a strong streak of idealism. He seldom put it into words, and then in a sort of aggressive, defiant manner, as if expecting to be doubted by cynics. But his feeling was real and deeply personal: "Baseball did a lot for me, and if I can give something back by selling baseball, why shouldn't I?"

In Stengel's scheme of values, loyalty ranked very high, especially the loyalty of an employee to an employer, and vice versa. When he was with the Yankees, winning pennants every year, there were half a dozen instances in which he insisted on keeping a player an extra year as a reward for past service. One example was Irv Noren, who wrecked both knees playing all three outfield positions for Stengel in the early 1950s, when others were hurt and someone had to play. Finally, Noren's mobility was cut far below pennant-winning standards, and Weiss would have dumped him in a minute. But Stengel insisted that Noren stay one more year, with a crack at several thousand dollars in World Series money instead of just a salary with some also-ran.

Casey, in turn, demanded absolute loyalty from others, and got pretty testy when he felt betrayed. This made his departure from the Yankees as bitter as it was; neither the players, by and large, nor the management had proved loyal.

As a winner with the Yankees, Casey became increasingly irascible. In the first few years, he seemed grateful for his success; as time went on, he appeared to become insatiable in his quest for perfection. There were so many good players on the Yankees that Casey couldn't stand watching some of them settle for whatever their natural abilities brought them.

As a loser with the Mets, he was much more patient, understanding, good-humored, gentle. He had his irascible moments as a Met, too, but usually during periods of better play, not during the frequent losing streaks. He is more tolerant of lack of talent than of talent going to waste.

"If a man has five good points, why wouldn't he work on the sixth point that can make him better? How many times have you seen a man practice scoring from third on a fly? How often can you practice it in a game? You gotta hit a triple, right? But in batting practice, you can go down there every time after you hit.

"If a pitcher has trouble keeping a man close, why wouldn't he study and master it? If a man can't hit a curve, why wouldn't he get the batting practice pitcher to throw him curves instead of just seeing how far he can hit it at noon?

"Some of 'em complain they can't get the signs on this or that play, but why do you have to see the coach? Why don't you know yourself, while you're on deck, what'll I do if he doubles, what'll I do if he triples, this is probably what they'll want. Then you won't be so shocked and taken by surprise when the sign is on.

"Or running a base. Why do you have to look at the coach? Second base is right where it always was, they ain't moved it, have they? And there's no hills on the basepath or obstacle courses, is there? So why not look at the ball in the outfield, and know what kind of arm the man has?"

So Stengel was a teacher, by inclination and conviction, by training and purpose. His phenomenal memory, his unmatched experience, were both devoted to passing on the things he had learned—from John McGraw, his model, and from the hundreds of other ball players and managers from whom Casey always absorbed information like a sponge.

Nevertheless, most players disliked working for him. Why?

First, Stengel was guilty of what has become the most unforgivable sin in the minds of the sensitive athlete of the post-

World War II period: Casey knocked players in front of other people. Of course, he did it partly on purpose and partly out of indifference. A man, no matter how forward-looking, can't simply slough off lifelong viewpoints. Until Stengel was 60, the issue of hurting a player's feelings by bawling him out in public never seemed to arise. Stengel believed, as the older generation did, that correction in public made a deeper impression, and that since the purpose of correction was to make the player (and the club) better, no resentment should result. Nevertheless, resentment did result, and in this one respect Stengel did not keep up with the times. Today, players' confidence, a necessary quality, seems more fragile than it used to be.

Second comes a closely related subject, second-guessing. Baseball is an endless succession of little decisions: pitch this man here, try to hit that pitch there. Sometimes, a man makes a wrong decision in terms of agreed-upon strategy; more often, a man who intends to do the right thing fails to carry it out physically—that is, a pitch intended to be low comes in high and gets hit over a fence (or, in Casey's famous phrase, "over a building").

Stengel did second-guess his men, at least in their opinion— but to Casey it was simply the manager's prerogative to keep searching for the right answer and to blame people for their mistakes to lessen repetition. Still, the players didn't like it.

Third, most players feared and resented Casey's talent for sarcasm. They felt that, as players, they had no comeback, especially to the press, which seemed largely pro-Stengel. Very few players ever stopped to think how much protection they got from Stengel's monologues, which monopolized the attention of reporters. Especially on the Mets, every word from or about Stengel, even if unfavorable to some particular player, was one less word addressed directly to the ineptness or problems of the same player. As a lightning rod, or as a diversionary force, Stengel was supreme.

Fourth, the less perceptive players considered him a joke,

and less perceptive ball players are in the large majority on any team. Those who didn't have the sense, or ambition, to try to listen and learn, found it easy to blame their own failures or limitations on Stengel's age, or mannerisms, or "meanness," or "craziness."

Many, on the other hand, did appreciate what Casey was. As Bauer summed it up one day, "Of course I learned about managing from Stengel. Who else did I play for?"

There was one criticism of Stengel that was more legitimate than most. He did have a tendency to force an injured man to play, to overuse a hot pitcher, to sacrifice an individual's welfare for the smell of victory. This form of selfishness is not the most admirable trait in the world—but it can be doubted that many successful generals throughout the history of mankind were free of it.

The press, by and large, liked Stengel, for obvious reasons: he was an endless source of good copy, he was exceptionally honest on serious issues, and he was not merely unselfish but positively overgenerous with his time. Still, since he could be stubborn, tactless, and sarcastic, he made some enemies among reporters, too.

The public, with few exceptions, liked Casey because he was fun—fun to read about, to listen to, to watch. Women and children seemed to find him particularly irresistible, and Casey returned the feeling.

Was he a clown? Only when he wanted to be, to evade giving a direct answer or to gain attention.

Was he a genius? Yes, in the public relations sense, and also a sort of half-genius in baseball strategy. He didn't invent platooning (which he learned from John McGraw, who platooned Casey into a .368 batting average in 1922), or half a dozen of his other trademarks, but he did refine them, and the testimony to his baseball brilliance is irrefutable: many managers today do as a matter of course what Stengel did as an exception 15 years ago—and it works.

A grand old man? Certainly to those who knew him at a distance. A senile fool? Not by a long shot. A father figure? To some. A tyrant? To many who worked for him. A symbol of fighting spirit? The best since Thermopylae. A publicity hound, and cantankerous? Sure. A peerless leader? As close to peerless as they come. A lucky stiff? Very often, but often unlucky, too. A wit? First-rate. A phony? Not in the least. A wizard? Alas, no. A myth? Yes, a glorious one, to last as long as baseball is known.

But beyond all these, he was that rarest and most estimable item among twentieth-century celebrities: completely himself.

21

The Greatest Pitcher

One of the silliest—and least resistible—baseball pastimes is picking the "best" something. It's silly because sensible comparisons can't be made if different eras or different leagues are involved. But it's irresistible because all who follow the game love to wallow in contemplation of the qualities and feats of the greatest players, to discuss and compare the greatest accomplishments, to share dreams of approaches to perfection.

One of the hardiest of these propositions is the question, "Who deserves to be called The Greatest Pitcher in the History of Baseball?"

Contemporary fans, especially younger ones, are apt to answer "Sandy Koufax" right off the bat. After all, by the time he retired at the age of 31 after the 1966 season, Sandy had broken just about every conceivable strikeout record; he had won the Cy Young Award, as the outstanding pitcher in the major leagues, three times in four years; he had pitched no-hitters in four consecutive seasons (an unparalleled feat), had led the league in earned-run average for five years in a row, and had pitched the Dodgers to three pennants in season-end showdowns.

No one doubts that Koufax was the outstanding pitcher of his time, and that his place in the Hall of Fame was assured even before he retired.

But is he the one who should be called "the greatest pitcher"? Or should it be someone from the distant past? Or from the not-so-distant past? Someone who is only a name to most present-day fans and players, like Walter Johnson, Grover Cleveland Alexander, Christy Mathewson, Cy Young? Or someone who remains a vivid memory from a more recent era, like Lefty Grove or Bob Feller?

Any answer to such questions is, naturally, intensely personal, which is probably why the whole unprovable business remains so popular. As a rule, the younger generation takes for granted that today's "greatest" anything is automatically superior. Older people, or at least those with longer memories, frequently insist that the "really great" ones were the heroes of antiquity—a period which, among sports fans, invariably coincides with the adolescence and early adulthood of the speaker. Because a privately defined "Golden Age" is embedded in each interested party, objective evaluation is difficult, and a thoroughly exhilarating, rip-roaring argument is always possible.

My choice is Johnson—a man I never saw pitch. Koufax and Feller were the best I did see.

To justify my choice, I must spell out how I arrive at it.

Longevity is one of the fundamental standards in selecting "the greatest." We are trying to single out one man, among the thousands who have pitched in the major leagues over many decades. However distinguished the achievements of any of them may be, only those who could maintain their superiority for the full span of career possibility—about 20 years—can be considered for the No. 1 ranking.

The man who made this point most vehemently was Koufax himself, in 1964. His season had been cut short by what was then called "an inflamed elbow," but it was already the chronic arthritis that was to be diagnosed as such only the following spring. Almost prophetically, Sandy said: "Before you compare me with the great pitchers of all time, let me be around awhile. Let me prove what I can do over a long period of time. Don't put me in a class with pitchers like Warren Spahn and Whitey Ford until I've shown I can win games for 10 or 15 years.

Spahn has been doing it for 20. That's what it takes to rate as a great ball player, not a couple of good years, but a whole career."

At that time, Sandy was 28 years old, and had been a full-fledged star for only three seasons. He signed with the Dodgers (then in Brooklyn) for a modest bonus in 1955, and never spent a day with any other team because bonus players had to be kept on the varsity, but he didn't become a consistent winner until 1961.

After 1964, of course, Sandy immensely strengthened his claim to a place among the full-career men. That's why, among all the records he set, the ones that meant most to him were career totals. He finished up having struck out more men than all but six other pitchers—Johnson, Young, Spahn, Mathewson, Feller, and Tim Keefe, who pitched back in the 1880s.

But if we accept a two-decade career (approximately) as a standard, we immediately rule out some famous names whose moments of glory were every bit as bright as Koufax's. Dizzy Dean, in 1933–1937, was as commanding a figure as any pitcher could ever be. But in the 1937 All-Star Game, a line drive broke his toe. When he tried to resume pitching too soon, he favored his leg and strained his arm, and was never great again.

Less celebrated, and certainly less remembered, is Addie Joss, who won 155 games for Cleveland in his first eight major-league seasons, and pitched two no-hitters, one a perfect game. But in 1911, at the age of 31, Joss died of tuberculosis.

A more recent example is Herb Score. Only a few years before Koufax, he was the magnet for all the same superlatives. After the 1956 season, the Boston Red Sox offered Cleveland $1,000,000 for his contract—and were turned down. But, the very next season, a line drive hit Score in the eye. His sight was saved, but he never could regain his pitching rhythm and soon developed a sore arm. He finally retired to become a broadcaster for the White Sox in 1963—still only 31 years old.

Those who can qualify, therefore, must be blessed with continued strength and good health. Pitchers' arms are notoriously fragile; the wear and tear are tremendous, the risk of injury always present—as Koufax has demonstrated.

All right, then, with the field narrowed down to the 20-year men, what are the other elements of pitching greatness?

There are four: stuff, control, craft, and poise.

Stuff is the physical element: how hard can he throw, how big is the break on his curve? Stuff is the product of strength and exceptional, hair-trigger coordination, and seems to be an innate quality, perhaps improvable by practice and technique, but not acquirable.

Control is the ability to throw the ball—with stuff on it—exactly where the pitcher wants to, with extraordinary accuracy.

Craft comprises the knowledge that comes with experience, analytic powers, meticulous observation, and resourcefulness. Craft is what tells a pitcher where and how to apply the stuff he can control.

And poise includes the ability to apply one's craft under the most severe competitive pressure, to rise to an occasion, and to produce best when the need is greatest.

Both the practice that perfects control and the experience that perfects knowledge and poise are time-consuming. In the process, age and the attrition of muscular strain take their toll. Usually, by the time a pitcher masters his craft, some degree of his physical gift has been lost.

It is very rare, therefore, to find a man who possesses the highest degree of stuff, control, and craft simultaneously. It is so rare, in fact, that our list of eligibles for the "greatest pitcher" designation is quickly reduced to quite manageable terms.

Spahn and Ford were the most distinguished pitchers of the post-World War II era. Spahn pitched until he was 44 years old and won more games (363) than any left-hander in baseball history. Ford, until the circulation in his arm (and his Yankee support) gave out in 1965, owned the best career winning percentage in the history of the game.

But neither of them, outstanding as they were, ever had speed and power even remotely comparable to that possessed by Johnson, Feller, and Koufax. The same was true of Carl Hubbell, Herb Pennock, Ted Lyons, and a dozen others. They were artists, fully worthy of Hall of Fame membership, but not contenders for No. 1.

Others, like Dean, Lefty Gomez, and Rube Waddell, did have overpowering stuff. But they never perfected the craft. Untouchable for a while, they became merely very good pitchers when their exceptional speed was lost.

That narrows the list to Johnson, Alexander, Mathewson, Grove, and Feller.

Cy Young must be considered a special case. He won more games than anyone else, 511. But his career began in 1890, when conditions of play (and rules) were simply too different to allow meaningful comparison. Only in 1903 was major-league baseball stabilized into its familiar form. All those being considered started to pitch after that (although Young did pitch until 1911).

Feller is the next to be eliminated, partly by fate. To his blinding fast ball, he added one of the biggest, most explosive curves ever used. He joined Cleveland at the age of 17, in 1936, and started breaking strikeout records right away. In all, he won 266 games, pitched three no-hitters and 12 one-hitters, and set a single-season strikeout record (348 in 1946) that stood until Koufax surpassed it in 1965.

But Feller was robbed of nearly four full seasons, at the very height of his powers, by World War II. He was only 23 years old when he went into service, and took up right where he left off when he returned at 27. Granted peaceful times, he might have posted 100 more victories and 1,000 more strikeouts. He might have made his claim to No. 1 undeniable. Even when his fast ball was long since gone, in 1951, he was able to win 22 games. But the lost years eliminate him.

Grove, according to most testimony, was faster than Feller.

"He was the fastest pitcher who ever lived," says Ford Frick, who was a baseball writer in the 1920s before moving up through the National League hierarchy to the Commissionership of Baseball.

Grove never had Feller's curve, but he kept his fast ball longer. In 17 American League seasons, he won exactly 300 games (and lost only 140) and was still the league leader in earned-run average at the age of 39 (in 1939).

But Grove did it all on power. Mathewson had that too, and more finesse. He used a famous "fadeaway," a pitch that would be called a "right-handed screwball" today. His career with the New York Giants ran from 1900 to 1916. Of his 373 victories, 365 came in a 14-year span, which means he *averaged* 26 victories per season.

Still, Mathewson was usually with a winning team. Alexander and Johnson were not.

"I would have to say," says Casey Stengel, who ought to know, "that Johnson was the most amazing pitcher in the American League and Alexander in the National. Alexander had to pitch in the little Philadelphia ball park, with that big tin fence in right field, and he pitched shutouts, which must mean he could do it. He had a fast ball, a curve, a change of pace, and perfect control. He was the best I batted against in the National League."

Alexander was 24 years old when he joined the Phillies in 1911. To a right-hander, the 250-foot distance to the right-field barrier in Baker Bowl presented a special hazard, since left-handed hitters were the ones who had a crack at it. It's true that the lively ball was not yet in use, but, by the same token, hitters who weren't swinging for the fences were much harder to strike out—and that fence could be hit even if the batter weren't particularly trying to hit it.

In his first seven seasons with the Phillies, Alexander won 190 games. He moved on to Chicago and St. Louis, and in 1926, at the age of 39, was the World Series hero for the Cardinals as they defeated the Yankees in seven games—well into the lively ball era.

Altogether, Alexander won 373 games. He pitched 90 shutouts, still the National League record, and this is a particularly significant statistic.

"A good pitcher's main job," Sal Maglie once observed, "is not to give up the first run." If a pitcher holds the opposition scoreless, his team can't lose. Once his own team scores, the pitcher's job is to give the other side one less. A shutout is proof positive that the pitcher has performed his team function to perfection.

Strikeouts are important in this respect, too. Base runners can't advance on a strikeout (generally), winning runs can't score from third, as they can on flies and ground outs. That's why stuff is so important. Alexander struck out 2,198 batters. (Grove, by the way, fanned 2,266, Feller 2,581, Mathewson 2,505, Spahn 2,584.)

At the same time, control is even more important than stuff —and Alexander walked only 951 men, averaging about one walk for every six innings pitched. And he pitched in 696 games.

If I were choosing the "most complete pitcher," Alexander would be it.

But Johnson was greater still.

Walter Perry (Barney) Johnson was strictly a fast-ball pitcher, the fastest of all. Eventually, he developed a pretty good curve, of which he became inordinately proud; but mostly, he just leaned back and fired the fast ball with a three-quarter-arm motion that was almost sidearm.

"You might know it was coming," says Stengel, "but you couldn't hit it. And he had perfect control, too."

"When I batted against him in 1921," says Fred Haney, who was a Detroit infielder then, "he looked so fast I couldn't believe it. When I got back to the bench, they told me, 'Hell, you should have seen him ten years ago, he was twice as fast then.' Hell, I was glad I *hadn't* seen him ten years before; I didn't want to see him the way he was right then."

"Johnson," says Frick, "always worried that his fast ball might kill someone if it hit him in the head. His control was so perfect, though, that he didn't even have to throw close to hitters. He just kept throwing it over the plate."

Johnson came out of Humboldt, Kansas, in 1907. He was 19. He went straight to the Washington Senators and never pitched for any other team in Organized Baseball until he worked one inning for Newark in 1928, when he was managing the International League club.

The Senators then, as ever, were seldom successful. During his first 16 years with them, they finished in the second division ten times. They were last or next-to-last seven times. He didn't get a chance to pitch in a World Series until 1924, when he was almost 37 years old. Then he lost two games to the Giants, but won the seventh and deciding game to give Washington its first—and only—world championship.

And, despite this minimal support, Johnson won 414 games —more than anyone but Cy Young.

"He was, besides, a wonderful man," says Frick. "The scene that sticks in my mind is the end of the 1925 World Series. Johnson was at the end of his career, and pitching the seventh and deciding game against Pittsburgh. Roger Peckinpaugh, a great shortstop who was having a terrible series, made an error. Then Kiki Cuyler hit a bases-loaded double, and Johnson was beaten.

"When the inning was over, he waited at the mound until Peckinpaugh came by on the way off the field—and he put his arm around Peckinpaugh's shoulders in a comforting gesture. That was Johnson the man."

And this was Johnson the pitcher:

He pitched 113 shutouts, a record that stands by itself.

He struck out 3,508 batters—about 1,000 more than anyone else.

He once pitched 56 consecutive scoreless innings—still a record.

He won 16 games in a row in 1912, setting an American League record that still hasn't been surpassed (although it has been tied).

He started, finished, and appeared in more games than any other pitcher.

From 1910 through 1919, he won 264 games, or more than one-third of all the games won by his team in those ten seasons (the Senators won 755).

To me, such statistics are beyond quibbling, even though I am suspicious of statistics by themselves. Anyone who calls Johnson "the greatest of all pitchers" may get an argument, but he can't be accused of being unreasonable.

In one way, however, Koufax was even more remarkable than Johnson for a little while, before the arthritis reduced his overwhelming aspects. Koufax, in his late 20's, probably had the greatest combination of stuff and craft ever seen. He perfected his control, and mastered his tactics, while he still retained all his phenomenal speed. Like Feller, he had both blazer and monster curve, but much finer control than Feller ever had. He must have been like Alexander—but only for those few peak years. Then the elbow gave out, and he retired—and, again like Johnson, enjoying universal respect for his personal qualities as well.

Finally, no discussion of this sort would be complete without mention of Babe Ruth.

Many fans, even today, are aware that Ruth was a pitcher before he became the home-run king, but few realize just how remarkable a pitcher he was.

From 1915 through 1919, Ruth was a regular starter for the Boston Red Sox. (He was a left-hander.) In 1915, his 18-8 record constituted the best winning percentage in the league. In

1916, his earned-run average of 1.75 led the league and his won-lost record was 23-12. In 1917, he won 24 and lost 13.

He pitched less than half as often in 1918 and 1919, posting records of 13-7 and 9-5. Then he was sold to the Yankees and became strictly an outfielder.

How good a pitcher would Ruth have been if he had remained one? Probably one of the best. He pitched in two World Series, in 1916 and 1918, and ran up a string of 29 consecutive scoreless innings, a record that stood until Ford broke it in 1961. Ruth's career earned-run average, for 163 games, was 2.28. He won 94 games and lost only 46, and was only 24 years old when he gave up pitching seriously. (Subsequently, at the end of a season, he would pitch an occasional game for the Yankees—and he never lost one.) At the age of 24, Alexander was just starting, Koufax had more defeats than victories, and even Johnson had only 82 victories (to Ruth's 89). Grove won his first big-league game at 25, and so did Spahn.

Certainly Ruth's native ability was prodigious. He might have become the greatest of all—but baseball history would have been inconceivably different.

22

There's Nothing New in Baseball

"There's nothing new in baseball," old-timers will tell you. They are right, to an amazing degree. Alexander Cartwright, in 1845, set the distance between bases at 90 feet. Players were sufficiently dissatisfied with their contracts to start their own league by 1890. A player hit four home runs in one game, and a perfect game was pitched, before the turn of the century.

To younger fans, baseball history really extends only as far back as the beginning of their interest. Every unusual event, experienced for the first time by some fan, seems "unprecedented." But if you stay around baseball long enough, you realize that it has all happened before—maybe not exactly the same way, but close.

But try this one on for size:

The first World Series involved the New York Mets.

In 1884.

And any present-day Met fan reading about the nineteenth-century Mets must experience a sensation of *deja vu* strong enough to make his hair curl.

The twentieth-century Mets became famous for self-inflicted defeat, bizarre situations and personalities, unaccountable popularity, and built-in inferiority caused by the discriminatory policies of older baseball organizations. Later, the Mets became something else—the all-time Cinderalla champions by actually winning a world championship in 1969, and an incredibly prosperous but harried contending team in subsequent years. But the lasting Met image, the one that provoked a library full of books when they finally did win, and the one future students of social history will try to resurrect and comprehend, is the original image of inept, lovable kookiness and, when least expected, success.

Well, that's just how it was with the old Mets, too.

"Now wait a minute, *wait a cotton-pickin' minute!!!*" the supposedly well-educated contemporary baseball fan screams at this point. "*What* Mets? What World Series? Eighteen eighty-what? Who's crazy?"

Ah, it's time to dispel some more myths.

Every fall, the baseball public is told that "the first World Series" was played in 1903, when the National League champion (the Pirates) accepted the challenge of the American League champion (the Red Sox); that there was no Series in 1904, but that starting with 1905, when the basic rules that still apply were devised, there has been such a series "for the baseball championship of the world" every year.

All that is true enough, except that history didn't begin in 1903. That was merely the first Series in which the *American League* participated; its major-league status was only two years old then. Naturally, since that time, baseball promoters have liked building up their present product by pretending that no other major leagues ever existed, and to a great entent this brain-washing has been successful.

But it's just not true. There *were* other major leagues, and they did meet in postseason championships.

The National League, still thriving, was formed in 1876. But from 1882 through 1890, there was another major league called the American Association (not to be confused with the minor league of the same name). A league called the Union Association tried in 1884, but didn't make it. The Brotherhood, or Players' League, was a full-fledged major in 1890, but failed financially. And the Federal League, which deserved major status in 1914 and 1915, finally yielded to the American and the National in a case settled by Judge Kenesaw Mountain Landis —whose participation in a compromise agreement had more to do than anything else with his eventual election as the first Commissioner of Baseball.

All these semiforgotten leagues had one thing in common: they lacked a firm working partnership with the older and stronger National; once the American League achieved that, "Organized Baseball" was on its way.

But that's the view looking backward; in the 1880s, people didn't know about such things. For all they knew, when the American Association started to succeed, there would someday be three, four, five, or ten major leagues.

And the Mets?

Here's how it all came about.

The first fully professional team, the Cincinnati Red Stockings, was formed in 1869. In 1861, a loose organization called the National Association of Baseball Players was formed. In 1876, the National League of Baseball Clubs was organized, embodying two new concepts: a set schedule centrally directed, and a partnership among clubs rather than players. In 1882, the American Association began play; and that fall, the Association champion (Cincinnati) and the National League pennant winner (Chicago) started to play a postseason series—but abandoned it after each team won one game.

The next year, no such series developed. But in 1884, a World Series to a decision was played for the first time. The National League pennant winner (Providence) accepted the challenge of the Association winner—the New York Mets.

Three games were played, all in New York, all won by Providence. Similar competitions were held through 1890, but no uniform set of rules was ever developed, so the World Series as we know it didn't really start until the twentieth century—but really in 1905, since the 1903 set was no different from the 1880s kind.

Now, what were these old Mets like? Were they merely namesakes, or true spiritual ancestors of the Casey Stengel Mets? Read on, and judge for yourself.

To begin with, the old Mets came into existence for exactly the same reason as the new Mets did: to fill the void created by the absence from New York of National League baseball for several years.

When the League started in 1876, it had a New York franchise. Late that season, the New York and Philadelphia (Athletics) teams refused to make their last scheduled western trips, because they could make more money playing exhibitions in their own areas. (Can you hear the cry? "All they think about is money. They're ruining baseball!") Since the basic principle of forming the League had been regularity of schedule, the League decided to expel New York and Philadelphia, the two most powerful teams in terms of following. By that strong action, the National League hurt itself financially but established its authority and its future.

For more than a generation, New York had been a hotbed of baseball interest. Now, in 1877, 1878, 1879, and 1880, there was no New York team in what was obviously a growing, well-functioning league. National League teams would book exhibitions with local clubs fairly frequently, and while that didn't make for perfect match-ups, it was better than nothing. Even without a home team rooting interest in the standings, New York fans could see, at least, National League stars on visiting teams.

There was, in short, money to be made.

In 1881, the Metropolitan Baseball Club was formed for the express purpose of playing exhibitions with National League teams. It was an immediate success at the gate. It played 60 games against League teams (winning 18, for a percentage of .300) and drew huge crowds. Receipts were $30,000—1881 dollars, with no income or admission taxes.

When the present Mets were formed, of course, the idea was

to bring National League stars (like Willie Mays and Stan Musial) back to New York. When they started to play in 1962, they played at the Polo Grounds.

The 1881 Mets also played at the Polo Grounds—the "old" Polo Grounds, at Fifth Avenue and 110th Street. And the crowds they drew could not be ignored by other National League teams. In 1883, the League awarded a New York franchise to John B. Day and moved in the players from the previous year's Troy (New York) team. If money was to be made, the National League wanted it.

But, the same year, the Mets acquired membership in the American Association, the rival major league.

And, who owned the Mets? The same Mr. Day who had procured the National League team, soon to be called the Giants.

There were three important differences between the leagues. The League had a 50-cent admission fee, no games on Sunday, and no liquor (or beer) sold on the grounds. The Association charged 25 cents, played on Sundays (where the law permitted), and sold beer. In fact, the Association was backed largely by beer interests (so today's widespread beer sponsorship of baseball on radio and television isn't new either).

Now Mr. Day, owning both the Giants and the Mets, had them both play at the Polo Grounds. But the Giant games meant 50-cent tickets and the Met games half as much; so, naturally enough, Mr. Day scheduled Giant games for afternoons, on the part of the field best suited for spectators; the Mets played their games in the morning, behind a canvas fence.

Equally naturally, but somewhat less justifiably, Mr. Day made another adaptation to the difference in price scales. When a Met player became very good and developed a personal following, Day would switch him to the Giants, thus strengthening the National League team at the expense of the American Association team—and just incidentally requiring the fans to pay twice as much to watch the same favorite player.

Such shenanigans, eventually, led to the demise of the Mets and the whole Association, but in the early years the Mets did have their one moment of glory—such as it was.

In 1884, the Association was a 12-team league. The Mets finished first, six and a half games ahead of Columbus. They had a great pitcher (Tim Keefe, now in the Hall of Fame) and a mighty slugger (Thomas Jefferson Esterbrook, a Staten Island boy). Later, both became Giant stars.

Providence had taken the National League pennant by a 10½-game margin over Boston (the Giants had finished in a tie for fourth). It had one of the greatest pitchers of early baseball history, Charles (Old Hoss) Radbourne. A curve-ball specialist, Radbourne's won-lost record that season was 60-12. (Overhand pitching had been allowed for the first time that year; pitchers were still expected to work every game; the pitching distance was 50 feet; and it took six balls to get a walk).

The World Series began on October 23, with the temperature in the 40's. The next morning's *New York Times* reported: "The long-looked-for series of games for the championship of the United States between the Metropolitan and Providence Baseball Clubs was begun at the Polo Grounds yesterday, and resulted in a bad defeat for the Mets. The curves of Radbourne struck terror into their hearts, and they fell easy victims to his skill. Some of the local players who have good batting records were like so many children in the hands of the pitcher of the Providence team. They made ineffectual plunges at balls that would reflect discredit on some of our third-string amateurs." (Note to modern players: they had writers who were "rippers" in those days, too.)

The details follow. The Mets made only two hits. In the first inning, Providence scored two runs off Keefe without getting a hit: he hit the first two batters and made two wild pitches; a passed ball and a sacrifice completed a typical Met inning—typical then, and typical 80 years later. Providence won, 6-0.

Underneath the box score, *The Times* account carried two additional statements:

"Both clubs play again today.

"The parade in honor of the Metropolitans has been indefinitely postponed."

So front-runners, ready to call off a parade, were in full flower, too, as far back as 1884.

The next day, Radbourne beat the Mets again, 3-1, but this time is was much more exciting. The score was 0-0 until the fifth, when, according to *The Times:* "In the fifth, Start, the first striker, was easily retired at first base and Farrell, who came next, made a base hit. The latter started to steal second. From appearances, Holbert threw him out by about five feet, but the umpire declared the runner 'not out,' a decision that failed to meet with the approval of the onlookers. Irwin 'flied' out to Roseman and Gilligan hit the ball to right field for two bases, sending in Farrell. Denny then followed and sent the ball over the picket fence in centre field, making a home run. This increased the score of the Providence Club to three runs. If the decision rendered by the umpire was unfair it proved very costly, as it defeated the Metropolitans."

It figured. As any present-day Met fan can tell you, those umpires never do give the Mets a break.

The next day, October 25, brought a denouement not even Stengel could have imagined.

Only a few hundred spectators showed up.

"When the League champions gazed on the empty seats, they turned up their noses and said they would not play," *The Times* reported.

After much argument, they took the field, but then tried to get out of playing the game by rejecting every umpire the Mets suggested. The Mets, "not to allow them any loophole by which to postpone the contest," said they'd accept any umpire Providence named—even the Providence manager.

But Providence did better: it picked Keefe, the man who pitched against them in the first two games, thus depriving the Mets of their best pitcher.

What followed could have been reenacted perfectly appropriately four-fifths of a century later at Shea Stadium.

The Mets made 10 errors. Their catcher (Charley Reipschlager, not Jesse Gonder) made six errors and was charged with two passed balls. After six innings, Providence had an 11-to-2 lead, having scored four runs in the fifth and four more in the sixth.

Keefe couldn't stand it anymore. He called the game on account of darkness.

And that's how the first World Series ended.

Two days later, that postponed parade was held, and it was a huge success. There was a torchlight procession that went from Columbus Circle to the Bowery and back to Union Square, snarling traffic and lasting for hours. Loyal enthusiasm had prevailed despite defeat.

(When the modern Mets won in 1969, official celebrations had had a lot more practice, and their ticker-tape parade up lower Broadway broke all tonnage records for confettied paper; but in the intervening 85 years, traffic congestion had evolved so spectacularly that the jams caused by the parade couldn't be easily distinguished from normal, daily Manhattan chaos.)

But before the 1885 season could start, Keefe and Esterbrook had become Giants, and Day had been forced to sell the Mets. They were bought by John G. Wiman, who moved them to Staten Island, where he had an amusement park, to promote his trolley car and ferry interests. In each of the next three years, the Mets finished seventh in an eight-team league, and after the 1887 season, they disbanded.

Many of their players wound up with the Brooklyn team in the Association—a team just starting to answer to the nickname of Trolley Dodgers. In 1890, this Brooklyn team moved into the National League and the Giant-Dodger rivalry began.

As it turned out, then, the first pennants ever won by the Giants (1888) and by the Dodgers (1890) were attained with important aid from former Mets.

It's something to think about, especially since the 1963 and 1965 Dodgers, and the 1964 Cardinals, won National League pennants (and the World Series) with help from ex-Mets of the modern era (pitchers Bob Miller and Roger Craig).

You see, it's true. There just never is anything new in baseball.

23

Whatever Became of the .300 Hitter, or, Where Did the Runs Go?

In 1930, the entire National League—including pitchers—had a batting average of .303. Bill Terry won the batting championship with .401, and 35 players hit .300 or better in 400 or more at bats. In the American League, there were 31 regulars who hit .300 and three complete teams.

In 1968, the National League had five .300 hitters and the American exactly one—Carl Yastrzemski, who won the batting championship at .301. The National League champion was Pete Rose, whose .335 beat out Matty Alou's .332, but no one else reached .320. The whole National League hit .243 and the American .230.

What happened?

These two points, 38 years apart, illustrate a real trend, not a statistical fluke. The game *has* changed, and numerical standards have changed with it. As always, the myth outlasts the reality, and the idea that .300 is the standard for distinguishing a good hitter from a bad hitter persists.

In today's baseball, that neat number is simply irrelevant. For any sort of sensible comparison between the 1970s and the 1940s, for instance, one must subtract about 30 points from the old averages. The .350 hitter of yesterday is the .320 hitter of today; the man who used to hit .300 now is doing well when he hits .270; the run-of-the-mill .250 hitter of tradition and legend now keeps his job by hitting .220; and the really weak hitters, who survive because of exceptional fielding ability, often don't reach .200.

How come?

Older players, and older fans, will often give the simplest answer: the players aren't as good as they were in the old days; nobody knows how to hit; the art has been lost.

This explanation can be dismissed as more simple-minded than simple, and as just plain silly. Athletes have improved in every measurable respect, and they have improved in baseball, too.

Other people offer a variety of pet ideas to explain the change, but no single factor is convincing.

Actually, there are perfectly good reasons for the change, almost inevitable reasons, and they are not hard to understand. One must simply recognize that each of the factors about to be listed, while insufficient in itself to account for the total drop in averages, points in the same direction. Their cumulative effect is tremendous.

These factors are:

1. Better pitching.
2. Distance hitting.
3. Bigger and better gloves.
4. More attention to defense.
5. Night games.
6. Coast-to-coast travel by air.
7. Lighter and thinner bats.
8. Bigger, more symmetrical ball parks.

Pitching is tougher in four distinct ways: (1) there are more "good" pitchers (but not "great") than there used to be, and, even more important, many fewer "poor" pitchers in the majors; (2) a much larger repertoire of pitches is used; (3) relief pitching has been developed as a specialty; and (4) more systematic attention is given to choosing the right pitch to throw.

There are more good pitchers than ever, and fewer bad ones, for one usually overlooked reason. Listen again to Eddie Stanky, who spent years developing minor-league players for the Cardinals and Mets before returning to managing with the Chicago White Sox: "You can teach pitching much more effectively than you can teach hitting," he said. "Therefore, as we spend more time and money on instruction, we produce a larger number of better pitchers, but we don't produce better hitters at the same rate. There is a lot you can show a pitcher; there is very little you can do to help a batter make contact with the ball."

Today, the major leagues are full of pitchers who have seen big-league baseball on television all their lives, who have had systematic instruction from Little League up, and ofter superior instruction in high school, college, American Legion, and rookie-league ball. In the minors, their managers are men chosen for ability to teach—not fading older players, as was so often the case in the old days.

Today's pitchers, at 19, are often thoroughly familiar with the philosophy of choosing pitches and studying hitters; they know the importance of keeping runners close to bases, and what to do in bunt situations; they have realized, from childhood on, the importance of good control instead of just throwing hard; and, on the average, they are physically bigger and stronger than their fathers.

All these things don't necessarily help a man throw harder, or more strikes, or give him a better breaking ball—but they contribute to poise and they help win ball games. Thirty years ago, pitchers had to learn the same things—but often, they learned them in the majors, in their mid-20's, and while they were learning, many hitters added to their personal records.

At the same time, the accent on youth, the careful handling, the reduction of the minors have left less and less place for the pitcher who isn't so good, or at least promising. In the old days, there were four or five regular starters, and the other five pitchers on any team represented quite a drop in ability; today, the relief men may be more talented than some of the starters.

In other words, while the best pitchers in any era were equally tough, the proportion of "patsies" is much smaller now than it used to be—and in the records, the hits off patsies are indistinguishable from the hits off good pitchers.

A generation ago, fast ball and curve, with a change of pace, constituted standard equipment. There were a few knuckleball specialists around, and Carl Hubbell was famous for his screwball. The slider was just coming into use.

Today, the slider is a standard pitch, and the pitcher who uses it increases the effectiveness of his fast ball and curve, since the slider comes right between. Various types of sinkers—including a mild version of the spitball—are also prevalent. Knuckleballers are somewhat more common, and left-handers who throw the screwball are plentiful.

Still more important, the pattern of pitching is more daring and more confusing. It is no longer possible to count on a fast ball with the count 3-0, 3-1, and 2-0; even young pitchers may throw breaking balls in such situations.

The biggest change of all is in relief pitching. A reliever used to be the man who took over when the starter failed, a measure of weakness. Today, the manager who has a good relief pitcher or two can't wait to get him into the game.

The hitter is affected adversely in three ways. First, the starters don't have to pace themselves, because they know (and the manager assures them) that relief will be available if needed, so they can throw "as hard as they can as long as they can." Second, the relief pitcher who comes into the game in the seventh, eighth, or ninth is fresh, so the hitter doesn't get a crack at a tired pitcher. Third, if the situation is crucial at the time of the pitching change, the relief pitcher is often chosen precisely because he is particularly tough for the particular hitter.

What this means to averages is readily seen. In 1930, the year of all that hitting, there were 538 complete games pitched in the National League and 560 in the American, a total of 1,098 games in which batters got to face the starter a fourth or fifth time. In 1968, with so much less hitting, there were only 897 complete games—even though there were some 400 more games played because of expansion and longer schedules. In 1930, almost half of all starters went the distance; in 1968, little more than one-fourth did. In other words, the 1930 hitters were getting a crack at a tiring starter 30 percent more often, even though the starters were getting hit harder in the first place.

Now do a little arithmetic: if a man gets one hit in his first three trips to the plate every day, and then makes out the fourth time, he is hitting .250. If he gets a hit the fourth time up every third game, he is hitting .333. In 1930, his fourth trip was against the starter approximately half the time; in 1968, he was facing a fresh and qualified reliever about three-quarters of the time. Thus the 1968 hitter, even if equal to the 1930 hitter in all other respects, might not get a hit the fourth time up every third game, but every fifth game. But that, over 150 games, would bring his average down to .300 instead of .333—and that's the 30-point difference we were talking about.

The above is an idealized example, for the sake of simplicity in numbers, but it illustrates a very real situation. The more times a good hitter can face the same pitcher in one day, the more of an advantage the hitter has (as a rule); not only does the pitcher get tired and increase his chance of making a mistake, but the batter gets more chance to adjust himself to that pitcher's motion and stuff. So the steady stream of relief pitchers has a definite effect on averages—and, in fact, that's precisely why relief pitchers are used so much: they get the job done.

All these factors—better pitching, more deliveries, more relief—are enhanced by the increasingly elaborate records managers keep, and the amount of scouting done. Outstanding pitchers always did study every opposing hitter—but many mediocre pitchers did not, or did so carelessly. And managers and coaches relied entirely on memory, which is fallible. Today, charts are kept of where every batter hit every pitch off every pitcher, and the conclusions are not left to the individual initiative of the run-of-the-mill pitcher. Managers make sure that *all* pitchers are told what only the better pitchers knew for themselves in the past.

So much for pitching. It's tougher, and it will continue to be tougher.

Almost as important is the psychology of the hitters. With very few exceptions, today's hitters are home-run minded, and have been from Little League on. They take a big swing, and a big swing means less bat control, which means a lower average —and more homers. There were plenty of homers in 1930, when Hack Wilson set the National League record of 56; but there are many more today. Through the 1930s, when the combined major league batting average was about .280, there were about 110 homers hit in every 100 games played. Throughout the 1960s, when the batting average was just under .250, there were about 160 homers for every 100 games, or almost 50 percent more.

So that situation is plain enough. Hitters, as a class, are sacrificing, quite consciously, average for power. If as many of them concentrated on just meeting the ball and going for singles as did in 1930, the averages of the 1970s would be higher.

Gloves are important in their own way. In 1930, fielders wore comparatively small finger gloves the only real function of which was to protect the hand. Today's gloves are highly effective traps that extend the fielder's range six inches or so. Infielders smother hotshots; outfielders snare long drives that would have gone off the fingers of the old gloves. To any individual hitter, this may turn half a dozen potential hits into outs during any one season—but if a man has 500 at bats, six hits is a difference of 12 points in batting average, or let's say the difference between hitting .303 (hurray!) and .291 (eh!).

Fielders not only have a better chance to grab a batted ball, they have a much greater chance of being in its path. Position play has been developed to a degree of accuracy undreamed of 20 years ago, when the "Ted Williams Shift" gave Lou Boudreau the reputation of genius. Today, extreme shifts according to batter-pitcher-pitch are routine—and again, it's not left up to the individual's initiative as much as it used to be, but centrally directed by the manager. The outstanding players, of course, always did place themselves properly; today, the ordinary players are made to do it as well.

In 1930, there was no night baseball. Since 1960, more than half of all games have been played under lights. Some lights are better than others, but no artificial lighting plant gives the batter as good seeing as normal daylight.

Combined with the visual factors of night baseball are the more important ones of irregularity in living habits. It's the combination of night game, day game, all-night plane ride, change in time zone, and mixed-up meal hours that wear a player down. A hitting *average* is a measure of consistency, and consistency is the one thing today's player cannot have. Whatever the hardships of the old days—broiling sun, no air-conditioning, bumpy train rides, and, in some cases, inferior hotels— the conditions were constant: you played ball every day, at about the same time. Today's routine (go back and look at Chapter 13) can't help but reduce a player's *average* efficiency.

In the search for home runs, players have turned to lighter bats, with thinner handles. These are easier to swing, and when they connect have a whiplash effect (like Fiberglas poles in pole vaulting, but not as extreme) that propels the ball farther. At the same time, the area of the bat that can meet the ball squarely is reduced. A heavier, thicker bat will produce a hit once in a while off the handle, but the thin bat won't. In this way, too, players have sacrificed average for power.

Finally, the parks are different, and the universally improved quality of pitching takes better advantage of them. In 1930, the National League included Ebbets Field, with a 296-foot right field; the Polo Grounds, with its 250- and 278-foot foul lines; Baker Bowl in Philadelphia, with a 280-foot right field; and Braves Field in Boston, with a 297-foot right field. In such parks, the danger of home runs in one direction often promotes a pitcher to risk giving up only a hit in another, and promotes walks. By 1972, the picture was entirely different. Of the 12 National League parks then in use, 11 had been built since 1960, all were symmetrical, and none had a foul line shorter than 330 feet. (The only "old" park, Chicago's Wrigley Field, was always a good hitting park, but its dimensions were symmetrical and reasonable.)

So far, all the factors we have mentioned have been part of an inexorable, long-term trend in favor of baseball defense. But there was also a special circumstance in the 1960s, quite unrecognized by baseball authorities until writers and statisticians beat them over the head with it.

In 1961, a record number of home runs were hit. Baseball old-timers were outraged at the idea that Maris broke Ruth's record of 60, and there was talk that the ball had been juiced up. There was also a relatively big offensive year in 1962 (although still far below the levels of the 1930s). At the same time, the competition of pro football on television was making baseball people sensitive to the charge (promoted by Madison Avenue people selling football to sponsors) that baseball was "too slow."

Someone got the idea that fewer walks would speed up the game, and the definition of the strike zone was rewritten. The actual wording didn't make much difference. The clear massage to the umpires, that their employers wanted a bigger strike zone, did.

The results were dramatic—and no one paid the slightest bit of attention. See for yourself:

	1962	1963	DIFFERENCE
Runs scored	14,461	12,780	1,681 fewer
Home runs	3,001	2,704	297 fewer
Batting average	.258	.246	12 points less
Walks	10,936	9,591	1,345 fewer
Strikeouts	17,567	18,773	1,206 more

Now, in the two adjacent years, exactly the same number of teams played the same number of games in exactly the same ball parks, with exactly the same dimensions and conditions— and with substantially the same players (taking the total population of both leagues). Also, for decades up to 1962, there had never been any change from one year to the next of the magnitude of the 1962–1963 changes, up or down.

So when, all of a sudden, there are 1,345 fewer walks and 1,206 more strikeouts, it's hard to believe in coincidence or a sudden mass hitting slump. Furthermore, the 1963 figures quickly became standard for the next few years—and in 1967 and 1968 plummeted still further. By 1968, the runs were down to 11,099, homers down to 1,995, batting average down to .236, walks down to 9,156, and strikeouts up to 19,143.

What had happened was simple enough for anyone willing to lift his head out of a sandhole to understand: a bigger strike zone gives the pitcher a bigger target, and it also forces the hitter to swing at pitches he shouldn't. Worse yet, umpires, being human, enlarged the strike zone down and away, as well as up and down, and it's the low outside pitch that causes all the trouble. All of a sudden one started to hear of strikes "on the black"—that is, on the black-rubber border half buried in the ground around the plate itself.

But if a hitter has a strike called on him on a low outside pitch, he is helpless. Now he doesn't know what's a good pitch and what isn't, and the whole art of hitting depends on avoiding "bad" pitches. Every pitcher hopes, 90 percent of the time, to hit that low outside corner. ("If a man could do that on every single pitch," Bob Lemon once said, "he'd win every single game.") Now that spot was a whole area, and a vague area at that. No wonder hitting died.

The ultimate ridiculousness of this situation was made vivid by the 1966, 1967, and 1968 All-Star Games. With the greatest hitters in baseball gathered together, and pitchers limited to three innings apiece, the games wound up 2-1, 2-1 in 15 innings (with 30 men striking out), and 1-0.

When the final figures for 1968 were in, even baseball officials couldn't ignore them. So they took a bold step: they restored the strike zone definition (which they didn't think was important), and they lowered the mound from 15 inches to 10 inches (which they did think was important).

Sure enough, in 1969 and 1970, offense revived—but only partially, because the umpires didn't shift back so quickly and, at least in part, because there was another expansion (which, temporarily, brings more poor pitchers into action).

By 1971, however, the long-term downward trend was asserting itself again; and finally, in 1973, the American League took the drastic remedy of the designated hitter rule.

Nevertheless, all the basic anti-offense tendencies of modern baseball remain in force, although their rate of effect will slow down because the big improvement in pitching has already taken place.

Perhaps the best frame of mind for the serious student of the game, or the hot-headed fan if he wants to cool off for a moment, is to apply to baseball averages the lessons learned so painfully from inflation: a dollar doesn't mean what a dollar used to mean—and a .280 average doesn't mean what it used to mean, either. Like prices, batting averages are important only in the context of the time, and the best rule of thumb for the fan of the seventies who wants to make comparisons with batting averages from the twenties and thirties is simply this: subtract 30 to 40 points from the old average before comparing it to the new.

Meanwhile, a still tighter strike zone would help bring back the kind of game that became so popular in the first place.

24

> • Yes, you hit .300, but how many runs did you knock
> in? Yes, you knocked in 100 runs, but what did you hit?
> Anonymous general manager in salary
> discussions with two players, 1912–19XX

Figures Often Lie

Statistics are the lifeblood of baseball. In no other sport are so many available, and studied so assiduously by participants and fans. Much of the game's appeal, as a conversation piece, lies in the opportunity the fan gets to back up opinions and arguments with convincing figures, and it is entirely possible that more American boys have mastered long division by dealing with batting averages than in any other way.

In one sense, baseball statistics are more valid than in any other sport (except track and field, in which, of course, they are "measurements" rather than statistics). Baseball is a game in which things happen one at a time, usually through individual effort. The batter's record is, essentially, his own, to a degree that a football player's yardage gained (thanks to blocking) or a basketball player's shooting (after being passed the ball at the proper moment) are not. The same is true for fielders and pitchers. It's not absolute, because interdependent factors do come into play, but it's much closer to absolute than in other games.

And, since all these statistics are merely elaborate ways of counting discrete events, they make some sense in a game compounded of individual happenings, rather than of a continuous flowing action as in basketball, hockey, or soccer.

In another sense, however, baseball statistics can be quite meaningless—and most of the time, they are used by fans and even players in this fashion. If one loses sight of what statistics really are, and how they operate, one can be led into marvelously logical-sounding nonsense.

The first thing to remember is that statistics merely count what has already happened; they say nothing about why.

The second is that the standard baseball statistics count only certain selected items, ignoring the effect of other equally countable items that are obviously related. For example, a man's total of runs batted in, which is recorded, is obviously influenced by his number of opportunities, i.e., the number of men on base when he batted; but this is not recorded.

The third is that many statistics have self-limiting factors, or other subtle mathematical relationships, that are universally ignored by baseball people. For example, if a team has a weak pitching staff, its total of double plays made may be high—because the weak pitching puts so many men on base that double-play opportunities are more frequent.

The fourth is that statistics, by their nature, are meaningful only for a large number of cases.

And the fifth, and by far the most important, thing is that baseball is played by human beings, whose actions cannot be described by simple numbers. A man's performance fluctuates whether or not surrounding circumstances appear unchanged.

Even with all these things in mind, however, the fiend for statistics can be led to totally incorrect conclusions, because there is one more fundamental flaw in the way standard statistics are kept. They record *how much*, but not *when*, and in the winning and losing of ball games, the *when* is all-important.

After all, the box score says that a man who got two hits in four times up had a good day. But the two hits may have been wasted singles, while the two times he made out, the bases may have been loaded with two out. His team lost the game, and he definitely did not have a good day. Another box score shows that a pitcher struck out 11, so he must have had "bad luck" losing the game, 3-2. But the box score won't show that with one out in the eighth inning, and the score tied, and a man on third, and a weak hitter at bat, our unlucky pitcher didn't succeed in getting one of his 11 strikeouts when he needed it, but gave up a long fly that scored the winning run.

The question of "when" permeates all baseball numbers, from the smallest to the largest scale. A run scored in the second inning of a game is not the same as a run scored in the eighth; scored early, it affects all subsequent strategy—it may keep a pitcher in the game instead of forcing him out for a pinch hitter, it may alter bunt situations and defensive alignments. A winning streak early in the season, putting a team in first place, is not the same as a winning streak of the same number of games in September, when that team is already out of the race.

Statistics, by their very objectivity, can't reflect such things, but the reality of baseball is built on exactly such factors.

Here are some common, almost universal, misuses of statistics, showing how myths are promoted and realities misunderstood.

Fallacy No. 1: Statistics can be used to predict. They can't, except in terms so broad as to be self-evident.

Fallacy No. 2: Statistics can be used to prove a point. They can *convince*, which is quite different and important in its own right, but they can prove only the event they record, not something else about it.

Fallacy No. 3: Statistics can be used to compare. Again, it is a question of scale. One can say, of course, that a .300 hitter is better than a .200 hitter, but one hardly needs statistics to see that. Attaching value judgments, however, to the difference between .310 and .290 is simply invalid, on the basis of statistics alone.

This third fallacy goes to the heart of the difficulty. The underlying assumption, in all statistical comparisons, is "other things being equal." But other things are *never* equal.

If one tries to compare figures for different eras, one is immediately immersed in different conditions, many of which the statistic user doesn't even know. In 1930, the ball was different from the one used in 1920, or 1960. Parks were different, styles were different, even rules were different. Until 1950, even the height of the mound differed in various parks. (It was then standardized at 15 inches.)

Such differences have small consequences, it's true—but it is precisely these small consequences that are being compared when one argues about players of different eras. One doesn't, very often, compare a star of today with a nobody of yesterday, or vice versa; one argues about a .341 of Ted Williams and a .367 of Ty Cobb, and within that sort of statistical range the differing conditions outweigh the difference in numbers.

But even within an era, and within the same season, comparisons must be made with care. An "average" is exactly that—an abstraction arrived at by "averaging out" a large number of cases. Only when a season is over is the true "average" for a player's performance known; the grestest of all statistical fallacies is extrapolation from insufficient data, the "at this rate" type of reasoning. A man who hits 10 homers in the first 20 games is *not* likely to hit 81 in 162 games, and, while every baseball fan recognizes the flaw in that example, dozens of similar mistakes are made every day in thinking about less familiar categories than homers.

Furthermore, even in the same season, players on different teams play a different proportion of games in various parks, which are shaped differently, have different ball-carrying characteristics, and are in turn affected by changes of weather and time of year. Also, individual hitters don't all face the same pitchers the same number of times, and neither hitters nor pitchers face each other under identical conditions of fatigue, health, and efficiency, or in similar game situations.

Take a particular pitcher. Let's say he starts against the Yankees six times (once in each series). Already, we're dealing with a very small number. In those six games, he may pitch to Mickey Mantle a total of 20 times. Suppose, this year, it happened that 18 of those times Mantle batted with no one on base, and that in two of the games a strong wind was blowing in. Our hypothetical pitcher, then, was usually able to avoid giving Mantle a really good pitch to hit, and when he did, Mantle hit two long flies that the wind kept in the park. That year, Mantle got one hit in 16 at bats, and four walks, off this pitcher—an "average" of .087.

Now this statistic becomes available to everyone (especially radiomen, who need such statistics to fill their word volume), and the pitcher has been established as being "tough for Mantle."

In reality, though, only Mantle can say if this pitcher was tough for him. The next year, things break differently: the pitcher has the same equipment, but now Mickey comes up often with men on base, and walks cannot be risked. The pitches are a little better, Mantle creams a couple for three-run homers—and suddenly the statistics are reversed.

This is the sort of thing that goes on all the time, and especially for players not as prominent as Mantle. It all *could* be recorded statistically, but it isn't—and it isn't worth the effort. The men who have to play know perfectly well how to allow for the immense number of variables involved; and the fans, who can get satisfaction from the illusion of order that rudimentary (but often invalid) statistics provide, would be merely overwhelmed by any attempt to give a truer mathematical picture of what goes on.

For this reason, many fans are perplexed, and hurt, when they find that baseball professionals pay little attention to some statistic the fan prized. On the other hand, players care passionately about those statistics that affect—they think—their salaries: batting average, home runs, runs batted in, errors, earned runs, victories.

The tone of the player's interest is quite different; he doesn't care what the figures prove, only what they say. He wants credit for a .300 average, does not want to be charged with an error or an earned run. But here, most players are just as misdirected in their attitudes as the fans. Actually, even these statistics—as distinct from slightly better statistics—don't have any effect on the player's earning power.

The fact is, ball clubs pay whatever they feel they have to. A star doesn't need statistics to prove his value, and the ordinary player has no bargaining power anyhow. What happens is that general managers, who are professional businessmen, *use* statistics as an arguing device when talking salary with players, very few of whom are professional businessmen.

The player, who probably grew up as a fan, has come to accept statistics at face value, and everyone who ever signed him to a contract did his best to keep his illusions intact. So the player believes, sincerely, that he might get that extra $2,000 if his batting average is ten points higher. But he is, of course, kidding himself. The club has decided, on whatever basis, what it is willing to pay this player. The manager, and through him the front office, certainly know what the player has contributed to the team's success, in the invisible as well as in the countable ways, and they know which statistics are quirks and which reflect real value.

The player may, and usually does, disagree about his value; but statistical demonstration of it is simply irrelevant, because for every positive statistic a negative statistic can be cited—and that's exactly how general managers work when a player falls into the trap of number citing.

Such conversations have become ritual:

"I hit .289," says the player, "more than any other guy on the club who played over 100 games."

"Sure," says the G.M., "but how many runs did you knock in? Only 44."

"But I was leading off most of the season," the player protests, "so how could I knock in a lot of runs?"

"But a lead-off man could steal more bases," says the G.M.

"Last year I stole twice as many, but you told me to lay off."

"You were getting thrown out too much."

They settle, and in comes the next player.

"You know I got to be worth more money," he says, "batting in 112 runs. Only two other guys in the majors knocked in that many, and how many hit 36 home runs?"

"You did all right," the G.M. admits, "but since when does a .262 hitter command that kind of salary? And you ought to knock in runs, with the lead-off man hitting .289 and getting all those walks. Besides, how come you got only 50-some walks? A slugger like you should get twice as many."

And so on. It is all what Nero Wolfe calls "flummery."

All this is not to imply that baseball statistics have *no* meaning. They have a great deal. The trick is to keep clearly in mind just which meaning is valid and which isn't. As a large-scale guide, they are quite sound. Over a period of several hundred times at bat, a man will perform quite in line with his lifetime average.

Also, to the professional baseball man, many implicit qualities go with the phrase ".300 hitter" or ".250 hitter" or "20-game winner," qualities not taken into account by the fan who uses the same terms. The fan's orientation, and knowledge, is focused at the numerical proportion involved; the professional is aware of a complex context—a certain degree of bat control and sensible hitting pattern, a certain proportion of luck, a balancing of hot streaks and cold streaks, a particular discipline and set of physical abilities—these make up a ".300 hitter." To the professional, an established .300 hitter whose average is .260 at the moment is still considered a .300 hitter; while a .250 hitter who has made 60 hits in his first 180 trips may have, incontrovertibly, a .333 average, but he is not yet a ".300 hitter."

The following checklist should help one keep the fascinating subject of statistics in perspective:

1. A man hitting .293 is not necessarily "hitting better" than

someone hitting .286, or even .276—although he certainly is hitting better than someone at .222; in other words, a slight difference is not significant at all.

2. Relatively small differences on the field can seem like big differences in numbers. For a man who has 300 official at bats with the season half over, the difference between .333 and .290 is 13 hits; the difference between .290 and .250 is 12 hits. Half a season is about 80 games. In other words, the difference between .250 and .290 is about one hit every seventh game—and lucky bounces, ball-park variations, scorer's decisions, luck of the draw in pitching opponent, and a host of other factors all must be figured in. Two slow hoppers and a fortunately placed pop fly, in the course of a month, can make the difference—or, in the other direction, four or five hard line drives that are caught.

3. All cumulative statistics—homers, runs batted in, strike-outs—should be considered in the light of opportunities, which are not included as part of the statistic.

4. Comparisons within one team are most valid; within one league, next so; across the two major leagues, of doubtful value; to previous years, increasingly unreliable the more years involved.

5. Players are not automatons; they vary in ability from week to week, and especially over the years. The most common mistake, made even by managers sometimes, is to keep thinking that because a man keeps his identity he keeps his ability, that the reliable name is still reliable in action. But a .300 hitter one year, even while relatively young, may not be a .300 hitter the next; and to distinguish between a slump, which is temporary, and a permanent change in effectiveness is the hardest judgment to make in baseball.

All these warnings apply to the use of statistics to prove, analyze, or determine a choice. The guiding idea is that statistics are a by-product, not a cause; a description, not a law; and an isolation of a few, almost arbitrary, factors from dynamic reality. In fact, that's the best thing to keep in mind: the word statistics suggests the word "static," and, in the real world, events are dynamic, not static.

Statistics as *records*, however, are another story. They are not merely valid; they are the whole business, by definition. Categories of records may be carried to ridiculous extremes, or to amusing lengths, depending on your point of view, but a record is a record is a record—and, strangely enough, in this one indisputably appropriate area of statistics, people still tend to go wrong by introducing the very value judgments they ignore when dealing in comparisons for analysis.

The Roger Maris case is the best illustration.

In 1961, Maris hit 61 homers, breaking Babe Ruth's hallowed mark. Two-thirds of the way through the season, Commissioner Ford Frick had issued his famous "asterisk" ruling, although he didn't use the word asterisk. In 1927, when Ruth hit 60 homers, the schedule called for 154 games. In 1961, it was 162 games. Therefore, said Frick, to break Ruth's mark, Maris would have to hit 61 homers in the first 154 games.

Now, if you say that fast enough, it may sound reasonable. But if you start to think about it, the argument evaporates.

Let's start with semantics: a "season" record is either a record for one complete season, or it is nothing at all. Yes, 162 games is more than 154, but 154 is more than 140, and it just happened that during the same season, 1961, Sandy Koufax broke the National League record for strikeouts—which Christy Mathewson had set in 1903, when the schedule called for 140 games. Why didn't Frick insist on "asterisking" Koufax's record? Because he wasn't aware of it, and no one had paid any attention to such a difference since 1904; but Ruth's record had strong emotional overtones, so this number-of-games issue was not only raised but widely supported.

But what about the numbers themselves? When a tie game is played, all the individual records count, but the game is replayed to a decision. Thus the very 1927 Yankees, for whom Ruth hit 60, played 155 games that season—and Ruth missed four of them. But the Detroit Tigers, back before World War I, had played 162 games in one season, although the schedule called for 154 (they had 10 ties, and two scheduled games were unplayed); what about records that might have been set by that Tiger team?

And what about logic? If 154 games, why the first 154? If some equivalence is being sought, when can the question of schedule balance be ignored? In the 154-game schedule, the Yankees faced each of seven other teams 22 times; in the 162-game schedule, nine opponents are met 18 times apiece—already an irreconcilable difference. But taking the first 154 games of a 162-game schedule means that eight games—with only two or three opponents—are to be arbitrarily ignored. For that matter, why not the last 77 games of one year and the first 77 of the next?

Anyhow, the whole idea of using the same number of games is an attempt to level off opportunities—but the real opportunities are measured by the number of times a player comes to bat, not by the number of games his team happens to play. Now, the 1927 Yankees had an exceptionally strong hitting team, which batted around more often, and players at the top of the batting order came to bat more frequently than the 1961 Yankees did. In fact, a little research shows that Ruth, in 1927, came to bat 692 times—and Maris, in 1961, came up 698 times.

Which standard should be used, then? Times up? Games played? Games scheduled? Official times at bat?

Why bother?

A season is a season is a season, and the Frick-Maris case—well-intentioned on Frick's part but quite unfair to Maris—is an instance of the mess that can result when statistics are used unthinkingly.

Which is how they are used 90 percent of the time.

25

· **See you at Grossinger's.**
Edward (Whitey) Ford, July, 1966

Department of Anticlimax: World Series and All-Star Games

To the fan, there is no question as to what constitutes the high point of the baseball season: the World Series. More Americans watch World Series games on television than any other sport event; more newspapermen cover it, and more words are written about memorable happenings in past World Series than about any other single sports subject.

To many fans, an important subsidiary climax comes in mid-July, when the annual major-league All-Star Game is played. The most glamorous and most successful players are gathered on one field, and the best-of-the-best generate a sort of excitement ordinary games can't provide.

To ball players, one word covers both subjects: overrated.

One of the greatest disillusions an ordinary fan can be subjected to is exposure to the real attitude of professional baseball people toward the World Series and All-Star Games.

It is disillusioning because, first of all, it comes as a shock, and then because this shocking attitude can be easily misunderstood in the other direction, so as to appear completely callous.

Most players *do* have some special, favorable feelings about these two extravaganzas, but the nature of these feelings is far removed from what fans imagine.

Consider the World Series. To the fan, winning it—the baseball championship of the world—certainly seems to be the most important goal a player can have.

But to the player—yes and no. The real trick, you see, is to get into the World Series. Everything after that is gravy.

There are two considerations: economics and a sense of proportion.

Ball players are making a living; their interest in victory is directly tied to their interest in income. And income is increased primarily by winning a pennant.

The difference, in round numbers, between a winning share and a losing share of a World Series is about $5,000. The difference between getting into the World Series, even if you lose it, and finishing first in your division but losing the playoff is about $6,000. And the difference between finishing first in your division, even if you lose the playoff, and finishing second is about $6,000.

So getting there is the important thing. If you finish first in your division, you get at least $6,000 extra, and maybe $16,000 if you go the rest of the way. But once you're in the World Series, you've already collected at least $15,000 in prize money, and the most you can get is another $5,000. Clinching first place, and then winning the playoff for the league championship, are the *really* tense and important situations.

But once it's won, the big battle is over. The big lump of extra money has been achieved, and the bargaining power and status for next year's contract discussion have been gained. After this long-term strain, the Series itself cannot avoid being something of an anticlimax.

A deeper self-interest than immediate dollars is involved. The player's long-run reputation, and his earning power, are tied to winning a pennant. He won't admit, easily, that this protracted achievement can be downgraded by losing a World Series.

That's where the sense of proportion comes in. Everyone who lives with baseball knows it is a game of averaging out, that "anything can happen in a short series." A 162-game schedule produces a "true" champion, although even so his margin of victory may be only one game; but a four-out-of-seven series, in any serious baseball sense, is too short to prove anything. To begin with, two outstanding pitchers can dominate it and nullify the 25-man balance it took to win a pennant; then, the normal complement of lucky bounces and other fortuitous happenings play a disproportionate role in determining the outcome. During a season, there is nothing unusual about the last-place team winning four out of seven, at some point, from the league leaders, and a World Series is no more meaningful than that.

Of course, it is nice to win. Winning a Series touches the mainspring of most professional athletes—competitive pride. The winners are properly delighted, but the losers are not nearly as despondent as the public expects—because they really haven't lost much. They got their pennant, the extra money, the reputation for the future.

And, perversely enough, this dampening of intense emotion is truest of the moment the fans consider the ultimate in excitement—a seventh game. Once a World Series gets to that point, there really is nothing left to prove; the record shows the teams were evenly matched. The players, who began spring training before March 1, are likely to feel, on October 20 or 21, fatigue more than anything else.

Let's return to the arithmetic. The players on any pennant-winning team can be divided into three classes: a superstar or two or three, making between $75,000 and $150,000 a year in salary; a group of established regulars, earning between $20,000 and $50,000; and the remainder, rookies and marginal players, making under $20,000.

To a man earning $100,000 a year, the $20,000 extra he may make by winning the World Series is a significant amount, worth working for all year. Such a player also makes considerable outside income through endorsements, and being on a pennant winner greatly enhances his value in this area.

But whether the final payoff for the Series is $20,000 or $15,000 doesn't matter very much. In his tax bracket, he probably can't keep more than half the difference anyhow. So, in real money, the difference between winning and losing that seventh game is $2,500—and he has spent about 10 extra days beyond the end of the regular schedule to play those seven games. The money, then, is simply not that important.

Pay no attention, then, when you read over and over about "money players" coming through in the World Series. They were "money players" getting there, perhaps, but by the time the seventh game comes around, they are almost pure amateurs: only the honor of winning is left.

And this is what is hard to emphasize correctly: the honor *is* important, it is an incentive, and pride runs deep—but failing to get it just doesn't carry the same disappointment that failing to win a pennant does.

On the other hand, to the man working for $20,000 a year, winning the World Series means doubling his pay, as well as establishing his status on a new level. To him, the financial difference between winning and losing is considerable; he may keep $4,000 of that $5,000 difference, and that's a very large portion of his total income. But it is precisely these low-paid, marginal players who get little opportunity to do anything decisive in a World Series, if they play at all. The spotlight is on the stars, most of the time.

The established pros in between, in the $50,000-a-year bracket, aren't as hungry as the newcomers, nor as blasé as the stars, but they too have been around for a while, and know that the big job was done when they got into the Series.

That's why you'll hear players say, over and over, with obvious sincerity: "I'd like to play in a World Series." They don't say they'd like to "win" one, although, of course, they would; but their ambition centers on "getting there," for both reasons —finances and permanent distinction.

And that's why, in dressing room celebrations by winners, you'll see the greatest animation being displayed by the least familiar faces, while in the losing dressing room a remarkable degree of calm well-being abounds.

But the World Series, however subdued, is still a contest with money at stake, along with prestige and the raw material of memory. The All-Star Game isn't even that.

In their hearts, most players look upon the All-Star Game as an only slightly mitigated nuisance. Financially, nothing at all is at stake—directly. The players who take part get gifts as mementos, but that's it. Emotionally, it's just plain silly: no matter how much a fan wants to consider it "a test of strength between the two leagues," and no matter how often baseball people (under pressure from their bosses) speak of it in such terms for promotional reasons, the idea that any one baseball game can "prove" anything simply can't be taken seriously. And it isn't even a real game: pitchers are limited to three innings.

Physically, it is a chore. The players must come from all corners of the country, often after playing a Sunday doubleheader, and scramble to get to their next assignment immediately after the All-Star Game. Just when a three-day rest would be most welcome to those players who have been working hardest— after all, that's why they're all-stars—they must put in two extra trips and one extra game.

Professionally, it is a risk. The list of players who suffered severe injury in All-Star Games is a long one, headed by Ted Williams and Dizzy Dean.

Injury, of course, is a constant risk in baseball; both sides, employer and player, accept it as a possibility in the line of duty. Neither, however, looks upon it in the same light in an exhibition game, because the club, as a business, doesn't stand to gain anything from an exhibition victory.

The All-Star Game is a glorified exhibition game, nothing more. The player who breaks a bone playing in it, and loses half a season of effectiveness, gets no appreciation from his own general manager in the next contract discussion. The club will agree it wasn't his fault, but there remains a large psychological gulf between facing the consequences of putting out for the club "in a regular game" and in an exhibition. Less drastically, the player whose record suffers a bit from accumulated fatigue doesn't really get consideration for his All-Star appearance, which robbed him of rest.

All these are legitimate reservations on the part of players. It is easy to castigate them as lazy or selfish, but their objections are valid.

The clubs, too, have no enthusiasm for the game. They make no money from it; it disrupts the regular schedule, indirectly causing some team to lose some desirable home date; it risks valuable property—the players—for no chance of gain; and it's a headache to the organization that plays host in any particular year.

Why, then, does it exist?

Basically, it is a benefit—a charity game with the receipts earmarked for the players' pension fund. As such, it is a sacred cow. And to the public, it is a sacred cow because the fans, apparently, love it. It would be terrible public relations to try to abandon it now.

In any case, to abandon it would require a majority vote among the 900 or so members of the Major League Baseball Players Association. Of these, 840 get a three-day vacation in midseason while the other 60 take part in an event that feeds a pension fund—and the ones who worry most about future pensions are the ones most unlikely ever to qualify for an All-Star Game. The situation thus created is not unknown to politicians, and any well-trained political scientist—or any man in the street, stopped at random—can tell you how that vote would come out.

But don't the players, the better players, that is, feel some sense of obligation, and enjoy the honor bestowed?

Yes, they do—some.

The honor, of course, consists of being *chosen*. Almost all players respond to this, and want to be tabbed "the best" at their position, at least a few times. But the fact is that, once chosen, going through with the playing of the game is just a chore.

It's a chore many players accept as an obligation, to their pension fund and to the public, with good grace. But an obligation is not the same as an enthusiasm, and the one thing that characterizes the whole All-Star operation, from the inside, is lack of enthusiasm.

When the World Series was young, and when baseball still had a monopoly on the attention of America's sports fans—let's say, up to the 1930s—what happened in the World Series was truly considered earthshaking. The "hero" or "goat" of a particular Series was remembered for years, and the sense of accomplishment that went with success was much greater. And, it should be realized, the relative value of winning and losing shares made a much bigger difference in an era of low regular pay and insignificant income taxes.

But this is an affluent world, and the competition for attention is ever increasing. The World Series hero is merely last week's television celebrity, quickly susperseded by other celebrities in other fields, and buried by the weight of baseball history even within his own. The memorability quotient of events in the 17th World Series ever played was necessarily higher than that of the 57th.

In short, almost all players, a great many fans, and the mass of nonfan population have become much more sophisticated about the meaning of sports "drama."

So don't look for real, as distinct from traditional, climaxes of "pressure" in the World Series, or in an All-Star Game, even when it is seen by 60,000,000 television viewers simultaneously. Interesting as they may be, these settings just don't involve the participants in the most intense forms of combat and tension.

Pennant races, however, do. That's the real, unadulterated excitement—the last couple of weeks of a closed race, involving perhaps four teams, with the whole season's success riding on every bounce, pitch, and decision. That's the real game for high stakes, and because it takes this tension so long to build, and because it is sustained so long and rises so gradually to the final resolution, baseball at that time provides a type of all-encompassing thrill, for both player and fan, that no other game can match.

26

The Changing Scene

When Babe Ruth hit 708 American League home runs, between 1915 and 1934, he hit all of them in nine ball parks: Fenway Park, Boston; the Polo Grounds and Yankee Stadium, New York; Shibe Park, Philadelphia; Griffith Stadium, Washington; Navin Field (now Tiger Stadium), Detroit; Comiskey Park (now White Sox Park), Chicago; Sportsman's Park, St. Louis; and League Park, Cleveland.

When Hank Aaron surpassed that one-league total by reaching No. 709 late in the 1973 season, he too was playing in his 20th season. But he had played (and cleared fences) in 23 different ball parks.

That's another measure of how rapidly baseball's physical surroundings have been changing.

The first great flurry of ball-park building was just before World War I. Between 1900 and 1915, virtually all the fields that made baseball legend were opened: the ones mentioned above in the American League—except for Yankee Stadium, which opened in 1923—and Forbes Field (Pittsburgh), Redlands (later Crosley) Field (Cincinnati), Wrigley Field (Chicago), Ebbets Field (Brooklyn), Braves Field (Boston), the Polo Grounds, and Sportsman's Park (which was shared by the Cardinals and Browns). Philadelphia's Baker Bowl, was older.

The romance in those names is completely uncommunicable to anyone under 30—probably under 40.

All these ball parks, with the exception of the Polo Grounds and Yankee Stadium, had similar topography. The playing area was more or less rectangular, with home plate in one corner, with a double-decked steel-and-concrete grandstand extending down each foul line. The outfield was backed by a high fence or bleachers. As time went on, some of the parks (like Ebbets, Comiskey, and Navin) had upper decks added behind the outfield. The Polo Grounds, essentially an oval, had home plate at one wide end, making extremely short foul lines and a very long center field. And Yankee Stadium, designed to make the most of Ruth's talents, had an odd shape like a bouquet of flowers with home plate at the narrow end, and right center field much closer to home than left center field.

But between 1923 and 1953—a space of 30 years—no new major league baseball park was built in America. (In Cleveland, a huge municipal stadium was built in 1931, but baseball fit into it awkwardly and only occasionally until the 1940s.)

In 1953, the Braves moved from Boston to Milwaukee, partly because a park was available: County Stadium, newly built but exactly like the existing parks in basic design. When the Browns moved from St. Louis to Baltimore in 1954, and the Athletics from Philadelphia to Kansas City in 1955, they occupied enlarged, existing parks—refurbished but not really new—that had already been used for minor league baseball and football. And when the Dodgers went west to Los Angeles in 1958, they occupied a football stadium, the Memorial Coliseum, while the Giants, moving into San Francisco, took over the existing minor-league park, Seals Stadium.

So it was 1960 before a truly new ball park was built: Candlestick, in San Francisco. It was hard to compare it structurally to older parks, but one thing could be said about it: it wasn't very good by any standard.

The new wave, then, really began with Walter O'Malley's new home for his Dodgers, in Chavez Ravine. He built it with private capital after the city gave him 300 acres of downtown Los Angeles for free, as an inducement to move. And O'Malley, enormously capable and alert, had a magnificent structure in mind. It was the first building designed exclusively for baseball since Yankee Stadium, and all the new ideas and technology of the 1950s went into it.

It was a lopsided oval, narrow at the home plate end like Yankee Stadium (putting the seats close to the foul lines), but perfectly symmetrical in outfield contour. It had no posts. It had eight levels. It was surrounded by a huge parking area, with parking locations related to seat locations. It had wide aisles, clean and extensive concessions stands, a couple of restaurants, and a stadium club for season-ticket holders.

It was referred to as the Taj Mahal on the Freeways, and it deserved to be. And it took him only eight years to pay it off, as the Dodgers made season attendances of 2,000,000 commonplace.

Almost all the parks that followed took their essential design from Dodger Stadium. And they followed rapidly: Washington in 1962, New York in 1964, Anaheim in 1966, and so forth, with Pittsburgh, Cincinnati, Philadelphia, and Kansas City coming with a rush in the 1970s.

But in Houston, where it was so humid, Judge Roy Hofheinz had a grander thought: a dome. An enclosed, air-conditioned ball park would avoid the possibility of a rainout and be the Eighth Wonder of the Modern World.

It was. It opened in 1965, and indoor baseball came to the major leagues.

But there were problems.

The dome consisted of thousands of little panes of glass, to let in the daylight for day games. But when the sun shone, these panes produced a blinding glare for any fielder who looked up. So they had to be made opaque.

That solved the problem of visibility. But it also killed the grass. Now you had a magnificent indoor baseball field, protected from the elements—and a plain dirt surface.

But technology, which was sending people to the moon

from a control headquarters only a few miles away, was developing on other fronts. Artificial grass-like surfaces were being invented, and one called AstroTurf was installed.

Purists hated it. But it didn't wear out, and you could easily play a football game one day and a baseball game the next. And that, of course, was exactly the economic answer for "multipurpose" stadia—which most of the new ones, built with local government funds, had to be.

Artificial turf is great for maintenance, but it's hard on the feet (because it gets so hot), and it makes the ball bounce more sharply. At first, it was taken for granted that the traditional dirt infield would remain. But the new parks in Cincinnati and Philadelphia were covered entirely, with just little dirt cutouts around each base, home plate, and the mound. This made the ball act faster still.

So the baseball scene in 1973 was efficient, comfortable, economical—and far less romantic.

Some of the old parks remained, especially in the American League: Boston, Detroit, Chicago, and New York—where Yankee Stadium was closed at the end of the 1973 season for a two-year modernization and reconstruction. Chicago had an artificial surface now, but the contours were the same.

In Cleveland, Municipal Stadium had been worked over several times, and had a modern, symmetrical interior. Minnesota had a park begun in the 1950s and enlarged when the majors came in 1961. Oakland's park—an unroofed oval, cold and uncomfortable, but off a freeway with good parking—dated from the mid-1960s. The Milwaukee Brewers were in County Stadium, the Angels in a miniature model of Dodger Stadium in Anaheim. Baltimore was still in its original stadium, threatening to move if a new one wasn't built. Kansas City had the newest park of all, with artificial turf and marvellous fountains. But the Texas Rangers, two years removed from being the Washington Senators, were still in a makeshift minor-league park between Dallas and Fort Worth.

As for the National League, everything had changed. Aaron, who had never changed teams (although the Braves themselves shifted from Milwaukee to Atlanta in 1966), saw all but one of the parks he played in as a rookie disappear.

The exception was Wrigley Field, which doesn't even have lights. It's a tribute to baseball's ability to cling to the past—in this case, to the attractive past. But the lovely, cozy ball park itself has a radical history: it was built for the use of a renegade Federal League team in 1914, and passed into orthodox baseball when the Federal League failed.

But in New York, it was now Shea Stadium instead of the Polo Grounds (where Aaron had once faced the Giants and later the Mets). Ebbets Field was gone altogether. In Philadelphia, it was the new Veterans Stadium (artificial turf) instead of Shibe Park (which he had known as Connie Mack Stadium). In Pittsburgh, it was Three Rivers instead of Forbes Field. In Cincinnati, it was Riverfront instead of Crosley. In St. Louis, it was Busch Stadium instead of the old Busch Stadium (which had been Sportsman's Park). In L.A., it was Dodger Stadium; and in San Francisco, Candlestick; and in San Diego, a beautiful new-style stadium; in Houston, the Astrodome; in Montreal, a "temporary" small park. These were places no one imagined, in 1954, would ever have National League baseball at all.

The new structures are truly marvellous, by and large, for sight lines, creature comfort, dressing room facilities, playing conditions, lighting, and access. They are all in the 45,000–55,000 seat range, which seems the optimum for daily baseball economics.

Most have, or soon will have, electronic "message boards" instead of straightforward old "scoreboards." They do give out-of-town scores, occasionally, and standard information on the current game; but they are, essentially, advertising and promotion devices—carrying ads, promos, blurbs, cartoons, acknowledgments of "groups" that bought tickets, and, once in a while, a bit of factual information. They are also used as cheer-leading devices, along with the organs that provide music at every break in the action.

And this, perhaps, is the saddest and most far-reaching change of all: the baseball customers of the 1970s seem to respond, docile and unthinking, to the organized cheer-leading and manipulation of the management.

There is much complaint among older fans that players today aren't as "dedicated," or "hungry," or "absorbed in baseball" as players used to be. But fans today, evidently, are less creative and less independent in their judgments than they used to be—at least wherever there are electronic scoreboards to tell them when and what to cheer.

It's just one more small step toward show-business-as-usual and away from the special quality that baseball, at its best, affords.

27

· **T'run 'im a fish!**

Requiem for a Bum
(Fan Prototypes)

In the final analysis, this whole complicated world of baseball exists for one reason: its audience.

Directly, every step in the development of this elaborate structure has been dictated by economics; but behind the economics lies the only thing that makes everything else possible, the continuing interest of the fans. In the long run, only what the fans accept is economically feasible. Indirectly, then, the fans dictate what baseball will be like, in a very real sense.

This has changed, and is still changing. In the 1920s, the fans proved, in the most convincing fashion (by buying tickets), that they preferred home runs and high scores to low-score slickness—and both the rules and the equipment (the ball) were changed. In the 1930s and 1940s, they showed that they would or could patronize night games more than weekday day games—and the game changed again. Today, the opportunity to watch television frequently, and to take a long automobile ride to a ball park occasionally, is constantly increasing—and baseball is catering more and more to television and parking needs.

And who are these fans? An amorphous mass? Interchangeable spectators? Simply "the market"?

To one who travels widely on the baseball beat, the particular character of fans in different cities becomes quickly apparent. Unlike an audience in a theater, which is essentially passive, spectators at a sport event are very much part of the action. They root; that, it can't be repeated too often, is the essence of spectator sport—rooting, not merely watching.

And they all seem to root a little differently in different towns.

In St. Louis, they are sentimental and sportsmanlike. *Gemütlichkeit*, the German word for a hard-to-translate homey fellowship, was often used in connection with Milwaukee, but it really applies to St. Louis. Cardinal fans would rather lose with familiar faces than see their established heroes uprooted in an attempt to build a better team. They want to win, of course, but they want to win with Musial, Schoendienst, Slaughter, and so forth.

In Philadelphia, they are knowledgeable and observant—and vicious. Home team players, as well as visitors, get their roughest verbal treatment in Philadelphia when the wolves are aroused, and, once aroused, nothing escapes the notice of these few but outspoken voices of the people. When it comes to throwing things, they're among the best, too.

In Detroit, the stands behind the outfield often contain better arms than those on the field. With a double-decked stand all the way around, the Detroit park makes outfielders ideal for target practice, and the amount of junk showered on them is hard to beat. The tenor of the crowd as a whole, however, tends to be reasonable. Detroit has a rich baseball tradition, the team is taken seriously but not quite as a life-and-death matter, and visiting stars are appreciated.

In Boston, visiting stars of the magnitude of Joe DiMaggio and Mickey Mantle are positively worshipped, but the dominant tone of the citizenry seems to be frustration. Perhaps that's why the home team has always had so much trouble with the press. Boston fans seem to demand reassurance, to seek recognition as "the greatest" on the flimsiest of evidence—and then to turn bitterly on their heroes when they turn out to be merely human (or, in recent years, even less).

In San Francisco, a large part of the population still seems to resent the fact that the Giants came from New York, a place toward which San Franciscans feel a certain amount of envy—not for what New York is, but for the relative importance the world assigns New York instead of San Francisco. The home players, therefore, get the sort of rough time they get in Boston, but not quite as bad, while the visitors don't really exist.

In Houston, they aren't baseball fans yet—just Texans. The Astrodome is the place to go, and the electronic scoreboard dictates every cheer and response, and those rugged individualistic Texans respond as dutifully as woolly Pavlovian lambs. That isn't to say they don't know baseball—they do, because Texas has always been one of the main areas of baseball activity; but they seem to disconnect themselves from normal reactions when they enter the roofed arena, even though they know better.

Minnesotans are the politest of all fans, the quietest, and, generally speaking, the neatest in appearance. They applaud more often than they cheer, and the time between climaxes—which is most of the time—is unusually peaceful for a ball park. They were the same way as basketball fans when they had the Lakers; they sat on their hands most of the time. They do root hard, and take great interest and pride in their team, but they just don't yell as much. And they don't throw things.

Yankee Stadium crowds must be divided into two categories: regular fans and transients. The transients make up a large portion of Yankee attendance, if one includes season boxes occupied by guests of the firms who own them. The regulars, however, can be described by one word: disrespectful. They are fickle, egging the opposition on as often as rooting for the Yankees; they pick some Yankees to hate (like Roger Maris) and never let up; they throw garbage for the fun of it, as well as occasionally in anger; but, unlike Philadelphians, they don't misbehave out of any deep (and perhaps hysterical) commitment to the fortunes of their own team, but out of a sort of impersonal banditry. As for loyal Yankees fans, they are uniformly chickenhearted—terrified of losing, and never secure with less than a ten-run lead in the eighth. Not even years of adversity, since the last Yankee pennant in 1964, have altered this essential moral cowardice, although a great deal of humility has been imposed. A new group of Yankee followers, attracted to underdogism, has been attracted since the team became second to the Mets in the New York picture, but even these are tinged with fickleness and are ready to drop away if the Yankees ever succeed again.

In Los Angeles, the passion of Philadelphians, the politeness of Minnesotans, the sentiment of St. Louisans, and the sheeplike instincts of the Texans are all combined with some peculiarly local characteristics. The crowd in Dodger Stadium is usually neat and orderly, and it roots heart and soul for the home team—but the most noticeable feature is the transistor radio. One's first impression is that two-thirds of those present are wearing hearing aids. In Hollywood, the psychology of which dominates the Dodger operation, it is always very important to know what to think, to know who's in and who's out, and to be up to date on the type of vital information that, everywhere else, is called gossip. So Dodger fans wouldn't dream of simply watching a game with their eyes; they have to hear it described, play by play. Among the consequences are some good ones: they are generally sportsmanlike, since that's the lead the broadcasters give, and they are exceptionally well informed on statistics, personal notes, and complicated plays (once they've been explained). In fact, it's hard to find anything to knock Los Angeles Dodger fans about—except by contrast to that unforgivably extinct breed, the Brooklyn Dodger fan.

If ever one type of fan symbolized baseball at its best and

worst, it was the Dodger fan at Ebbets Field from the 1920s through 1957, the black year of Exodus.

He was certainly not neat; in fact, he would seldom bother to be insulted if you called him a slob.

He wasn't especially sportsmanlike when in pursuit of a Dodger victory, although he did show honest respect for such visitors as Carl Hubbell, Mel Ott, and Stan Musial. He hated them—but he respected them and acknowledged their greatness.

As a litterer of the field, he was right up there with Philadelphians and Bronxites in volume, but without quite the hostility of Philadelphia or the aloofness of Yankee Stadium.

But he was dedicated, informed, sharp, and above all verbal. He knew as much as the Los Angeles fans know, but from his own indescribable research, not from spoon-feeding from the club's publicity department. His opinions, right or wrong, were his *own*.

He was an individualist, superstitious, rude, joyful, long-suffering, enthusiastic, original, and—a word that was an up-to-date word in his era—hep.

It is not a coincidence that Casey Stengel's character was forged in Brooklyn, nor, on a more serious level, that Jackie Robinson was able to break the color line there.

The ball park itself was tiny and intimate, with the spectators close to the field. It was in a cozy residential neighborhood. Its open archways let sunlight pour in from various angles into early evening (which made problems for the players).

Irreverence pervaded the atmosphere. The ushers were fans —and experts—instead of merely hired help. Everyone present, not only a hard core as in other parks, was a critic.

Everyone has his own impressions from childhood, particular incidents that make personal some general condition. My memory of Ebbets Field is rooted in one such impression. In 1935, when I was 11 and Casey Stengel was managing the Dodgers (the year after they had shown Bill Terry they were "still in the league" by knocking the Giants out of the pennant in the last two games of the season), they had a shortstop named Lonnie (Linus) Frey.

Linus Frey was to go on to become an all-star second baseman for the Cincinnati Reds, to help them win two pennants (one at Brooklyn's expense). At this time, though, he was a youngster and ill-equipped to play shortstop. He would make an error, it seemed, every single day, and, since the Dodgers were down around sixth place, it was fair enough to say that he was helping to keep them there.

The crowds, in those days, were numbered in the hundreds, not thousands. Any strong voice could be heard clearly throughout the small ball park—and, of course, on the field.

Every time a grounder would be hit to Frey, this man (whom I never met) would call, "T'run 'im a fish!" just as Linus was trying to field it.

I decided that he must mean Frey fielded like a seal—whatever that might mean—and that this was a particularly clever and apt and irreverent and amusing remark.

To this day, I don't know what the man really meant, but ambiguity was very much part of the Dodger syndrome—noisy, uninhibited ambiguity.

In Ebbets Field, you see, nothing *had* to make sense, but almost everything *was* fun—and that's the little three-letter word that baseball is letting slip away. And the danger of that can't be underestimated. It all rests on the fan, and, by the rules of the game, only a small portion of the fans can have victory— but most of them have to have their fun, and abandoning places like Ebbets Field was a damaging step. The Mets, in their Shea Stadium, have inherited some of the spirit and some of the fun, but only some.

Met fans, of course, deserve a whole book to themselves, but only some high spots can be touched here. They did more than any other single factor to save baseball in the 1960s.

Sociological, and anecdotal, aspects of the Met fan have been dealt with in countless articles. Boiled down, the elements of their uniqueness were a vacuum, an identity, a stacked deck, novelty, association, and cultural climate.

Because the Giants and Dodgers, during 50 years in New York, had created a rivalry unmatched in intensity, a tremendous vacuum was created when they left. Giant and Dodger fans, nurtured on National League baseball, were hungry for more of it. The five years between the departure of the Giants and Dodgers and the beginning of the Mets was long enough to make hunger acute but not so long as to cause lethal starvation. So, when the Mets began, there was ready-made interest in them.

A more important factor, in the long run, proved to be the fact that they were brand-new. Younger fans adopted them as their own, precisely because they could be in at the beginning; one could get awfully fed up with listening to fathers and brothers talk of former greats, or tagging along on some older person's enthusiasm for the Yankees. In the Mets, the youngsters had something private, and, if older folks sneered at it, that only made it more precious. In this sense—the temporal sense —all Met fans were created equal.

Hand in hand with this proprietary feeling went ultimate underdogism. Americans love underdogs under any circumstances, but here was a team *created* as an underdog, doomed to failure by the conditions of its creation. Anyone could see that the Mets had to be inferior because they were given the worst players, and told to play against the best. Since most people feel, in one respect or another, underprivileged, the Mets immediately generated a community of interest. They had been dealt a stacked deck.

And this, in the climate of the 1960s, tapped deep places in the culture as a whole. Large groups felt victims of a stacked deck, and one of the largest such groups was teen-agers, in time-honored but exceptionally open rebellion against adult standards. Another such group was intellectuals, who found themselves deliciously able to become involved in rooting for a hopeless cause just because it was hopeless, when they would have felt silly rooting for a hopeful cause in so trivial an area as baseball. Also, this was a time of pop art, theater of the absurd, social protest—all forces into which the condition and the behavior of the Mets fit admirably. What could be more absurd than, in an activity devoted to victory, rooting for someone who *had* to lose?

So the Mets became in, and developed their own type of followers—above all, loyal; passionately interested, but compassionate as well; able to indulge in a sort of one-way vision, buoyed up by any positive Met action regardless of context. It was as if the other team never came to bat; one day, the Mets were losing, 17-4, with two out in the last of the ninth and two strikes on the pinch hitter, Tim Harkness, and throughout the Polo Grounds they started yelling, "Let's Go Mets." The Met fan was able to blot out the six runs the other team had just scored, and could derive joy from one run the Mets scored in return.

Such fans had one additional, unusual, overriding asset: a sense of humor. They could laugh at themselves and at their plight, and retain a sense of proportion. This crowning quality created the tangible characteristic of Mets fans—their famous signs.

It was not the artistic workmanship (although some had it) nor the rooting element in these signs that made them catch the national imagination; it was their point. What they had to say was terse, clever, funny, sardonic. As imitations proliferated in other ball parks, the contrast between authentic Met signs and the imitators was driven home. Anybody could, and did, paint signs saying "Let's Go Braves," or "Beat the Dodgers," or "We Love Willie Mays," and things like that.

But only Met fans could produce banners that read: "When?" and "Pray" and "To Error Is Human" and "Eamus Metropoli" (Latin for "Let's Go Mets") and "Marv Throneberry Is Alive and Hiding in Argentina" and (when the Cubs finally usurped last place in 1966) "God Bless the Chicago Cubs." And since the customary medium for this art was the ordinary bed sheet, stolen or sacrificed at home, a group inevitably produced a banner reading: "The Bed Sheet Manufacturers of America Love the Mets." And not even victory, so blissfully experienced in 1969 and so elusive since, has changed the underlying mood of the Met fan, despite the inescapable bourgeois respectability acquired since the move from Harlem to the edge of the suburbs in Queens.

It is this attitude—humorous, quick-witted, antistuffy, involved but not taking oneself *too* seriously—that baseball must generate in its fans to survive. Before the Mets, creeping pomposity was choking baseball to death. Met fans have had a salutary effect, and a great influence, in other cities, and the example of their profitable numbers has not been entirely lost on baseball executives.

Fun.

That's the essential word—fun. Baseball rooting must be fun for the fans, in their various ways. Fewer professional baseball men understand this than ever before, but people like Bill Veeck and Frank Lane, who mingled with their crowds instead of sitting in isolated offices and air-conditioned boxes with guards at the door, grasped it fully. Veeck, of course, was the master of stimulating the fun to be had (it was he who invented the performing scoreboard, which shoots off fireworks when the home team hits a homer at Comiskey Park). But all baseball executives, to some degree, must try to be conscious of this if they are to be successful.

And fun is a key word for all the other aspects of the game we've been discussing. Big business though it is, it must be fun to play, or a man can't play it well; it must be fun to live with and work with day after day, or the executives and writers and other auxiliaries would find equally profitable and less wearing occupations; it must be fun for the owner, in some way, or he'll find a better use for his money and for his image; and it must be fun for the fan, or he won't come at all.

And it must be, I suppose, fun to read about, or we wouldn't be here at the end of this book, would we?

- **Don't any of you people ever get hungry?**
  Shout of a peanut vendor in Fort Lauderdale Stadium

Under the Stands

Just for the sake of completeness, and to underline the idea that the baseball business is a pretty big business, let's make a quick, superficial survey of all the people who work in a ball park.

There are hundreds.

Some work for the club all year round, others just when the stadium is in use. Some are employed by the concessionaire, who may be an affiliate of the club or may have a free hand. Some work for the city or county, if the stadium is municipally operated.

Among the year-round employees are all the front-office people of the club. Nowadays, the club's offices tend to be in the ball park itself, although in some cases a downtown office is still maintained.

A typical organization is the New York Mets. It has, as working executives, on the job daily, a president, an assistant to the president, a vice-president and administrative assistant (who looks after player affairs), and a vice-president and business manager (who is in charge of the stadium and other physical properties).

There are two public relations men, five promotion people, a traveling secretary, a comptroller, a ticket department manager and assistant, a maintenance supervisor, a head grounds keeper, and a four-man farm-system department. There are telephone switchboard operators, secretaries and stenographers, and two receptionists. There are bookkeepers and ticket-handlers, messengers, and office boys.

The grounds-keeping crew, which converts the field from baseball to football or other events, as well as keeping the field in playing condition, numbers about 20.

The maintenance forces include electricians (who must help operate the public-address system and scoreboards), plumbers, carpenters, and various types of repairmen.

When a game is being played, there have to be ushers, ticket-sellers, ticket-takers (at the turnstiles), rest-room attendants, private police, parking-lot attendants, a nurse, elevator operators, some city police, and special-assignment people (like press-room attendants, a knowledgeable supervisor at the press and pass gate, doormen at various private points).

In the concessions machinery are: vendors, who circulate in the stands with their baskets of beer, hot dogs, peanuts, etc.; behind-the-counter salesmen at refreshment and souvenir stands; checkers, who issue the wares to and collect money from vendors; men to move the immense amount of foodstuffs and supplies from storage to distribution points; and a full range of kitchen help.

Where there are stadium clubs of one sort or another (and all the new parks have them, as well as some of the old), all the appurtenances of a high-quality restaurant and bar are on hand: captains, waiters, busboys, bartenders, cooks, dishwashers, cashiers, and so forth.

Then there is the matter of cleaning up. All the indoor portions—the restaurants, offices, clubhouses—must be scrubbed and cleaned in the ordinary way, by people who have permanent jobs of this sort. And after every event, the stands themselves are swept through by a swarm of temporary workers, who collect the tons of paper and assorted debris a large crowd can leave.

Down in the dressing rooms, along with the ball players, coaches, managers, and trainers we already know about, are the "clubhouse men"—usually, two for the home team and one for visitors. These are essential to the care and comfort of a ball club: they keep the locker room clean, supply minor items to the players (shoelaces, socks, sandwiches, soft drinks), shine shoes, look after equipment, take messages, run errands, and maintain a level of discretion that would do credit to British Intelligence.

Up on the press-box level, there are newspaper reporters, Western Union telegraphers, broadcasters with their engineers, the scoreboard operators, the club's publicity man, and (in many parks) the person who plays the organ for pregame and between-innings music. The public-address announcer is here, and the electrician who operates the phonograph for recorded music.

If the game is televised, half a dozen television cameras, each with a cameraman, may be scattered around the stands, and a technical crew (consisting of a director and a couple of assistants) will work in a permanent installation under the stands or out of a portable television truck.

In a special booth are photographers: newspaper, magazine, and newsreel, often with special heavy equipment.

The broadcasting business brings its own fallout. In addition to the announcers and engineer, who are obviously necessary, there is a whole chain of directors, ad agency people, station or network representatives, and persons connected in one way or another with sponsors. The club's statistician usually sits with the radio crew, although he services the press as well.

All these people, to some degree and in many cases totally, earn their living from major-league baseball.

So do the 25 or so scouts employed by each club, men who scour the country for playing talent.

So do the managers and some executives of minor-league clubs, supported by the big-league team.

This, then, is the part of the baseball iceberg seldom noticed by the fan—for whose satisfaction all these jobs must be performed. In addition, periodically, the seats and stands must be painted and repaired, gates must be fixed, traffic flow along ramps must be planned and directed, signs must be devised, produced, and placed, nameplates must be installed on season boxes—the details are endless, and expensive.

Many of the workers involved (in New York, almost all) are unionized. Supplies—paint, sod, lumber, pipe—are constantly more expensive to buy and install. It's a big and expensive operation.

Of all these activities, one has a direct effect on the game on the field, and deserves more discussion: grounds keeping.

Like so many aspects of baseball, grounds keeping is more art than anything else. There have been some wizards at it, and when the job is done carelessly, the consequences are felt quickly.

To be played well, baseball requires two ground conditions: a smooth-dirt infield, and an even carpet of grass on the infield and outfield. Providing these basic conditions, through drought and flood, despite occasional ground-tearing football games or the erection of a boxing ring (with ringside spectators trampling the ground and temporary bleachers denting it), in the face of unfavorable grass-growing conditions, is not easy.

But beyond these generalities, fields can be tailored to the competitive needs of a ball club.

If the ground is very hard, balls will bounce harder, higher, and faster—and many hits will bounce through a hard infield. If you have a fast team, without too much power, that's what you want. However, if your infielders are slow, you want the infield grass to be cut higher (slowing down a batted ball on its first bounce) and a softer dirt portion.

If you have good bunters, you want the dirt paths to first and third tilted slightly in—so that a bunt down either line will tend to roll fair. If you don't, and think the other team does, you want them tilted the other way, to make bunts roll foul.

You want hard, firm footing for base-stealing, which is why Alvin Dark, managing the San Francisco Giants, got the name "Swamp Fox" in 1962. He had the infield around first base soaked before a game against the Dodgers, so that Maury Wills couldn't get a good start. The Dodgers complained bitterly to the umpires, who forced the Giants to fill the man-made puddles with sand to dry them up—which was exactly what Dark wanted, because the loose sand provided bad footing for the entire game, whereas the puddles would have dried up within a couple of innings: hence, Swamp Fox.

Tall outfield grass can help slow-footed outfielders in one sense—it will keep some drives between them from bouncing through for extra bases—but can be a handicap on hits in front of them if the base runners are fast.

The height of a pitching mound is specified now—10 inches above the level of the base lines—but it used to be permissible to have it range in height from 12 to 18 inches, and many a mound was tailored to a home team pitcher's stride or delivery. The slope from the mound can still vary somewhat, so that one can appear "higher" than another.

Usually, the ruts, bumps, and other inconsistencies of the playing surface, infield or outfield, cannot be recognized from the stands. The players, however, are intimately concerned with this at all times, and rate fields as carefully as they rate opponents. Many tactical situations take the condition of the field into account.

The grounds keeper and his crew have one other important game function: response to rain. How quickly they can cover the infield with a tarp, and how well they can repair puddles afterward, will often determine whether or not a game can be resumed—and therefore can determine the result.

One could go on and on describing the specifics of all these baseball-related jobs. The idea is clear: it's not just a matter of finding nine guys who can play and buying them uniforms.

Let's leave this subject with one final thought: all old-fashioned ball parks, and some of the new ones, display flags from poles on the roof whenever a game is played. Somebody has to go up there at the beginning of the day and pull them up—and at the end, pull them down. He, too, is "in baseball."

Chronology of Major Rule Changes

Here is a chronology of major rule changes since 1876, when the first major league was formed.

At that time, the rules were:

> Only underhand pitching allowed, with the pitcher permitted to move around in a box (6 feet by 4 feet) 45 feet from home plate.
>
> Batter could call for a high or low pitch.
>
> Nine balls for a walk.
>
> Two chances for a called third strike.
>
> The home team chose which half inning it wanted to bat.
>
> The ball was essentially the same as now.
>
> The bases were stakes driven into the ground.

1877—Canvas bases, 15 inches square, adopted, and home plate put entirely into fair territory.

1880—Eight balls for a walk.

1881—Pitching distance increased to 50 feet.

1882—Seven balls for a walk.

1883—Foul must be caught on fly for an out.

1884—Overhand pitching allowed, and six balls for a walk.

1886—Seven balls for a walk, bases placed in fair territory, umpire permitted to use new ball at any time (instead of at end of inning).

1887—Batter's right to call high or low eliminated.
   Hit by pitcher entitles batter to base.
   Five balls for a walk.
   Four "called strikes" for an out (this year only).
   Walk scored as base hit (this year only).
1888—Three strikes is out.*
   Walk scored as no time at bat.*
   Batter given a hit when runner is struck by batted ball.*
1889—Four balls for a walk.*
1891—Substitution permitted at any time.*
1893—Pitching distance set at 60 feet 6 inches, and pitcher's
   rear foot must maintain contact with a slab, 12 inches
   by 4 inches.
   Flat bats prohibited.*
   Sacrifice scored as no time at bat.*
1894—Foul bunt is a strike.*
1895—Foul tip is a strike.
   Infield fly rule instituted.
   Bat limited to 2¾ inches in diameter.*
   Pitcher's slab made 24 inches by 6 inches.*
1899—Balk rules adopted.*
1900—Five-sided home plate used (to help umpires).*
1901—First two fouls count as strikes (National League only).*
1903—American League adopts foul strikes.
1904—Pitcher's mound limited to 15 inches in height.
1910—Cork center ball.
1911—Home teams wear white uniforms.
1917—Earned runs added to official records.*
1920—Spitball forbidden (and other trick pitches).*
   Runs batted in added to official records.*
1925—Minimum home-run distance set at 250 feet (instead of
   235).
   Cushioned cork center ball.*
1931—Home run is fair ball where it leaves the playing field,
   not where it leaves the umpire's sight.*

*As in present rules.

1934—Both leagues adopt the same ball. (There had been differences in the stitching.)

1973—Designated hitter (American League only).

How to Compute
the Standard Averages

BATTING AVERAGE: Divide At Bats into Hits, to three decimal places.

An "At Bat" is an "official" time at bat; in theory, a time in which the batter was given an opportunity to get a hit. Thus, it is *not* an "official time at bat" when a batter walks, is hit by a pitch, makes a successful sacrifice bunt (advancing the lead runner), hits a sacrifice fly (scoring a man), or is awarded first base because of interference by the catcher.

A "Hit" is any ball hit so that the batter reaches base safely without the aid of an error by a fielder. Every single, double, triple, and home run counts as one hit for computing batting average.

EXAMPLE: 365 AB, 97 H

$$
\begin{array}{r}
.265 \\
365\,)\overline{97.000} \\
730 \\ \hline
2400 \\
2190 \\ \hline
2100 \\
1825 \\ \hline
275
\end{array}
$$

Ave.—.266

A man who got a hit on every official at bat is batting 1.000.

A man who has no hits is batting .000.

SLUGGING AVERAGE: Divide At Bats into Total Bases, to three decimal places.

Total Bases is the sum of bases accounted for by base hits—one for a single, two for a double, three for a triple, four for a home run. It indicates a batter's "power."

EXAMPLE: 365 AB 97 H   (14 2b, 3 3b, 12 HR)
To the 97 hits, add 14 (extra bases on doubles), 6 (two extra bases for each triple), and 36 (three extra bases for each home run). The "Total Bases" is 153.

$$
\begin{array}{r}
.419 \\
365\overline{)153.000} \\
1460 \\
\hline
700 \\
365 \\
\hline
3350 \\
3285 \\
\hline
65
\end{array}
$$

Sl. Ave.—.419

A man who hits a home run on every official at bat has a slugging average of 4.000.

ON-BASE AVERAGE: Add to Official At Bats the number of walks, hit by pitch, sacrifices, sacrifice flies, and first on interference. This sum is called "Total Appearances."

Add to Hits the number of walks, hit by pitch, first on interference, and reached base on error. This is "Total On Base."

Divide Total Appearances into Total On Base.

In computing an On-Base Average, *do not* include in the Total On Base the times a batter reaches base on a fielder's choice on which another man was retired.

WON-LOST PERCENTAGE: Divide the total number of games (victories plus defeats, ignoring ties) into the number of victories, to three decimal places.

EXAMPLE: Won 87, Lost 62, Tied 1

$$
\begin{array}{r}
.583 \\
149\overline{)87.000} \\
745 \\
\hline
1250 \\
1192 \\
\hline
580 \\
447 \\
\hline
133
\end{array}
$$

Pct.—.584

An all-winning team is playing 1.000.

A team that wins half its games is at .500.

(The terms "average" and "percentage" mean exactly the same thing, both inaccurately by mathematical standards. In baseball usage, simply by tradition, it is customary to speak of batting "averages" and won-lost "percentages." Strictly speaking, a .300 average means 30.0 percent of the time, with 1.000 equivalent to 100 percent.)

EARNED-RUN AVERAGE: The full name of this standard for rating pitchers is "Earned-run Average Per Nine-Inning Game."

An "Earned Run" is one for which the pitcher, *by his pitching*, is responsible. If an error or a passed ball contributes to the scoring of a particular run, which would not have scored otherwise, it is an "unearned run." Once a team has had the opportunity to make three outs in an inning, but has prolonged the inning by making one or more errors, all the subsequent runs are "unearned." A run, earned or unearned, is charged against the pitcher who allowed that run to reach base originally.

Divide the number of Innings Pitched into the number of Earned Runs Allowed. (Ignore thirds of an inning in Innings Pitched, taking the nearest complete inning.) Then multiply the result of this division (to three decimal places) by 9.

EXAMPLE: 184⅔ IP, 55 ER

$$
\begin{array}{r}
.297 \\
185\overline{)55.000} \\
370 \\
\overline{1800} \\
1665 \\
\overline{1350} \\
1295 \\
\overline{55}
\end{array}
$$

(this is "earned runs per inning")

$$
\begin{array}{r}
.297 \\
\times\ 9 \\
\overline{2.673}
\end{array}
$$

ERA—2.67

Earned-run averages are given to two decimal places. Since the average score of all baseball games is 5-4, any earned-run average under 3.00 is considered excellent.

FIELDING AVERAGE: Add number of putouts, assists, and errors made for Total Chances.

Divide Total Chances into sum of putouts and assists, to three decimal places.

EXAMPLE:

$$
\begin{array}{r}
.967 \\
424\overline{)410.000} \\
3816 \\
\overline{2840} \\
2544 \\
\overline{2960} \\
2968
\end{array}
$$

fielding average—.967

A man who makes no errors is fielding 1.000.

Major-leaguers' fielding averages are invariably well above .900.

Batting Averages, Slugging Averages, Won-Lost Percentages, Earned-run Averages and Fielding Averages are the only ones that are officially kept as part of baseball records.

On-base averages are gaining increasing acceptance informally. Other proportions are often used by baseball people, on a do-it-yourself basis, with illuminating results. Among the common ones are:

PITCHING: Hits per inning ratio: less than one hit per inning is good.

Strikeouts per inning: one per inning is sensational.

Walks per inning: one walk, or less, for every three innings is good.

Walks-to-strikeouts ratio: Two strikeouts for every walk indicates good control.

BATTING: Walks-to-strikeouts: more walks than strikeouts is good.

Runners driven in: Runs batted in, minus home runs, gives the number of *other* runners the hitter drove home.

Hits per game: one hit per game is average.

Home runs per time at bat: one homer in 20 or less is top-grade slugging; one in 100 or more is subnormal.

The standard statistical categories, with their usual abbreviations, are:

W—Games Won
L—Games Lost

BATTING:
- G—Games played
- AB—Official At Bats
- R—Runs scored
- H—Hits
- 2b—Doubles
- 3b—Triples
- HR—Home Runs
- RBI—Runs batted in
- TB—Total Bases
- S—Sacrifice bunts
- SF—Sacrifice Flies
- SO—Times struck out
- BB—Times walked
- BBI—Times walked intentionally
- HB—Hit by Pitch
- SB—Stolen Bases
- CS—Caught Stealing
- GIDP—Grounded into double play

PITCHING:
- G—Games participated in (as a pitcher)
- GS—Games Started
- CG—Complete Games
- IP—Innings Pitched
- H—Hits allowed
- R—Runs allowed
- ER—Earned Runs allowed
- BB—Walks issued
- BBI—Intentional Walks issued
- SO—Strikeouts
- WP—Wild Pitches
- HB—Hit Batsmen
- ShO—Shutouts
- Saves—Games Saved
- ERA—Earned-run Average per 9-inning game

FIELDING: G—Games played
                  PO—Putouts
                  A—Assists
                  E—Errors
                  DP—Double Plays (participated in for individual; total for team)
                  TC—Total Chances
                  PB—Passed Ball (catchers only)
                  TP—Triple Play

MINIMUMS: In professional baseball, minimum standards have been set to make individual league championships meaningful, in recognition of the fact that an *average* is valid only for a reasonably large number of opportunities. These minimums are:

To qualify for a batting championship, a player must come to bat 3.1 times the number of games scheduled for his team —that is, his "total appearances" (including walks, etc.) must match or exceed this number. In the major leagues, with a 162-game schedule, this minimum is 502 plate appearances. In a minor league playing a 140-game schedule, it would be 434 plate appearances. This rule dates only from 1955, so before that, there were batting champions who didn't meet the requirement.

To qualify for an earned-run pitching championship, a pitcher must work at least the same number of innings as games on the schedule: 162 in the majors.

To qualify for fielding average championships, players must take part in two-thirds
of the games scheduled, except catchers,
who must take part in half, and pitchers,
who must pitch as many innings as games
scheduled.

How to Keep a Scorebook

Because baseball has a slow tempo, with plays happening one at a time, it is possible to keep a detailed record of what has happened. Writers and others professionally concerned must do this; a very large proportion of fans do it simply because it adds to their enjoyment of the game.

The traditional method of keeping score is a type of shorthand worked out basically before the turn of the century. Like all shorthand systems, regular users develop their own preferences and minor variations on the accepted base. Among baseball writers, no two scorebooks look identical in every detail, but by and large anyone can read anyone else's book for 90 percent of the plays recorded.

The variations concern the symbols used to record hits and the system used to follow each player's path around the bases. The universally accepted basis for recording outs is the numbering of defensive positions. These are identified as follows:

1—pitcher
2—catcher
3—first baseman
4—second baseman
5—third baseman
6—shortstop
7—left fielder

8—center fielder
9—right fielder

Thus, an entry 6-3 indicates a ground out, short to first; an entry 8 means a fly out to center.

Since numbers refer to the position, they are not affected by substitutions; to find out who "6" or "8" was in a particular inning, one looks at the batting order.

It is convenient, therefore, to avoid the use of numbers for anything else in the shorthand portion of the scorebook, to avoid confusion. A system of letters, either as abbreviations or symbols, can provide the remaining information, and can be combined with numbers to avoid ambiguity.

For instance, the traditional symbol for strikeout is "K." Probably this is because "S" is so needed in other connections. Usually "S" is used to indicate a stolen base; "SAC" or "SH" is used to indicate a sacrifice; "BB" or "W" will serve for base on balls, or walk; and so forth.

Such symbols are essential, because they deal with the play itself. Others are optional, depending on how detailed a record one wants to keep. For example, one can use "L" before the number to indicate a line-drive out instead of a routine fly; "D" to indicate a deep fly; "P" to indicate a pop-up.

If a man makes out, the notation for that time at bat is simple enough. It becomes complicated only when he gets on base.

There are two approaches, both widely used. The older, more traditional record visualizes the box alongside each name, under the appropriate inning, as a map of the diamond. Whatever brings the batter to first base is placed in the lower right-hand corner; whatever takes him to second, in the upper right-hand corner; to third, the upper left-hand corner; and home, the lower left-hand corner. The diamond in the center of the box can be filled in, or a heavy dot made, to indicate that the man scored.

Nowadays, it is just as common to fill in the box in ordinary reading terms—starting in the upper left-hand corner, going across, then back to the lower left-hand corner and across. In this case, the box is not a map but a diagram.

In recording a hit, you must know how many bases it was worth; you may want to know in what direction it went, and whether it was a grounder or a fly. The simplest way of doing this is to use a horizontal line for each base—one for a single, two for a double, three for a triple, four for a home run. Direction can be indicated by using the fielding position, so that $\underline{7}$ can mean a single to left. By placing the number above or below the line, fly or grounder can be indicated: $\overline{\overline{9}}$ is a ground-double to right; $\underline{\underline{1}}$ is a fly-ball triple to left; $\underline{6}$ is a ground single through short.

Such a system, even though it uses numbers for plays that are not outs, is better than the one I use myself—but in the extremely personal area of scoring shorthand, early habits are hard to break. The hit symbols I learned first were crosses, with dots to indicate direction: $\dotplus$, ground single to left; $\ddagger$, home run to right. This catches the eye better when one glances quickly at a scorebook while writing a story. But for fine detail, that is, to distinguish between a ground single through the left side and one that went off the shortstop's glove, I still have to use a small number, where the dot would normally be: $\dotplus$.

The scoresheet itself is a grid. Down the left-hand side are listed the names of the players and their positions, in the proper batting order; when substitutions are made, they must be inserted on the proper line, so that the batting order is always correct. (When space becomes a problem with several substitutions at one position, the new men can be entered at the bottom, with arrows leading to their proper place.)

Across the top, the innings are numbered consecutively, from left to right. Thus there is one box in each inning for each spot in the batting order.

When there is a pitching change during the inning, a heavy

horizontal line below the box of the man who last faced the outgoing pitcher can mark the change.

When a pinch hitter or pinch runner is used, a circled letter of reference ("A" or "B" or "C," or "Y" or "Z") can be placed just to the left of the box affected, and the same code letter entered alongside the name of the substitute in the batting order.

As a man progresses around the bases, within his own box, some provision must be made for showing how he went from base to base. The hit, walk, force-out, or whatever, as the original entry, tells how he got on.

In the vast majority of cases, his subsequent advance is self-evident. If the next man doubles, naturally he went to third, and it's enough to mark by a line (if you're using the diamond-map system) or any other notation that he reached third. A common method is to use a number—the number of the subsequent man in the batting order whose action caused the advance—to note each step.

This, in my opinion, is a bad way of doing it. It introduces a set of numbers—the position in the batting order—unrelated to the defensive position numbers, and is therefore confusing. Since I use crosses for hits, I'm free to use simple horizontal lines ($\equiv$) to indicate that a man reached third, with further explanation by letters if necessary. That's why it is better, if you use horizontal lines for hits, to use the positional, "map" idea of assigning each corner of the box to a specific base.

In my system, when a player drives in a run, I draw an arrow from his box to the box of the man who scored, thus making runs batted in stand out.

As with everything else, the best method is the one that's geared to the needs of the user. To a newspaperman, the most important factor is quick reference with minimum ambiguity: he's going to glance at his scorecard while writing a story. To someone keeping records, greater detail that can be read back with careful attention a long time in the future is more important. To a fan, only a sketchy record of hits and outs may be of interest.

So far, we have talked only of the play-by-play portion of the score-sheet. It also contains, at the right-hand side and at the bottom, space for summaries—the traditional "box score" material—totaling at bats, hits, double plays, etc. Working newspapermen seldom fill this in completely, noting only the categories they're interested in (the pitching records, for instance, and extra-base hits). But a well-kept scorebook, when used over a period of time, is greatly enhanced (for research purposes) by neatly totaled summaries.

Here are all the symbols I use. They are neither recommended nor authoritative, but representative and self-consistent:

REACHING BASE:

∴+	single to left (line drive)
≠	ground double to right
≢	triple to left center
≢ᵛ	Home run into the upper deck in right
⊛	Home run, inside the park, to center
BB	Walk (circled, on four pitches; boxed, on full count)
HB	Hit by pitch
B .	Bunt single, toward first
FC	Fielder's choice (usually a force-out)
BFC	Bunt fielder's choice
BBI	Intentional walk
A 6	Error (fumbled grounder by shortstop)
M 8	Error (muffed fly by center fielder)

W 5	Error (wild throw to first by third baseman)
4 *E* 3	Error (grounder to second, throw to first dropped by first baseman, with an assist for the second baseman on the play)
⊁*PB* or ⊁*WP*	First on missed third strike

ADVANCING BASES:

S	Stolen base
PB	Passed ball
WP	Wild pitch
B	Balk
T	Took extra base on throw to another base

OUTS:

K s	Strikeout swinging (circled, on three pitches; boxed, on full count)
K c	Strikeout called
K t	Strikeout on foul tip
s⊁ 2-3	Strikeout, catcher dropped ball, threw to first
XX 4-6	Forced out, second to short (in box of the base runner putout)
OS 2-6	Out stealing, catcher to shortstop
CO 1-3	Picked off base, pitcher to first baseman
DP 4-6-3	Double play, second to short to first
TP	Triple play
SAC. 1-4	Sacrifice bunt, pitcher to second baseman covering first
SAC. 8	Sacrifice fly, to center (always a run batted in)

F 5   Foul out to the third baseman

IP 6   Pop-up to short

TL 4   "Texas Leaguer" (looping fly between infield and outfield) caught by second baseman

8 D   Long fly to center

4 L.   Line drive to the second baseman

Any outstanding fielding play is circled.

Any exceptional occurrence (such as interference) is marked by an asterisk and explained in the margin.

In general, any series of numbers indicates how the ball was handled, with a putout for the last one and assists for the others. Thus, 8-4-2-5-2-5-1-5: On a hit to center, a runner from second scored, but this man, who started from first, made too wide a turn at third and was caught in a rundown which involved the catcher, pitcher, and third baseman.

The Baseball Hierarchy

Organized Baseball is the name adopted by the self-governing structure that has evolved in professional baseball. The hierarchy has been constructed by a series of agreements, entered into by clubs to form leagues and by leagues to form associations.

The cornerstone is a five-page document called the Major League Agreement. It is signed by the two major leagues, and by each of the clubs in them. It sets up the commissioner's office and spells out his duties, and in other ways establishes the fact that the National and American Leagues are to operate jointly and to subscribe to common rules. It is this agreement that makes possible the World Series, honoring of contracts, uniform playing rules, and so forth.

Appended to the agreement is a 60-page, detailed document called the Major League Rules. This defines the membership of each league and all the regulations for signing, exchanging, and controlling players, as well as all the other agreed-upon practices. It is both the constitution and the main body of legislation of major-league baseball.

The Professional Baseball Agreement forms the link to minor-league baseball. This agreement is between the Major Leagues (an entity set up by the Major League Agreement) and the National Association of Professional Baseball Leagues, which contains all the sanctioned minor leagues. The minors thus accept the jurisdiction of the commissioner, the major-league playing rules, and all the business regulations that must be kept consistent with what the majors have decided between themselves.

Then, the Professional Baseball Rules parallel and extend the Major League Rules where they apply to relations between the majors and the minors.

Finally, the minor leagues are bound together by the National Association Agreement (adopted originally in 1901), which spells out inter-league relations among the minors. It is signed by the leagues and individual clubs that comprise the minor leagues. The minors are grouped into classes of ability, with AAA the highest and Rookie Leagues the lowest.

The ultimate power in baseball, therefore, resides in the 24 owners of the major-league clubs. They select the commissioner, and pay him, through the Major League Agreement; and through the other interlocking documents and the commissioner himself, they control the minors.

Structurally, the Office of the Commissioner is the top of the pyramid. It includes the commissioner, who has the power to rule in any dispute on any level; an administrator, who is the right-hand man and baseball-experienced assistant to the commissioner; a secretary-treasurer, whose primary concern is the technical operation of the office (pension plan questions, draft meetings, waiver technicalities, and so on); a public relations officer; a director of radio and television; a director of liason with college and amateur groups; and a coordinator of Inter-American affairs.

The commissioner, with his staff, therefore, is analogous to a combination of the President and Supreme Court.

Baseball's "cabinet," to carry out the simile, is the Executive Council. This consists of seven members: the commissioner, the presidents of the two major leagues, and two club owners from each major league.

The next step down is the major-league president level. Each league president's office controls the umpires in that league, makes schedules (which are coordinated with the other league), approves contracts, and handles all intraleague regulatory functions.

Each league has its own public relations office, a board of directors (composed of owners), and staff.

The next step down is each individual club, as represented by its ownership. However, the club owners collectively constitute the legislature of baseball: they make and amend the laws when they meet in individual league meetings, and then in a joint meeting of the two leagues (presided over by the commissioner).

Below the owners are the general managers, who deal with the day-by-day operation of each individual club. They act as advisers (and immensely influential ones, of course) to the owners, but actual rules can be adopted only by the owners.

At the top of the minor-league structure is the President of the National Association. Each minor league has a president, who is more powerful, with respect to his own league, than the major-league presidents are; however, since most minor-league teams are owned outright or subsidized by major-league organizations, there is no effective independence for any of the minors when major-league interests are in any way involved.

The major-league players have an Association, which acquired a full-time executive head, Marvin J. Miller, in 1966. This is the closest thing to a union that baseball has. Each team has an elected player representative, and the representatives in each league choose one of their number to be league player representative. They, with Miller, confer with the owners about pension problems, scheduling, working conditions, and various grievances, but here again, they can only ask. The owners are sovereign—reasonable, even benevolent, but absolute in their powers except for the new salary arbitration provisions.

Minor-league players have no effective representation of any kind, nor any pension plan.

Also affiliated with Organized Baseball are:

The Association of Professional Baseball Players of America, a benevolent organization that looks after indigent or ill former players, umpires, and trainers.

The National Baseball Hall of Fame and Museum, a private organization that has baseball's sanction, in Cooperstown, New York.

A Baseball Umpire Development program.

A Major League Promotion Corp., which handles movies and authorized emblems on various products.

An amateur baseball coordination program operated out of the commissioner's office.

Official statistician for the National League, and many minors, is the Elias Sports Bureau, in New York City. The American League handles its own statistics.

The annual meetings of both the minor and major leagues, and joint meetings, take place in late-November–early-December.

Roster Regulations: Limits, Trading, Deadlines, Waivers

Baseball "law" is as complex, and as subject to technicality, as any other kind. Some of the regulations, however, are of immediate interest to the fan, because they affect directly the part of the game he can follow. Most of these rules have been developed to promote even competition, by limiting rosters and maneuverability of players, so that it is no longer possible for the wealthiest team simply to buy whatever player it needs at any time. It used to be possible, and it did happen.

The primary limitation is that a major-league club can have only 40 men on its roster at any one time.

Of these 40, only 25 are eligible to play for the major-league team on opening day. The rest must be farmed out or otherwise disposed of. However, from September 1 to the end of the season, all 40 may be used in games.

A player can be disposed of in the following ways:

He can be released. This makes him a free agent, able to sign with anyone on any terms.

He can be sent "on option" to a team in the minors. That means he still belongs to the parent team, and can be "recalled" at any time (with certain restrictions). Once a man is on a major-league roster, he can be optioned out only three times. After that he must be kept, released, or offered to another major-league team.

He can be traded (or sold) to another major-league club, but if he has 10 years of major-league service, the last 5 with one club, he must agree to the move.

Up until June 15 of every season, any player may be traded or sold to any other team in the same league, without restriction. However, before he can be passed on to a team in the other league, all of the other teams in his own league must be given an opportunity to buy him for a set price. This is the "waiver" rule: other clubs must "waive their rights" to the player before he can be transferred out of the league.

The waiver system works according to the reverse order of the league standings: the lowest team gets first choice, the next-to-last team goes next, and so forth. In recent years, the waiver price has been $20,000, a relatively insignificant sum. Players can be put "on waivers" and then withdrawn, and kept by the original club; but that can only be done once with any one player in any one year. The second time, the waivers are "irrevocable."

Of course, in order to claim a man on waivers, the club that claims him must have or make room on its roster, since the limits still apply.

After June 15, through the end of the season, no trading is permitted except by means of waivers, even within each league. And to trade a man from one league to the other, one must go through the waiver ladders in both leagues.

Shortly after the World Series, in mid-October, major-league rosters are "frozen," and no further movement of players to and from the minors is permitted until after the draft of minor-league players takes place at the winter meetings. However, from the end of the season until the next June 15, there are no restrictions on trading within one major league.

Interleague trading, without restriction, is permitted for a five-week period which overlaps November and December.

The "regular" draft is designed to assure progress upward

for players in the minor leagues. Each fall, all players with 2 or more years of professional service on a minor-league roster can be drafted, for a set price of $25,000, by any major-league club. Players in lower minor classifications can be drafted (for smaller amounts) by teams in the higher minors.

This sweeping "unrestricted" draft came into being only in 1965. Now only the 40 men on the parent roster are exempt from the draft; in the past, dozens of men could be out on option and not subject to draft, so the draft never became an important feature in talent-stocking. It is more of a safety valve for the player being covered up in a well-stocked organization than a source of strength for major-league team building.

Another innovation, drastically altering traditional baseball procedures, was the "free agent draft," also begun in 1965. This covers all players not yet signed to a professional contract, essentially high-school graduates and college players. The major-league teams draft the "rights" to negotiate with the players they have scouted, thus eliminating the competitive bidding for the more desirable prospects, a bidding that pushed bonuses as high as $250,000 in the case of Rick Reichardt and the California Angels.

An injured player can be placed on a "disabled list," so that he doesn't count against the active 25-man roster while recuperating; but he must then remain idle a minimum time (the rule has fluctuated from 60 to 15 to 21 days), although, of course, he may stay on it indefinitely. That way his place can be filled by an able-bodied player.

Players who enter military service go on a special list and don't count against any roster limit until a stipulated time (15 or 30 days) after they rejoin their club.

Veteran players—those who have had eight years of major-league experience—cannot be sent to the minors without their consent.

In releasing a player completely, the "$1 waiver" procedure

is used. Any team, following the waiver list sequence, can claim the player's contract for $1, a formality that permits the weaker teams to get first crack at any player. However, when a contract is claimed in any fashion, the club that claims it assumes its obligations, such as salary. If no claim is made, the club is free to negotiate from scratch with the player in question.